ARABIA FELIX

THE FIRST CROSSING OF THE EMPTY QUARTER DESERT BY A NON-ARAB

BERTRAM THOMAS
COMPILED IBN AL HAMRA

CONTENTS

INTRODUCTION – THIS EDITION

This edition has been completely retyped, images from the original books were scanned to improve print quality, and place-specific modern photographs included for context. Punctuation and spellings, though occasionally at odds with current usage and often inconsistent within the book have generally been kept as in the Bertram Thomas text.

After several years of anticipation and planning Bertram Thomas achieved the first crossing by a non-Arab of the Rub Al Khali, the Empty Quarter desert, in 1935. It was the culmination of his years in the Sultanate of Oman as a minister for the country's ruler, Sultan Taimur bin Faisal Al Said. His taking employment in Oman was the means to his achieving this ground breaking crossing, as he writes 'when I left the Administration of Trans-Jordan for the Court of Muscat and Oman I already cherished secret dreams'.

The book, Arabia Felix, is written by Bertram Thomas in a detached tone and its full of phrases that today are at the least politically incorrect and certainly derogatory. His phrasing may simply be the every-day terminology used 100 years ago, with no meaning to be assumed, much as today's language is full of terms that are very easy to be offended by.

Bertram Thomas demonstrated a profound understanding of both the people and customs of Iraq (Thomas used Mesopotamia - though the name had changed to Iraq) and Oman (as described in his book Alarms & Excursions in Arabia), indeed his work in Iraq entailed him acting as judge. His ability to achieve his aims, or rather the British government's aims, in Iraq and in Oman show that he in fact maintained a very positive relationship with all he met. In Iraq, where he was the sole British administrator in a remote district, he ensured through his strong personal relationships with the local population that there was effectively no uprising against British rule by the area he administered. In Oman he needed to negotiate for escorts and camels for transport at several stages on his journey down the east coast of Oman to Salala.

Most of that route was in areas only nominally under the administration of Oman's ruler the Sultan Taimur, and neither the Sultan Taimur or Britain would be in a position to offer a lone British traveller any timely support, or even be aware if he needed it.

Thomas lived in Iraq from 1916 to 1922, and usually was the only Englishman in town. Perforce, he spoke in Arabic after his appointment as a British Assistant Political Officer and also learnt the culture of his region. His subsequent time in Trans-Jordan, though shorter and part of a larger British team, must also have reinforced his awareness of the fundamentals of the culture in northern Arabia. Moving to Muscat for 5 years, from 1925, and living and travelling by camel through Oman built on these insights. It's clear that he had an enquiring mind-set, as the pages of his

Bertram Thomas

writings are full of either his questions or explanations by his companions about some aspect of a location or culture.

Despite his remarkable life, from working in Iraq then becoming a minister for the Oman government, and the achievement of being the first non-Arab to cross the Rub Al Khali, Thomas has been eclipsed in fame by his contemporaries. Reading his correspondence with the British Raj bureaucracy, it is quite possible that he resented the restrictions put on him. Following his request put to British regional officials for their permission for him to write column for a newspaper, he was advised that each piece should be present to the British Political Agent in Muscat . Thomas replied that he regretted causing them a waste of paper and withdrew his request, suggest his irritation at the least.

After his crossing of the Rub Al Khali which was the subject of the book 'Arabia Felix', there was some correspondence about awarding him a knighthood as suggested to the British Prime Minister Ramsay MacDonald, by an un-named government Minister. In May 1931 the Viceroy of India, the Earl of Willingdon, on the advice of the Persian Gulf Resident (this term and Political Resident were used interchangeably in the region for the same position), advised the Prime Minister that it was to be 'deprecated'. Key reasons given were Thomas's 'deceptive' organisation of the Rub Al Khali crossing; though when this was planned earlier in the year by Thomas it would have been made during his holiday at the end of his 5 year contract and before the start of his expected additional 3 years employment, not at the termination of his employment by Britain. Additionally, his 'lax' handling of the Sultanate's finances was mentioned, noting that 'he has taken little interest in his work'. No mention was made of his singular achievement in Musandam or indeed that both he and the Sultan were subject to a chain of command stretching through various levels of British administration up to the Viceroy of India. It's clear that the establishment, after declining offering him any honour connected with the crossing of the Rub Al Khali, would have been unlikely to enhance his reputation as an explorer at all.

It is often assumed Wilfred Thesiger was the first non-Arab to cross the Rub Al Khali desert, despite doing so over a decade after Thomas and relying on the very Bedouin who Thomas used to guide him for the crossing. Indeed, the areas Thesiger subsequently travelled within Iraq overlapped with Thomas's administrative area and Thesiger dealt with the son of a Shaikh who was a prominent character in Thomas's book Alarms and Excursions. Harry St John Philby who had a career that in many respects was similar to the career of Thomas, working in Iraq and becoming closely associated with the ruler of Saudi Arabia, King Abdul-Aziz, but unlike Thomas has been the subject of a biography and widespread interest. Perhaps the most notable person whose fame eclipsed Thomas is T.E. Lawrence (Lawrence of Arabia) with his remarkable media presence. Lawrence was chosen to write the forward to Arabia Felix precisely because of this fame; though perversely he did so under the pseudonym T.E.S. (Thomas Edward Shaw).

Bertram Thomas was born on 13 June 1892 in a large village, Pill, near Bristol the city and port on the River Avon in Somerset western England. A rail line, between a new port for Bristol at Portishead west of Pill (on the south bank of the River Avon) and the city to the east, served the village. The adjacent port of Avonmouth on the north bank of the Avon made the area of Pill ideal for sailors and workers at these ports, and the village became well known for the mariners living there. Bertram Thomas's father, William, a master mariner who worked as a pilot (as did many of his family), lived at Avon Villa, 5 Springfield Road in Pill, one of a row of modest houses near the village centre.

When Bertram Thomas was 16 his father died, leaving his widow with five children. Enabling his mother, Eliza, and his siblings to remain living in Avon Villa, Thomas started working at the Post

Office the same year. As with so many men in Europe, the 1st World War changed his life. Thomas joined the North Somerset Yeomanry serving in Belgium, 1914-15. He then was posted with 4th Battalion Prince Albert's (Somerset Light Infantry) to Iraq, the start of 34 years association with the Arab world.

In origin, this regiment was founded during the reign of the British King James II in 1685. The rapid growth in the British military for the 1st World War also increased the size of Prince Albert's (Somerset Light Infantry) to 18 battalions. After the Ottoman Empire sided with the German Empire, Britain, through the British Raj in India, invaded Ottoman ruled Iraq with large numbers of Indian troops involved. After the major Ottoman victory against Britain in the January 1916 Siege of Kut in central Iraq, and a series of connected British military failures in the country, a wholesale reorganisation of Britain's military in Iraq was undertaken. They were to be overseen from London, rather than India, with new Generals and after the death or wounding of 23,000 men and capture of 13,000 by the Ottoman's at Kut, new forces were required.

The 4th Battalion Prince Albert's was originally based in India from 1914 and its repositioning into Iraq was when Thomas joined it; he became one of some 150,000 British troops in the country. Britain eventually overwhelmed the Ottoman forces and occupied Baghdad in March 1917. At the end of the 1st World War the number of soldiers were substantially reduced, however Britain then had a new role in Iraq, that of the League of Nations mandatory power.

In spring 1918 Thomas became part of the administration of the British Mandate of Iraq. Arnold Wilson, who wrote the preface to Alarms and Excursions, was the Civil Commissioner for Iraq and also acting Persian Gulf Resident (the regional governor within the British India Raj). Wilson however had an approach at odds with the growing attitude in London, which was that Iraq should become independent. A revolt in Iraq during 1920, described in Alarms and Excursions, was partly a result of Wilson's methods, following which Wilson was removed from his job.

Thomas eventually became Assistant Political Officer (a local governor) at Al Shatrah, an Ottoman-era town in the southern Iraq marshes, which are formed by the Euphrates and Tigris rivers. The town was a key centre for the al-Muntafiq tribe, Iraq's largest and most influential Iraqi Shia tribe. Small numbers from the Jewish and Mandean (monotheistic Gnostic religion) communities also inhabited the area. Thomas was not only the political administrator for the town and its surrounds, but the policeman and judge, an unenviable situation for the only British representative in the area. The previous Ottoman practice of hearing court cases was in the imperial power's language, Thomas heard all his cases in Arabic, testimony to his fluency in the language. Remarkably during the 'Iraqi Revolt' between May–October 1920 which was widespread against British rule, his district did not rise against the administration, therefore his official role can be considered a success.

For a time Thomas lived in the same Baghdad compound as Gertrude Bell, attending various events with her and others. Despite Thomas being an official in the country, the book Alarms and Excursions does not cover the next key event in Iraqi history, the installation of King Faisal as King of Iraq in August 1921. Thomas's abilities were however recognised with the award of an O.B.E. He then transferred to Trans-Jordan in 1922 as Assistant British Representative. He was a rising part of the British administration in the Middle East, his next position was confirmation of their confidence in him; it would be life changing for him.

A general slump of trade in the Arabian Sea region in the early 1920s impacted custom's revenue in Muscat and Oman. Customs revenue was the chief income source for the finances of the ruler, Sultan Taimur. The market for Oman's dates in India also dropped, which compounded the drop in state income. An assumption, by some British officials, was that the State would be bankrupt in 1924. General friction between Sultan Taimur and British officials revolved around finances, especially a subsidy paid directly to him by India. Against all this was a consideration of Britain withdrawing its active involvement in Oman, and effectively making the state rule itself independently.

The first British contact with Oman dates to AD1613 when a ship, the Expedition, anchored off Dhufar, southern Oman, with an ambassador from King James I (IV) to Persia, Sir Thomas Powell. A treaty with the English East India Company was signed in AD1646 by Philip Wylde with Oman's ruler, Imam Nasir bin Murshid Al Yarubi. This gave the English exclusive trading rights and religious freedom along with extraterritorial jurisdiction, and additionally the exclusion of any other Christian nation to have supply rights at Sohar which at the time was the principal Arab port in northern Oman. Further treaties were concluded between Oman and Britain over the decades, however the most momentous event in the relationship was not directly between Oman & Britain but came with the death of Oman's Sultan Said bin Sultan Al Said. He had ruled Oman its colony Zanzibar, and their various dependencies. An agreement, supported by Britain, between two sons of Sultan Said bin Sultan formalised the separation of these two regions, with one son becoming ruler of Zanzibar and its dependencies which included coastal East Africa and another ruler of Oman and its dependencies that included Gwadar in Pakistan. With the stroke of a pen, Oman was separated from its wealthier former colony and from that date became increasingly reliant on Britain for financial, political and military support.

This reliant relationship between Oman and Britain was thrown into sharp focus in 1920, when the Treaty of Seeb, an agreement between Sultan Taimur and an independently minded religious leader, Imam Salim ibn Rashid al-Kharusi, was signed. The Imam's supporters controlled the northern mountain regions including Al Jabal Al Akhdar southwest of Muscat. This area, noted in The Times 18 September 1913, had been in revolt against the Sultan's rule for several years. The 1st World War had impeded any general support Britain might be able to offer to Sultan Taimur however, in general there was a disinclination to become militarily involved in Oman, and this policy continued after the war. The Treaty of Seeb was directly negotiated between the Imam's representatives and the British Political Agent Ronald Wingate, Sultan Taimur being in India. The treaty agreed that the Imam could rule in the mountain areas under his control and the Sultan in the coastal and others areas under his control but that only the Sultan would conduct the foreign relations of either side, which were in any case only through Britain.

Sultan Taimur bin Faisal Al Said, who Thomas would be working for, became the ruler of Muscat and Oman in 1913 after his father Sultan Faisal bin Turki died. Sultan Faisal had become increasingly reliant on Britain for income, and both internal and external security; a state of affairs that continued after the accession of 27-year-old Sultan Taimur. The relationship between the two countries was clearly not one between two independent states.

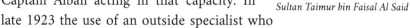

Sultan Taimur bin Faisal Al Said

From 1922 Britain had attempted to employ a person as Financial and Military advisor to the Sultan with a Captain Alban acting in that capacity. In late 1923 the use of an outside specialist who had worked in Bahrain was being considered. He was unable to take up the offer.

In March 1924, Sultan Taimur made it clear to Lieut Col A.P. Trevor, Political Resident in the Persian Gulf, that he had 'no suitable person in the State to advise him in reforming the administration'. The Sultan 'wanted to get an Englishman who would advise him'.

Reginald Graham Hinde, the British Political Agent (a form of British ambassador but here also power behind the throne) in Muscat, started a search for a financial adviser/minister for the Sultanate of Muscat and Oman and its ruler Sultan Taimur on 17 March 1924. He noted that Sultan Taimur hoped to interview the applicant in Dehra Dun, the north Indian summer resort, during June. A person under 40, who had experience in Egypt or Iraq was preferred and fluency in Arabic was essential. The salary would be Indian Rupees (INR) 1,500 a month, rising by INR100 annually (INR10 – 15 to GBP1 appx), with an annual holiday of one month and furnished accommodation.

Other people, including H.M. Monk, collector of customs at Basra, were considered but for various reasons were not suitable. However, on 24 May, Sir Arnold Wilson, a senior official in Iraq, 'depreciated' Monk and highly recommended Bertram Thomas, Assistant British Representative in Trans-Jordan. Thomas's fluent knowledge of Arabic was noted, and it was stated that 'no one can compare with him for knowledge of the revenue business'. Wilson also noted that Thomas had impressed the Emir of Trans-Jordan, Abdullah bin Al-Hussein, and his father, King Hussain bin Ali (of the Hejaz).

Thomas hand-wrote a letter to Francis Bellville Prideaux, the new Persian Gulf Resident, on 26 May that he was interested in the position. Prideaux set his recruitment in motion on 6 June. Thomas arrived in Basra Iraq from Trans-Jordan on 2 July and by 11 July, had broadly agreed his contract after meeting with Hinde in Srinagar, India. Thomas wished to start in September. He left for Bombay on 27 July to meet Sultan Taimur at the Taj Mahal Hotel with Hinde. The meeting was a success, and on 30 July, the Sultan confirmed his wish that Thomas was appointed, in effect from September. However, there was one more hurdle, Prideaux the Persian Gulf Resident also needed to approve Thomas's appointment. So Thomas sailed on either the Vasna or Varsova (he named it Varsova, Hinde called the ship Vasna) to meet Prideaux at Bushire, under the misunderstanding that a meeting would be possible around 6 August. When Thomas arrived, Prideaux advised him a meeting was not possible; indeed Prideaux was still corresponding with an alternative candidate, Monk, as late as 21 August. On 24 August Hinde, requested by Sultan Taimur, contacted Prideaux regarding a decision. By 6 September, the most senior British official in Trans-Jordan enquired through the British government's Secretary of State for the Colonies in London to Prideaux about the situation. The decision was made by 24 September 1924 that Thomas would be appointed from 1 April 1925, and both the Political Agent in Muscat and the Secretary of State in London were advised. The government in London was asked to contact the authorities in Trans-Jordan. Thomas accepted the offer on 2 October, having already assumed that his application was unsuccessful and therefore had sent his travelling expenses claim on 12 September.

The new British Political Agent Charles Gilbert Crosthwaite asked for confirmation of Thomas's appointment on 7 December. Bertram Thomas planned to leave London, where he was staying, on 27 February 1925, arriving in Bombay on 23 March and berthing in Muscat on 1 April (he actually arrived on 2 April). His accommodation was to be a 'comparatively', new house, in Muscat about 80 meters behind the British seafront 'embassy' and close to the home of the new British Political Agent Charles Gilbert Crosthwaite. Both embassy and Thomas's house, Bait Kharajiyah, were demolished in 2005, and the new guest palace in Muscat lies over their location. The only thing missing from Thomas's new home was its furniture. This was purchased in Bombay, the shipment included cutlery and a bed, the allowance was given at INR4,000. Thomas's draft contract was drawn up and initialled by him and sent for various approvals on 14 April 1925.

Thomas presented a comprehensive Six Month Financial Report (1 January - 30 June 1925) on 23 July. This report was forwarded by Crosthwaite, then Persian Gulf Resident, for the attention of the Foreign Secretary to the Government of India. Thomas's employment contract was agreed and signed by Sultan Taimur, Captain Alban, the Political Agent in Muscat and Bertram Thomas, dated 23 July 1925.

Thomas continued to draw up financial reports, for approval by the British Political Agent, with Budget Estimates dated 6 December 1925 and other reports produced to schedule after that.

Muscat is a coastal town hemmed by arid mountains, on one of a series of sea bays including its own and a larger one at the nearby town of Mutrah. The town walls of Muscat secured it and enabled some control over the comings and goings of people. The Sultan's palace and adjacent British Political Agent's building (the embassy) dominated the seafront. On either side of the harbour two crumbling Portuguese forts offered some semblance of power. Muscat had changed little for a century, there was no road connection between Muscat and Mutrah or any other farther location, though one was constructed in 1927 (it remained unpaved until 1962). In its heyday, 70 years earlier, Muscat was by far the most important port in the north Arabian Sea, however trade had long ago moved to other ports in the Arabian Gulf.

Thomas was clearly unused to the bureaucracy his role in Muscat entailed. He sent a letter to Sir Arnold Wilson the former administrator in Baghdad, now the manager of the Anglo-Persian Oil Company's Middle Eastern operation, and Thomas sped up delivery by using the British official delivery service. The letter was returned to Muscat on 12 August 1925 attached to a letter from a secretary at the Persian Gulf Residency in Bushire to Reginald Alban, the Political Agent in Muscat with an official request that all such letters be sent through the Political Agent. A personal covering letter by Charles Crosthwaite, who had worked in Muscat and who was now in Bushire, to Alban was also sent, noting that Thomas is 'now apt to forget his own place in the scheme of things'. Wilson subsequently wrote the preface to Alarms and Excursions in Arabia. Later in the year, when Thomas was approached to be a part-time newspaper correspondent in Oman, he asked permission from the Persian Gulf Resident in Bushire to undertake the work. The approval was granted on 17 September 1925, subject to any written articles being shown to the Political Agent in

Muscat. Thomas withdrew his request on 20 October and noted he regretted causing a 'waste of the Political Resident's (Persian Gulf Resident's) time and stationery'.

Thomas, however, did adapt to his place in the scheme of things and adapted them to his ambitions.

Francis Bellville Prideaux, the Persian Gulf Resident wrote, between February and April 1926, to the Secretary to the Government of India in the Foreign and Political Department. He noted that the Sultan of Muscat wishes Mr B.S. Thomas, at present Financial Adviser to the State, to be recognised as a member of his Council of Ministers (Prideaux wrote State Council), and to be referred to in correspondence as 'Wazir (Minister)', not Mr. In Prideaux's letter, consideration was given to the requirement for official gun salutes by British government vessels to members of the Council of Ministers in the absence of the Sultan. It was noted that 'Mr Thomas should not be the minister in question can definitely safeguarded against'. Prideaux concluded by writing 'In these circumstances I recommend that the Sultan's request be agreed to'. A letter dated 18 June from Prideaux to the Secretary to the Government of India in the Foreign and Political Department, said 'In my opinion no objection exists at the present time to the Sultan's request about Mr Thomas. This officer understands his position thoroughly and, so far, has executed his duties to the entire satisfaction of all parties in Muscat'. The point about gun salutes was again emphasised in an additional letter on 18 July, which concluded by agreeing to the Sultan's request. The British Consulate and Political Agency confirmed this on 22 July, 'subject to the condition that in no case should Mr Thomas alone pay an official visit to a British Government vessel'. There were no restrictions on his accompanying any other member of the Council of Ministers. Was there concern that receipt of a gun-salute would allow Thomas to rise above his place in the scheme of things.

Thomas seems to have won widespread approval with the work he did. Barrett, the new Political Agent in Muscat, wrote on 5 August 1926 that 'The finances of the Muscat State have been passing through a time of depression, and it is due to the unceasing vigilance of Mr Thomas that expenditure has not exceeded revenue to a much larger extent than has been the case'.

Not withstanding his role as finance minister, Thomas's pleasure does seem to have been exploration of the country. In Alarms and Excursions in Arabia he wrote 'But the bondage of an office stool …. was less to my liking than the comparatively free life — most of it spent in the saddle — of a District Political Officer'. In 1926, he travelled along the coast northwest from Muscat and, from this coast, cut through the mountains to The Gulf coast town of Sharjah, in what was then termed 'Trucial Oman'.

Thomas had planned his Rub Al Khali crossing for several years and made clear his desire to Sultan Taimur by 1926. In winter 1927-28, he travelled from Suwaiah, south of Sur Oman, down the coast to Salala. He had to negotiate safe passage from the major tribes on his route, and include within his team *rabias* (a tribesman of an area to act as protector) along the way and moving south towards Salala obtained three sets of replacement fresh camels and their bedouin owners at Bani bu Ali, Khaluf and Wadi Ainain.

Later during 1928 he had visited Kuwait and met Harold Dickson whom he had known from Iraq and was previously British Political Agent in Kuwait, but was then working with the Kuwait Oil Company. According to Wilfred Thesiger, recounted in 1992, following his meeting with Dickson in Kuwait, Dickson had told Thomas that he (Dickson) planned to cross the Empty Quarter & Thomas replied: 'I should consider that a most unfriendly action. I intend to cross the Empty Quarter and live the rest of my life on the proceeds'. Thesiger's negative recollection of his own conversation with Dickson may have been coloured by Thomas having achieved the first crossing, and Thesiger relying not only the Bedouin who Thomas had recruited but also on Thomas's own maps. These maps were so detailed that Thesiger could successfully plot a route to a water well on his journeys in the Rub Al Khali by merely relying on the map.

Visiting Dhufar in January 1930 with Sultan Taimur Al Said, the two now being on very friendly terms, the Sultan recommended Thomas to key shaikhs. He then left Salala on what was an exploratory journey in Dhufar with 40 camels and a total of 31 people. They included 25 Bedouin from the Bait Kathir, Ar Rashid and Bait Imani tribes who would be a key to his expected travel into the Rub Al Khali later in the year. The party ascended the well-vegetated Jabal Qara before descending through arid foothills to travel north, along the eastern edge of the sands of the Rub Al Khali.

In January 1930 the leader of the main tribe of Musandam, a region in the north of Oman on the Strait of Hormuz, sent a letter to the Council of Ministers, announcing that the region was independent from the Sultan. Thomas then played a substantial, if not critical, role in Musandam remaining part of the Sultanate. After unsuccessful negotiation, by Thomas on his arrival in Musandam, with rebellious inhabitants in Musandam a short naval bombardment, by British naval ships, was organised in April; its success was detailed in his book Alarms and Excursions in Arabia.

Both Bertram Thomas and Sultan Taimur had wished that Thomas would remain in his position for a further three years after his five-year contract ended (in April 1930) with Sultan Taimur writing to the British Political Agent in Muscat during March 1930 after his Dhufar trip. However, in May the Persian Gulf Resident at Bushire was looking for a replacement for Thomas, the purpose to save INR500. In July, Stuart Hedgcock had applied for the position. Hedgcock had worked in the British political service Iraq for over 12 years, joining as Thomas had done after the 1st World War. Though having obviously stayed after April 1930, in anticipation of his employment being extended, Thomas would be unemployed on Hedgcock's arrival. On 3 October 1930 Thomas wrote detailing that he would leave his employment on 1 January 1931. The Persian Gulf Resident in Bushire wrote to the British Political Agent in Muscat that Stuart Hedgcock, who Thomas must have known from Iraq, should arrive in the last week of December. Thomas left Muscat for Salala on the night of 4 October. On 30 November Thomas wrote from Salala, to the Political Agent in Muscat, that the Council of Ministers had agreed an unpaid leave of absence from 1-31 December and that 'This will bring an easement to the Muscat Treasury of INR2,000 so I hope you will have no objection'. The letter arrived in Muscat on 18 December, Thomas by then was approaching Shisur on the edge of the Rub Al Khali.

While crossing the desert with his guides, Thomas made little attempt to reduce the differences between him and the Omani's. He used a Bikaner-pattern saddle, a camel saddle used by soldiers from the British Raj. A heavy piece of equipment, it sat over the camel's hump and was far less practical on this journey compared to the light south Arabian style that was placed behind the hump. As he noted, it meant that he rode a different camel almost daily to rest a camel after carrying both him and the saddle. Under his turban he wore a shallow flying helmet with the brim removed, though unfortunately he gave no indication the benefit of using it. Throughout the journey Thomas was accompanied by his servant Muhammad, this alone must have created a barrier between him and the Bedouin he relied on. Muhammad must however been required as Thomas travelled with what may have been enough scientific equipment to require five pack camels, indeed the expedition seemed to have been partly organised to support Thomas in collecting plant and animal specimens, enabling him to create a report to scientific bodies in London. In this he achieved some success, for a species of lizard, *abu qursh*, 'the father of the dollar,' was new to science and is now named in his honour *Uromastyx thomasi*. Possibly the most separating aspect of his behaviour was that he travelled 'with head callipers to make and record skull measurements, for such measurements are vital to anthropologists', he was practicing the now obsolete & discredited practice of craniofacial anthropometry. This must have been a degrading experience for the people whose skulls he measured as he also included fairly detailed physical measurement and recording of the subject.

Despite all these separating habits the crossing itself was not only remarkable in itself, it illustrated his ability to maintain the cohesion and loyalty of his group. Thomas was travelling with a group of independent people, who hardly acknowledged any authority of the Sultan of Muscat and Oman, let alone being in thrall to a strange Englishman travelling with them. Wilfred Thesiger made use of broadly the same guides over a decade later.

The route of the journey took the party north from Salala and over the leafy Jabal Qara mountains. They then tracked northwest, over the rocky plain, past Shisur and into the dunes of the Rub Al Khali at Shanna. From there it was a journey north, through the dune-fields until reaching the Sabkhat al Manasir, the water-logged sand-flats which are coated with a salt crust, near the Qatar peninsula.

Thomas succeeded in his attempt to become the first non-Arab to cross the Rub Al Khali on 5 February 1931, and the journey forms a major part of this book 'Arabia Felix'. After time spent in Doha Qatar, Thomas landed in Bahrain on 22 February 1931 and returned to Muscat, arriving 7 March, to then depart Oman forever.

As a postscript to Thomas's departure from Muscat, Hedgcock, the replacement as Financial Advisor to Thomas, resigned in June 1931. Sultan Taimur, after many years of expressing his wish to abdicate did so on 10 February 1932.

Alarms and Excursions, in Arabia, Thomas's first book, was published in 1931; Arabia Felix, the second, was published in 1932 and included a dedication to Sir Arnold Wilson.

After leaving Oman, Thomas gave a number of talks on Arabia in Canada and the U.S.A., as well as Britain and published papers on Arabia. He married Bessie Hoile in London July 1933 with a daughter, Elizabeth, born in September 1934.

Thomas completed a PhD thesis at Cambridge University in 1935 "The Geography and Ethnology of Unknown South Arabia".

After the outbreak of the Second World War, he served for a time as public relations officer in Bahrain (1942- 43), and in 1944 became director of the Middle East Centre of Arabic Studies, of which he was the effective founder, first in Palestine and later in Lebanon.

Bertram Thomas died in Cairo, 27 December 1950 and was buried in a churchyard at Pill, not far from his childhood home.

ARABIA FELIX

ACROSS THE EMPTY QUARTER OF ARABIA

by BERTRAM THOMAS

O.B.E. [Mil.]; formerly Wazir to H.H. the Sultan of Muscat and Oman, sometime Political Officer in Iraq, and Assistant British Representative in Trans-Jordan. Founder's Medallist of the Royal Geographical Society; Burton Memorial Medallist of the Royal Asiatic Society; Gold Medallist of the Geographical Society of Antwerp; and Cullum Gold Medal of the American Geographical Society

WITH A FOREWORD BY

T. E. LAWRENCE (T.E.S.)
FIRST PUBLISHED 1932

FOREWORD - T.E. SHAW

Thomas shocked me when he asked for a foreword to his great journey-book, not because introductions put me off (he may as reasonably enjoy them, perhaps) but because he had recourse to me. It took some while to think out so strange a lapse.

T E Lawrence (left of the Amir's shoulder) at Versailles with Amir Faisal

You see, in my day there were real Arabian veterans. Upon each return from the East I would repair to Doughty, a looming giant, white with eighty years, headed and bearded like some renaissance Isaiah. Doughty seemed a past world, in himself; and after him I would visit Wilfrid Blunt. An Arab mare drew Blunt's visitors deep within a Sussex wood to his quarried house, stone-flagged and hung with Morris tapestries. There in a great chair he sat, prepared for me like a careless work of art in well-worn Arab robes, his chiselled face framed in silvered, curling hair. Doughty's voice was a caress, his nature sweetness. Blunt was a fire yet flickering over the ashes of old fury.

Such were my Master Arabians, men of forty, fifty years ago. Hogarth and Gertrude Bell, by twenty years of patient study, had won some reputation, too; and there were promising young officers, Shakespear and Leachman, with a political, Wyman Bury, beginning well. To aspire Arabian-wise, then, was no light, quick ambition.

They are all gone, those great ones. The two poets were full of years and in high honour. Naturally they died. The war burdened Hogarth and Gertrude Bell with political responsibilities. They gave themselves wholly, saw their work complete and then passed. The three younger men died of their duty, directly; and that is why Thomas must come down to me.

I suppose no new Sixth Former can help feeling how much his year falls short of the great fellows there when he joined the school. But can the sorry little crowd of us to-day be in the tradition, even? I fear not. Of course the mere wishing to be an Arabian betrays the roots of a quirk; but our predecessors' was a larger day, in which the seeing Arabia was an end in itself. They just wrote a wander-book and the great peninsula made their prose significant. (Incidentally, the readable Arabian books are all in English, bar one; Jews, Swiss, Irishmen and What- nots having conspired to help the Englishmen write them. There are some German books of too-sober learning and one Dutch.) Its deserts cleaned or enriched Doughty's pen and Palgrave's, Burckhardt's and Blunt's, helped Raunkiaer with his Kuweit, Burton and Wavell in their pilgrimages, and Bury amongst his sun-struck Yemeni hamlets.

Our feebler selves dare not be Arabians for Arabia's sake - none of us save Rutter, I think, and how good, how classical, his book! The rest must frame excuses for travelling. One will fix latitudes, the silly things, another collect plants or insects (not to eat, but to bring home), a third make war, which is coals to Newcastle. We fritter our allegiances and loyalties.

Inevitable, of course, that these impurities should come. As pools shrink they stench. Raleigh could hearten my ancestor - 'Cozen, we know but the hand's-breadth of our world' - but since him Arctic and Antarctic, the wastes of Asia and Africa, the forests of America have yielded their secrets. Last year I could have retorted — 'There is but a hand's-breadth we do not know' - thinking of that virgin Rub Al

Khali, the last unwritten plot of earth big enough for a sizable man's turning in twice or thrice about, before he couches. However, only these few paragraphs of mine now stand between appetite and the tale of its conquest. To-day we know the whole earth. Would-be wandering youth will go unsatisfied till a winged generation lands on the next planet.

Few men are able to close an epoch. We cannot know the first man who walked the inviolate earth for newness' sake: but Thomas is the last; and he did his journey in the antique way, by pain of his camel's legs, single-handed, at his own time and cost. He might have flown an aeroplane, sat in a car or rolled over in a tank. Instead he has snatched, at the twenty-third hour, feet's last victory and set us free. Everything having been once done in the slowest fashion we can concentrate upon speed, amplifying the eye of the tortoise by the hare's and the bird's. All honour to Thomas. The Royal Geographical Society itself forgives, bemedals its supersessor ... also he has an O.B.E.

I will not say how much I like this book, lest Jonathan C. dig out the odd, sentence for his blurb. Thomas let me read the, draft, and I then did my best to comment usefully; once remarking that the tale was good enough for his journey - no faint judgment, set against what I think the finest thing in Arabian exploration. As he tells it, the achievement may read easy, because, he is a master of every desert art. Here once more is the compleat Arabian traveller enshrined. Not twice but twenty times his tiniest touches set me remembering that wide land which I liked so much, twenty years ago, and hoped never to feel again. Thence, I suppose, the reason of my writing him this useless foreword; that and my understanding of his risks. Only by favour of a propitious season could this very rare individual, after infinite care and tact in preparation, have gambled his life upon the crowning solidarity which the desert owes to Ibn Saud, and won through. Thomas is as fortunate as deserving. T. E. S.

PREFACE

In the preparation of this book I have made no attempt to collate the scanty scientific observations of earlier travellers in adjoining regions which may, or may not, have some scientific bearing upon the problems I have touched upon. To have done so, indeed, would have been beyond the scope of a personal record. Hence the reader is spared an impressive bibliography. My endeavour has been to set forth as a straightforward narrative the things that I saw and heard, and the experiences that befell me. If in the fulfilment of that task I have fallen short of standards that have been set me by my predecessors in the sphere of Arabian travel, I would plead that the narrative has been written amongst many other preoccupations in the few months since my return from Arabia. Where, in recording conversations and folk stories, Arabic, Mahri or Shahari words are used, I have transliterated them in accordance with the local dialects in which they were spoken, and have eschewed the Arabic lexicon. shaikh

I have to thank the Royal Geographical Society for much assistance in collating my astronomical observations on this and on previous journeys, and in the preparation of the map which accompanies this volume; and especially the President, Admiral Sir William

Goodenough, the Secretary, Mr. A. R. Hinks, and the Map Curator, Mr. A. S. Reeves.

The laborious task of reading the manuscript has been undertaken by friends — Aircraftman T. E. Shaw (Colonel Lawrence), who has been so good as to contribute a foreword; Professor H. A. R. Gibb, to whom I am also grateful for a number of valuable comments and suggestions; Mr. R. W. Bullard, H.B.M.'s Consul-General at Leningrad and formerly H.B.M.'s Consul at Jeddah, and Sir Arnold Wilson, my former chief in Mesopotamia. But for their advice and help it would not have been possible for me to have passed this book through the press without considerable delay.

BERTRAM THOMAS
East India United Service Club,
St James's Square,
12th December 1931.

INTRODUCTION

Arabia Felix! Strange that the epithet 'Happy' should grace a part of the earth's surface, most of it barren wilderness where, since the dawn of history, man has ever been at war with his environment and his neighbour. Yet there can be no mistaking the classical geographers. To Strabo, Pliny, and Ptolemy, the term Arabia Felix served for the entire peninsula south of the Syrian desert (Arabia Deserta) and the mountains about Sinai (Arabia Petraea). True, the term consorts ill with the horrid wastes of Rub Al Khali that form no small part of Arabia, but there lies in the central south, bordering the Indian Ocean, a land at once of rare physical loveliness and of ancient fame. If there be any region in Arabia entitled to the epithet 'Happy,' other than the Yemen, whose glories were well known to the ancients, it is this province of Dhufar, an Arcadia of luxuriant forests that clothe steep mountains overlooking the sea, of perennial streams and sunny meadows, of wide vistas and verdant glades. Here, according to the writer of Genesis, Jehovah had set the limit of the known world 'as thou goest east unto Mount Sephar'; hither came the ancient Egyptians for frankincense to embalm their sacred Pharaohs; here, may be, were hewed the pillars of Solo- mon's Temple, if indeed Dhufar be not the site of

Ophir itself, and the traditional market for ivory and peacocks' feathers.

I have attempted to set down in the pages that follow a narrative of my recent camel journey across Rub Al Khali, and of my researches in this fair province of Dhufar, the gateway of that journey, and to me the true Arabia Felix of to-day.

The virgin Rub Al Khali, the Great Southern Desert! To have laboured in Arabia is to have tasted inevitably of her seduction, and six years ago when I left the Administration of Trans-Jordan for the Court of Muscat and Oman I already cherished secret dreams. The remote recesses of the earth, Arctic and Antarctic, the sources of the Amazon, and the vast inner spaces of Asia and Africa, have one by one yielded their secrets to man's curiosity, until by a strange chance the Rub Al Khali remained almost the last considerable terra incognita which is surprising considering the great antiquity of settled Arabia, the border lands of which touched the early civilisations of Egypt and Babylonia.

Yet Arabia has remained the forbidden land. Through- out the centuries scarce twenty European explorers have been able usefully to penetrate to her inhospitable heart. For this there are two main reasons. First, lack of rain and the merciless heat of the Arabian desert permit of but scattered and semi-barbarous nomad societies, which are at such perpetual war that, even for themselves, life is insecure. Secondly, the religion of these desert men, at least in practice, is fanatical and exclusive. From time to time they hold it virtuous to enforce Islam with the sword. In Arabia proper all European visitors have been individual men, and only once in all her history, and that in Roman times, has she — the then supposed Eldorado — excited the cupidity of European invaders, so that among her inhabitants, left so severely to themselves, insularity, bigotry, and intolerance are indigenous growths with a long pedigree. Hence an area equal to half the superficies of Europe had remained a blank on our maps.

It had fascinated Richard Burton, who in 1852 offered his services to the Royal Geographical Society for the purpose of what he termed 'removing that opprobrium to modern adventure,' but he succumbed to official obstruction and never put his plans to the test. I enjoyed advantages. Thirteen years of post-war service in various political capacities on three sides of Arabia enabled me to acquire a peculiar knowledge of tribal dialects and of Arab ways, and to become acclimatised. I had addressed myself for years past to two problems - how to find an avenue of approach to the interior and how to cultivate the tribes there. As a Minister of the Muscat and Oman Council of Ministers, my name came to be known throughout south- east Arabia; it was because I was the Sultan's Wazir and because of the cordial relations existing between the Ruler and myself that I was brought into personal touch with the most influential Arabs of that part. Hence a general attitude of tolerance towards me, an Englishman and a Christian, without which I could never have dreamt of moving off the beaten track.

Then, too, I knew the mind of authority and so avoided the pitfall of seeking permission for my designs. Was not the lesson of Burton before me? The British official attitude, with which, let me add, I am in general sympathy, is, in view of the anarchy that normally prevails in Desert Arabia, inimical to exploration. The good official must avoid responsibility and commitments, and to learn of, and not forbid, an expedition implies tacit authorisation. So my plans were conceived in darkness, my journeys heralded only by my disappearances, paid for by myself and executed under my own auspices. Throughout my service in Muscat I elected to spend my summers there, to save my local leave (intended by authority to be spent in India to escape the heat of Muscat), for exploration of Arabia during the winter, the only time when it is physically possible.

In this way piece by piece I began to explore and map the Rub Al Khali. In the winter of 1927-28 I made a 600-mile camel journey through the southern borderlands from the toe of Arabia nearest India to Dhufar; in 1929-30 I explored the steppe for 200 miles north of Dhufar to the edge of the sands. On these occasions I dressed as a Badu, spoke nothing but the local dialect, lived as one of the people, and eschewed tobacco and alcohol to win a reputation for orthodoxy that would ultimately help me in the crossing of the Great Desert from sea to sea.

These journeys showed me the error of the common impression that this part of Arabia could be best explored by the modern means of cars and aircraft. It had been proposed that our ill-fated R.101 should fly over this unknown desert on her return journey from India. Three years earlier an enterprising American millionaire had conceived a similar plan, for which he proposed hiring an airship, and I was tentatively approached to be a member of his expedition. I was not sorry when his plan failed to mature, because my experience taught me that, useful as such transport could be in its time and place, no positive scientific results could be anticipated from it. Problems that awaited solution were the discovery of the structure and slope of South Arabia, its drainage and geological formation, and the filling in of the great empty spaces on the map; the fauna, the human inhabitants, their racial and linguistic affinities, their manners and customs, and way of life. These objectives could not in any single instance have been usefully investigated by an air survey, not a name would be added to the map, not a single fact of anthropological, zoological, or geological and few of geographical importance be established.

Also there seems something indelicate in the intrusion of Western machines into these virgin silences; a feeling not to be confused with the thrill of the unknown, bounded here by the rim of the inverted bowl of the heavens, or with the mental stimulus that comes from plans in the slow process of precarious accomplishment. But all these things count. And to one who has experienced them, who has learned to talk with his only companions for months on end - rude and unlettered brigands of the desert though they be, and to admire some of their virile qualities, the camel-back and the long marches go to make the magic of Arabia.

ARABIA

Far are the shades of Arabia,
Where the Princes ride at noon,
'Mid the verdurous vales and thickets,
Under the ghost of the moon;
And so dark is that vaulted purple
Flowers in the forest rise
And toss into blossom 'gainst the phantom stars
Pale in the noonday skies.

Sweet is the music of Arabia
In my heart, when out of dreams
I still in the thin clear mirk of dawn
Descry her gliding streams;
Hear her strange lutes on the green banks
Ring loud with the grief and delight
Of her dim-silked, dark-haired Musicians
In the brooding silence of night.

They haunt me — her lutes and her forests;
No beauty on earth I see
But shadowed with that dream recalls
Her loveliness to me:

Still eyes look coldly upon me.
Cold voices whisper and say —
'He is crazed with the spell of far Arabia,
They have stolen his wits away.'

WALTER DE LA MARE

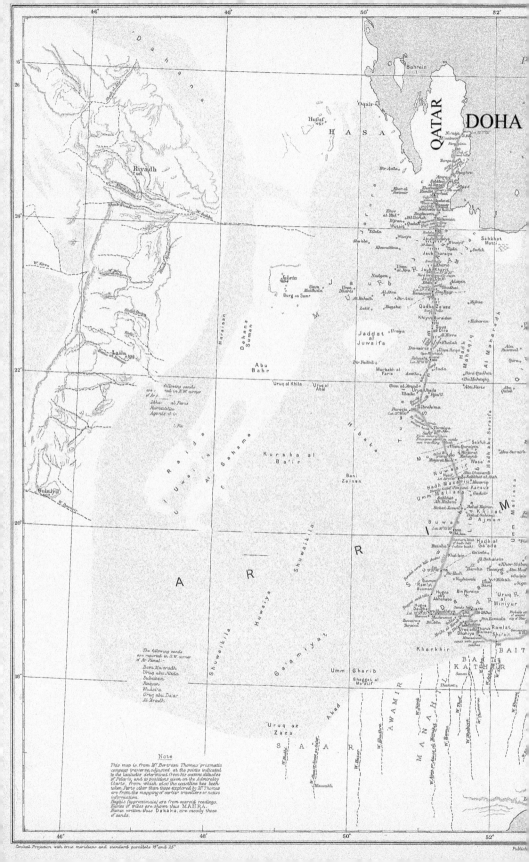

Musandam

Abu Dhabi

Sharja

TRUCIAL 'OMAN

Ramlat al
Khatam

Jabal
Hafit
5000

Dhafra

AWAMIR

AL BU
SHAMIS

Zaharont

Ibri

Halil

W. al Ain

W. Aswed

Abu Ghar
Zaraytan

DARU

Al Hamra

Soliar

Muscat

HAJAR

O

M

A

N

Turuf

Kutla

W. Batha

Sur

R. al Had

HARASIS

AFAR

Ramlat
Ghasaiwara

W. Musallim

W. Halfayn

Adam

Adaba

Bala Beni
Bu Resen

Ja'a'lan

Balad Bani
Bu Ali

YAL WAHIBA

Habil

R. Jibsh

L

Uruq bin
amaisha

Ramlat Ghafa

Ghor Naqa

Umm
as Samim

W. Rauf

Ghaifan

Sar

R. Ruwais

Da'sai

MANK

Ramlat Umm
Bakhur

Qarn as
Sahama

Raqi

Khaluf

Masira I.

Musira Channel

Ramlat Umm
at Tabul

Waterless stony plain

Dhirib

Abu Dhur

Thamilal

Abu Dhur

Maran

Labuk

Jaddat

Bughara

Sabkhat
Mijora

Sabkha

Harasis

100

J. Askalai

Gulf of Masira

Ablotan

Bughara

Ba'ida
Mandar

Al Ain

Murausdig

Ramlat
Mughshin

W. Batha

W. Bani

R. Madraka

Wadi Mughsin

W. Baghar

Suwira

Ramlat
Aradh

W. Andham

Umm
Dharta

Al Quran

W. Andam

J. Lisk

7100

Kaeir

Sauqira Bay

ARABIAN

Hanfit
1028

W. Andhh

R. Sharbitat

Dhimir
Ghara

Al Kh

KHARA

Qamr

DHUFAR

Kuria Muria Bay

R. Naeik

R. Nus

Kuria Muria
Islands

SEA

SALALA

Strait of Hormuz

PERSIA

Adam

Gulf

SIAN

1

A PROPITIOUS START AND AN EARLY CHECK

It was midnight of the 4th-5th October 1930. The little Arab port of Muscat lay asleep. Only one of its inhabitants, albeit Prince amongst them, Saiyid Sa'id bin Taimur, had, in the absence of his father the Sultan, been taken into my confidence and made privy to the activities of the beach. There, a *badan* (small country rowing boat) was hauled close inshore and my faithful servant Muhammad bore to her his master's mysterious boxes, his gun and camel saddles. I was secretly embarking on my long-cherished ambition to unveil the unknown southern Arabian desert. To-morrow, the news of my disappearance would startle the bazaar and a variety of fates would doubtless be invented for me by imaginations of Oriental fertility.

H.M.S. Cyclamen lay twinkling in the inner anchorage, and I went alongside to collect a mascot which Pemberton, her pilot, who had just been supping with me, would, he had said, leave with the 'hand' on watch. Thence my Baluchi boatmen, sworn to future secrecy, pulled on into the open sea.

Muscat harbour - with Jalali Fort and official buildings

The brilliant light of the full moon allowed immediate introduction to my mascot - it was Walter de la Mare's poem, 'Arabia' - and, of more immediate importance, I could reassure myself of the contents of the cable in my hand:

'*s.s. British Grenadier* arriving 6.0 a.m. Sunday three miles off-shore Muscat - Master.'

The dark mass of the 10,000 -ton oil tanker came looming up. A flag which I flew by arrangement did its work; I was quickly transhipped, and the British Grenadier, homeward bound, was on her course again ere four bells had struck, bearing me away from Muscat.

I planned to be landed at Dhufar half-way along the southern coast of Arabia if weather conditions at the end of this south-west monsoon season would permit, or failing that, to be dropped into the first Arab dhow we encountered. Next day the freshening wind slightly reduced our speed, and the prospect of making Salala in daylight grew doubtful. To 'stand off' all night was not to be entertained, and so it was an Arab dhow that we made for when we saw one. Her crazy little dinghy came along- side in response to our siren; Muhammad and I, dressed in Arab kit, slipped over the side and down the pilot ladder. My boxes made a precarious load, but she was equal to our demands, and carried us safely over the long undulations of the swell to the anchored dhow. The *British Grenadier* signalled 'good luck' and went forging ahead, soon to be hull-down in the grey watery solitudes where the sun had set.

The Arab captain of *Fath as Salaam*, for that was the dhow's name, shook his head when I spoke of landing; he had, in fact, quite other views. A ground swell, even in the mildest weather, runs vigorously along these gently shelving beaches, and sends huge rollers crashing inshore. A whaler or other English-built boat would surely capsize and break up, but the local *banush* (of sewn timbers), craftily handled by the fisherfolk, comes riding safely through, despite moments when it seems to stand giddily on end and one looks on apprehensively, knowing that the sea, a boiling cauldron in the vicinity, would show small mercy to a swimmer.

Mindful of my chronometers, I persuaded the captain, after much argument, to make for Risut, a sheltered bay down the coast. Two hours after the lug had been bent and hoisted, it still flapped listlessly, while the un- changing view of the white fort and mosque, midst a coco-nut grove backed by the blue Qara Mountains, which consti- tutes all that is to be seen of Dhufar from the sea, showed that we had scarcely moved one way or the other.

A playful whale helped to beguile the moments - a ponderous dark green monster that came and lay alongside us like a submarine beside its parent ship, proud to prove itself not much smaller than the '*Fath as Salam*'. It seemed to me perilously friendly as it dived just under us, to rise but a few feet away and break surface with a snort, before sinking heavily again, with a little wash and a multitude of bubbles to mark its going. Nor were our sailors unconcerned. With an eye on our dinghy, which lapped about astern of us, they kept up a fright- ening din by drumming empty kerosene tins. The wind freshened to deliver us, and by noon we came close hauled to Risut [1] where I landed.

And so into the saddle. We hugged the shore till we passed Auqad (Abkid), a small village in the plain, and thence rode along the edge of a coco-nut palm grove to make the fort of Dhufar at sunset on 8th October. Here, very tired after a sleepless twenty-four hours, I was to occupy my old room in the keep. But it was not a kindly night.

Mosquitoes were legion and a swarm of yellow hornets were building themselves a house in the rafters above: a tiny insect, too, invisible as a sandfly but not less of a torment, took toll of my blood.

Salala knew of my presence: it must not know of my plans. Secrecy was imperative. To disclose them would be to invite hostility and the news would spread abroad, as all news spreads in illiterate Arabia, with the speed of the telegraph and unauthorised accretions that would not disgrace a London evening newspaper.

Where was Sahail the Rashidi? So much for a Badu's pledged word. I had heaped riches on this member of my last year's caravan and made a secret agreement that he should meet me at Salala in this mid moon of *Rabi'a al Awwal* with a camel party to take me into the great sands. He had sworn that only death would prevent his coming. Devious enquiries showed that he had not been heard of in Dhufar since he had gone off to his tribe with the two hundred dollars and a dagger - immense fortune - I had secretly given him then. If this and the promise of more had failed to bring him to fulfil a solemn promise I despaired of my prospects. The Rashid, to which he belonged, is the only genuine tribe of the southern sands, and without their assistance any dream of a crossing were vain.

The desert news in Dhufar was bad. War! The Rashid and the Sa'ar were fighting, the former my hoped-for friends, the latter their powerful hereditary enemies of the northern Hadhramaut - an ancient blood-feud. It followed that the immediate hinterland was menaced by raiders or worse. It seemed that Sahail, with the best of intentions, might be unable to raise a party of his fellow-tribesmen to run the gauntlet to the coast for me. His tribe would either be engaged in offensive operations in the Hadhramaut or have withdrawn themselves for refuge into the depths of the sands. Here was a deadlock. For me the door to the sands seemed bolted and barred.

I could see no way out. Two Rashidi tribesmen, Ma'yuf and Khuwaitim, had come to Dhufar for the frankincense harvest, and I sent for them, for though without camels and out of touch with the tribe, they might yet be knowledgeable. However, it is difficult to gain an Arab's confidence without giving him yours, and it would have been perilous to show my hand prematurely, so we conferred daily for some days till I gathered that the Rashid tribe might be distant a month's march anywhere from north to west, and certainly indisposed to leave their sandy sanctuary.

I should be obliged in the happiest event to arrange a separate caravan, if I could, to take me to some water-hole on the edge of the sands (there were but three possible ones) and trust to the Rashidis' ability and willingness to come there to meet me and carry me forward. But the unpleasant experience of my journey of the year before had taught me the limitations of mountain caravans, of men's alarm for themselves and their camels even when there was no war in the air. The Acting-Governor to whom I dared reveal only this part of my plans tried cajolery, but there is no compelling authority in these mountains and I detected an undercurrent of hostility that would have made it madness to embark with such allies into the desert. My ambitious plans so carefully laid and secretly cherished for the year past seemed to be utterly at an end.

Would it be safe to confide in these two Rashidis? The only hope was to inspire them with confidence and gain their loyalty by offering them the right inducement to run the risk of taking a message to their shaikh, and the right inducement to the shaikh to carry his tribe with him. It was the moment for bold courses. I unfolded my plans under their sworn oath; those plans were for the shaikh's ear only. There were to be glittering rewards. A pact was sealed. They would do it. If Allah delivered them from the Sa'ar, they would search the sands, and if they found the Rashid, they knew their mission and payment was to be by results.

Their parting remarks in true Badu vein showed what manner of men they were.

'Here, Khuwaitim,' I said, 'you have no rifle. Take this one. It is a small present for you.'

'What,' came the reply as he took it from my hand and examined it critically, 'you are not going to give me any ammunition with it?' Badu ingratitude or Badu casualness? Bounty coming to him he ascribes to the will of God. My gift of the rifle had little to do with any volition of mine; it was inevitable; it was what Allah had ordained.

The departure was postponed till after the midday prayer in the mosque. I, restless under delays already, had suggested leaving at once. They would not. 'Are we not Muslims?' retorted Khuwaitim.

And so they set off on foot to the mountains where, by a secret arrangement with an old fellow-traveller of an early journey, Salim al Tamtim, they would be furnished privily with his own best riding camels and so, none knowing, disappear into the drought-stricken desert.

They knew not when they would return. Perhaps in thirty or forty days, perhaps not at all.

If they could bring a party of men and camels from the sands well and good; if not, I must accept failure.

On so slender a thread hung the prospect of even a start to my cherished journey.

I must be resigned in any case to wait here long weeks with no very strong hopes.

2

AT DHUFAR: ANARCHY, TREACHERY AND HOSPITALITY

Below my window in the fort the palm-fringed beach shelved down to the sea. At anchor rode a dhow just arrived, eager from Basrah, with the first fresh cargo of this season's dates, announcing, by her gay bunting and firing of her muzzle-loading mortar that she was no stranger to Dhufar.

Along this seaboard the province of Dhufar [2] extends from Hadhbaram to Dharbat Ali. It consists of a massif 3000 feet high running right down to the sea on east and west, and retreating in the centre, to embrace the crescent- shaped maritime plain of Jurbaib.

Judged by Arabian standards it is a province favoured by Providence. It owes a unique climate to the 'Indian' south-west monsoon, which here makes a preliminary call and during the summer months sprinkles these mountains with a drizzling rain so that the region flows with milk and honey. Just over the mountain divide flourish the famous frankincense groves of Arabia. This precious product, sent to the temples of India, wins back rice and cloth, coffee and spices for its owner's booths, and has been the prosperity of Dhufar through the ages, though it were well not to confuse it with the Dhufar of Arrian near Sana' in the Yemen, a mistake made by Abul Fida'.

Meadows below Khiyunt

The two main settled tribes of the province are the Qara in the mountains, where they live by raising herds and the rewards of frankincense; and Al Kathir, who fish and farm and trade from villages in the plain. For the rainy months of summer when the seas are too stormy to be usable by native craft, there is a general exodus [3] from the plains to the mountains, where frankincense groves require harvesters and milk is in abundance.

Well water is plentiful, generally at a fathom's depth round the villages, and but for the paralysing hand of a wayward tribalism, artesian wells would probably make the whole plain blossom. Beneath the coco-nut groves wells, mostly served by slaves, bulls or camels, minister to fields of lucerne, sugar cane, plantains, wheat, millet, cotton and indigo. A sixteenth share of each crop must go as taxes to government, whose coffers otherwise receive only a nominal 5 per cent, share of the mountain produce. Here prevails the 'good old rule, the simple plan, that he shall take who has the power, and he shall keep who can,' and if the Sultan's writ runs strong along the coast, in the mountains it is a doubtful and variable quantity.

Ethnologically Dhufar is as much an enclave as it is geographically. Tribal tradition is one of anarchy — of long internecine strife, alternating with short periods of sporadic government. No recorded history is to be found among the natives, though I was at pains to enquire from every literate resident. But illiteracy is general, and only the old *Qadhi* could tell a coherent though disconnected story of Dhufar's past. The people, composed of warlike and rival tribes, have always found law and order irksome. They love unfettered personal liberty more than life, and glory in their hereditary wars. The alternative of an extraneously imposed authority has in the past been acceptable to them only by force, or else as the lesser evil after periods of exhaustion and, as the lessons of one generation had to be re-learned by the next, no dynasty has been able to entrench itself.

Historical landmarks are few. They begin in post-Islamic times with the ruler Muhammad bin Ahmad al Mingowi, whose ruined capital lies on the lagoon of Khor Ruri. [4] Mingowi is an ancient name that comes more readily to these people's lips than any other, and almost every ruin in the country is ascribed to him.

After him, in A.D. 1279, came Salim bin Idris al Habudhi. Driven by drought from his native Hadhramaut he put into Dhufar, first to covet, then to conquer it. In the sixteenth century rose Saif al Islam al Ghassan, a scion of Sana', whose palace was the citadel of Balid, to-day the most extensive ruins of the Dhufar plain. A hundred years of tribal anarchy was ended by a Kathiri master of the land, followed by yet another age without a name, lasting for the whole of the eighteenth century. An independent Saiyid, revered son of the Prophet, raised his standard successfully in the first years of the nineteenth century and endured for twenty-five years until the Qara killed him. Fifty years later, about 1880, the scene was braved by Fadhul bin Aliyowi, a Hadhramauti, who came claiming authority from the Ottoman Government, but he could not maintain himself and was expelled.

Then it was that the people of Dhufar turned to the Ruling House of Muscat to take over their country. Though that was scarcely more than fifty years ago, *Al Sa'idi* influence grew to its present considerable proportions, and if there is no part of the Sultanate to-day where authority is wielded with more difficulty, nowhere is authority wielded more salutarily. Yet the foundations were laid in blood. That story is worth the telling, not so much as a sketch of recent history, as for the light it sheds on the psychology of tribal governors and governed in remoter Arabia.

Saiyid Turki bin Sa'id, the grandfather of the present Sultan, was the Ruler of Muscat to whom the Dhufaris had turned for protection. Now Turki had a slave, one Sulaiman bin Suwailim, a man in whom he reposed complete trust; he had manumitted and exalted him to be Counsellor, and Commander-in-Chief of his forces - not an impossible destiny for a slave in Arabia. Sulaiman enjoyed an immense prestige among the tribes of Oman for his personal qualities. He was fearless, unscrupulous and strong. If the lawless reputation of the Dhufaris was deserved, no lesser man could be expected to establish Muscat influence, with the little backing Muscat could give. Sulaiman, therefore, it was that the Sultan sent to Dhufar as his first *Wali* (Viceroy).

Did not the Ruler habitually address his slave as *abana* (our father)? said my informant, an old pensioned soldier who had come to Dhufar in those far-off days with the original Army of Occupation and remained ever since. 'Abud bin 'Isa was a Nejdi, a fine old veteran with brown flashing eyes, a heavy jowl and large ears that showed he was no South Arabian. Like many of his kind, to Omanis known as *ahl al gharb* (people of the west), he had left his native country as a boy to come and take service in the army of the Muscat Ruler, lured thither by the attractions of the pay - three dollars a month to a Badu of Inner Arabia was in those days a glittering reward. And this mercenary army was a pillar of strength to the Ruler of a country riven by rival claimants to the throne; it was not merely of good fighting stock, but of unswerving allegiance because unaffected by local loyalties.

Eighteen of these Nejdis arrived with the Wali Sulaiman to occupy Dhufar. It was a small force, but it enabled a start to be made, and before the arrival of the Omani garrison of a hundred *askaris*, Sulaiman had taken in hand the building of a fort-prison at Salala on the Omani model, impressing slave and *dhaaf* [5] labour for his purpose.

But the vigour of his activities, to which had been added the collection of taxes, was not to tribal liking and discontented murmurings soon arose from among the Qara. A man of less resolution would have been intimidated. Sulaiman was not to be deflected; his acts knew no moderation, he behaved arbitrarily. Now came a challenge. One of his soldiers was ambushed and murdered at Hamran, where a picket had been placed over the water. But even Sulaiman dare not imprison Finkhor, the powerful shaikh of the Qara section involved, though he must parry the affront. A fight at Taqa, in which the government askaris were supported by elements of Al Kathir, produced no casualties on either side - not an unusual state of affairs in Arab warfare with shots exchanged at long range. But it brought a feeling of relief, so that both sides could honourably endure a peace. The place was in favour of Sulaiman, for with the oath of allegiance came the present of a hundred head of cattle.

With insufficient power to rule magnanimously, Sulaiman continued to employ the terrorist methods that better suited his character, and it was not long before the tribe were once more on the warpath. A tribesman had indulged in a time-honoured foray (the fear of raids from the mountains is a daily dread in the plain to this day) and Sulaiman imposed some exemplary punishment. This was disproportionate in the tribal mind, which thereupon flared up, and only a blockade of the mountains [6] — an extremely bold course - brought them to their knees.

The cup of tribal wrath against Sulaiman was full, but did not overflow till he left for Oman on leave, with every apparent reason to be satisfied with the masterful accomplishments of his three years' efforts. He set his two sons Ali and Mas'ad to rule in his place, and then the Al Kathir, whose support of Sulaiman had made possible his dealing with their old rivals, the Qara, now saw their opportunity in Sulaiman's absence and in the cellars of the fort which were full of tithe and customs levies - butter, rice and dates. The instinct of avarice, abnormally- developed in the Badu, was astir. A plot was hatched. One party of Kathir would bring a petition against another, and as the case proceeded more Kathiri witnesses would be sent for until the town was possessed by an army of them. And so it happened. Suspicion would have arisen had they come in any other circumstances. As it was the government troops remained scattered over the plain on their daily duties. This morning, like every other, the two young governors sat at the gateway of the fort holding the morning reception. The coffee cup had gone round the large assembly of Kathir tribesmen present. The moment had come. Consummate treachery! On a signal from the leader the Badawin leapt up and fell upon their hosts, sword in hand. Ali and Mas'ad, Sulaiman's sons, with their wretched soldiers were pitilessly murdered, the Badawin rushed down and ransacked the cellars and then razed the new government fort to the ground.

All that was left of Muscat government in Dhufar was one Bakhit bin Nubi and forty soldiers who fled to Murbat to take refuge with some friendly Qara. This Bakhit was a negro and a character withal. He was a slave of Sulaiman, for a slave may own another slave or other chattels, though without the power of bequest, so that on his death his goods revert to his master. Four months must elapse - the south-west monsoon having cut communication with Oman - before news could reach Muscat and reinforcements be sent. Bakhit took upon himself to act, and his actions must have been wise and courageous, for as the days passed and the menace of retribution approached, he induced the rebels to see that to support him was their safest course. Events in Oman had necessitated the retention there of Sulaiman, so that when later he came to Dhufar it was on a temporary visit to discuss future dispositions. A British man-of-war brought an Ambassador of the Sultan, the erring tribes were punished, and their leaders abased; it was too late for restitution except that the old fort doorway was returned to adorn the bigger and stronger government fort to be built on the site of the old one, where it stands to this day. Bakhit was installed as Governor. His old master Sulaiman (who was himself to die by the hand of an assassin in Oman soon afterwards) left with him this message: 'If I hear that Bait Kathir have chosen a shaikh amongst them and he lives, your head will be cut off.' Bakhit did not falter. During his seven years of office the ten ringleaders of the troubles were one by one quietly despatched by slaves sent for the purpose. True, these shaikhs had been granted a general amnesty by the Envoy from Muscat, but that scarcely affected either party's conscience, for where treachery is a habit of mind, men are actuated by the stern necessities of the moment, not by any principles of morality.

Instability is the chief characteristic of any regime in tribal Arabia. It is inherent in the Arab genius, and springs from the preponderating part played by personalities and the relative unimportance of the machine. Where the strong personality is of the government or is well disposed to government all will be well. Where stronger men are without, trouble lurks. Thus when in the course of time Bakhit's rule was replaced by that of 'Abdullah bin Sulaiman, a free man of weak character, the prestige of government declined and the tribes ceased to pay their dues. They despised the new Wali for his weakness rather than admired him for his benevolence, so that he died unregretted by good men, leaving to his successor - the present admirable incumbent - whose guest I was for the moment, the task of re-establishing that authority which he had so supinely relinquished.

As I stood on the old battlements reconstituting in my imagination scenes such as these, horses were brought for me to the gateway below from the Court stables - the only specimens of their kind to be found within three hundred miles. They were selected from a dozen or so which the Sultan has brought from time to time, for he was much attached to Dhufar, its gazelle-hunting and hawking, and spent more than one summer there during my term of office.

To-day I was riding out to Salala to call on Sa'ad bin Abdul 'Aziz, the wealthiest merchant in the place, a man of humble and obscure parent-age, as the Arab merchant prince often is. Our way lay past the tiny bazaar, out of the town gateway, and through a deep coco-nut grove (in Dhufar the coco-nut palm takes the place of the date palm found else-where in Arabia) on through fields of cotton and indigo and so across the strip of plain that fronts Salala town. Imposing indeed are the lofty

many-storeyed houses of dazzling whiteness - the stone hewn from the
plain where they stand - the ornamentation [7] giving them a semblance
of dignified age which accords ill with the dingy and squalid interiors.
Sa'ad's house rose like a palace midway along the front of the town; but
even there we found its courtyard hot with flies and heavy with the
smell of its stalled cows. The narrowest of steps led thence to the guest-
chamber at the top of the house, a large room with a fine central beam
of Malabar teak upholding the ceiling and admirably ventilated with
many small unglazed windows, for window-panes are unknown. [8]
The furnishings were few but luxurious. Every inch of floor space was
covered with carpets, pleasant individually, but inharmonious in the
mass; a dozen mirrors at least, all life-size and gold-framed, adorned
walls as vain as those of any tailor's closet; alcoves were stuffed with
silver incense burners, coffee appurtenances, and gaudy bric-a-brac. We
trooped in and sat in line round the four sides of the room, I being
motioned to a corner where there were a few extra cushions, tough as
medicine balls, but glad to the Oriental eye in their bright scarlet or
emerald-coloured trappings. Only our host and his sons and domestic
slaves stood to do the honours beside a table arrayed with bottles of
almond syrup, coloured sherbets and fancy tumblers. As in all social
gatherings in Arab tribal towns, no woman was to be seen or
mentioned. Those of any standing at all had, as always, hidden themselves till strange men should have left their house, and any furtive
unveiled figure to be seen in the courtyard was surely that of a slave girl.

Next to me sat old Salim al Sail, another merchant, a God-fearing
man and a Solomon among his kind. Human frailty made him claim
descent from the noble Bait Ghassan, while all men whispered that he
was a foundling child of low Shahari origin that a mountain torrent
had swept down in a summer freshet. [9] Salim's eyes, as became his
eighty years, were growing dim, though they were still capable of a
twinkle when he begged in secret for an aphrodisiac. At other times,
as now, he showed a wider interest in mankind. 'Are any of the
nations at war. Sahib?' 'What has happened to the Germans?' And,
'Are the *Italiyaniyin* your friends?'

Exorcism of the Evil Eye

Dhufar's propinquity to Somaliland and Italian influence in the Yemen may account for the fact that the Italians loom larger in their minds than any other Europeans, and I have never heard aught but good spoken of them and their administration.

And now a mountain shaikh at my side was brightening the conversation.

'Why are you such big men, and we so much smaller?'

'Perhaps on account of our soil and air,' I said.

'But *Allahu Alim* (God is the knower) we are much smaller than our forefathers. Look at their graves at Khor Ruri - twenty paces long. They were that great.'

'God is the knower,' I returned, being careful not to offend religious susceptibilities, for one commentator on the Qur'an gives Adam's height as thirty-six feet, and other patriarchs in proportion (a figure modest in comparison with those given by others). 'Is it not God's mercy?'

'How?' said he.

'It is difficult enough,' I replied, 'nowadays, with so many men in the world, for all to find nourishment for stomachs this size' (and I held out an imaginary football): 'had we kept so big we should have needed a sack of rice at every meal; think of the cost!'

A general titter went round, and my questioner's silence showed that he was satisfied that the subject was exhausted.

A sailor, one Khamis of Auqad, was brought to my notice as having visited my country. (The native has no idea of the direction of Europe and points to the east, to India, supposing that to be the Englishman's home). Khamis, a free man, yet was the father of a slave-born child, for he had taken to wife another's slave woman, so by local canons the child belonged to her owner. The three hundred dollars he had paid for the woman was the price of her hand, not of her freedom, and he was now engaged in paying a further five hundred dollars to her master, to buy the freedom of his own offspring. [10]

Fuwala, the light refreshment which is a feature of any visit of courtesy, was brought in by a slave - a large dish- laden tray of fids of beef grilled crisp and black, spaghetti drenched in tomato sauce, and slices of pineapple. Coffee went round after the tit-bits, and lastly the frankincense burner which, however, was not held under the nostrils for a few brief seconds, and handed thus from person to person by a slave as in Oman, but left smouldering at my side. And in this land of true frankincense, unexcelled in the world, my host was surpassing himself by using an imported substitute, inferior to my mind, but here more costly. This was *aud*, a kind of sandal-wood which I understand serves for frankincense in European churches, *al aud la tagud* runs an Arab jingle, which means 'After the incense do not tarry.' The offered incense is indeed a sign not to be mistaken, so after a minute or two of courteous silence one mutters 'tarakhkhus' (with your permission) and rises to go.

'We hope you are making a long stay,' says my host, partly by way of courtesy, partly to tempt a disclosure of my plans.

'Yes! I am on two months' leave,' I reply. 'Shaikh Hasan has agreed to take me up into his mountains for some shooting next week; he has promised me a panther and an ibex.'

I had barely risen the next morning to wind and record my chronometers when throbbing tom-toms and raucous female voices attracted my notice. Soon through the prison courtyard below came twenty young negresses, dancing a sensuous measure, their heads poised in snake- like detachment balancing full water pitchers. Here was the Bathing Chorus, a recognised institution when the Sultan or I was in residence, and the tank in the bathroom must needs be replenished daily. As they filed past the doorway of my room they ceased to sing; a young one, confident in her youth and greatly daring, risks what may be almost a wink in my direction, for in their world of Dhufar, they were none of them better than they should be. On filing out each halts to turn and make obeisance. A motherly old negress among them loiters to ask after brothers and husbands in the Muscat Court, and have I brought letters? She soon turns the conversation to the question of customary payment, but with all the black beauties agog in that expectation she is clearly no undisputed representative. Two parties at least are evident, both animated by the single idea of *bakhshish*.

'Have you counted us, O Wazir?' shouts one. 'Four and twenty here, and four downstairs,' says another (this an unblushing lie).

'Count us, O Wazir! Let your servant Muhammad count us!'

I smilingly promise them a basket of dates and some dollars for the morrow, and they gaily respond by lining up in my upper courtyard as for 'Here we come gathering nuts in May,' descending the stairway after a final rollicking ballet, to more drum fingering and chanting. And so I turn complacently to enjoy the bath they have prepared for me while their strains grow fainter and fainter, and at last are no more to be heard.

3

SKULL-MEASURING AND DEVIL DANCING

'From what Arabs are you?' Thus has the question been put to me in the desert, by natives conscious that I was of a race different from theirs, for the word Arab is used by them to denote 'people' rather than the particular race we mean.

But is it so certain that the Arabs are themselves racially one? Neither Glaser the scholar, nor Burton the traveller thought so. The former held the South Arabian to be Hamitic and not Semitic. The latter declared that he had found proof of three distinct races. Whatever the case, Burton's anticipation that 'physiological differences sufficient to warrant our questioning the common origin of the Arab family would be found' was a sound one. Such differences I discovered in abundance in this central region of South Arabia: not merely physiological, but cultural and linguistic differences that constitute collectively a serious challenge to the conception of a single racial entity for the entire peninsula.

I came indeed prepared with head callipers to make and record skull measurements, for such measurements are vital to anthropologists. Of importance too are visual observations of the foreigner domiciled for some years in Arabia, for his mind becomes unconsciously stamped with the physical characteristics of the natives, and is therefore acutely aware of aberrations from racial types when he meets them. Thus it was that after continuous residence in Arabia from 1915 onwards, serving in capacities that brought me into close touch with the Arabs of Mesopotamia, Trans-Jordan and the Persian Gulf, I was impressed on meeting the natives of central South Arabia - the Dhufar 'bloc,' with a feeling of some fundamental difference. The Political Resident in Aden, Major-General Maitland, recorded a similar impression in the following terms:

'The people of Arabia belong to two distinct and apparently quite different races. The common idea of the Arab type . . . tall bearded men with clean-cut hawk-like face. The Arabs of South Arabia are smaller, darker, coarser featured and nearly beardless. All authorities agree that the southern Arabs are nearly related by origin to the Abyssinians. Yet strange to say it is the Egypto-African race who are the pure Arabs, while the stately Semite of the north is Musta'rab . . . Arab by adoption and residence rather than by descent.'

Arab scholars themselves have inherited a tradition that their race is derived from two stocks, Qahtan and Adnan, but tribes scattered over the peninsula to-day claiming descent from one or other of these ancestors are of indistinguishable racial types. On the other hand, differences noted by Burton and Maitland and Glaser, and in our own generation by Rathjens, are well marked, and the tribes thus differentiated do not coincide with the Qahtan-Adnan demarcation.

None of these Europeans, moreover, could have been familiar with the group of Dhufar tribes I encountered, which there is very strong anthropological and linguistic evidence for regarding as at most racially peculiar, at least racially different.

Inscriptions and ruined cities in South-west Arabia bear witness to ancient Minaean and Sabaean civilisations that decayed before the rise of Islam in the seventh century of our era. We know too of early Abyssinian and Roman invasions and of Greek and Aramaean settlements. Who are these South Arabians? If the answer to the problem rests with anthropologists, as it assuredly does, the collection of relevant data was of never-failing interest to me on my travels.

I had early entertained hopes of unearthing and sending home ancient skulls, but the dangers of offending religious susceptibilities in Arabia were great. To disturb a body that has been given Muslim burial is the worst desecration, and has been a fruitful source of trouble as when, for instance, in Mesopotamia during the war, someone un- wittingly drove a car through a derelict Arab cemetery. Hence also the rock tombs faced with loose stones which I had come upon in the Wadi Dhikur in 1927-28 were forbidden ground. On my 1929-1930 journey I had met with better fortune, for at Hasik we passed a cave whose entrance had been forced by a wolf or other wild animal. It was daylight and the presence of my Arab companions imposed restraint, but I contrived to halt near by, and no one knew next morning that a skull found in the cave was in my bedding - though the jawbone was missing and the rest of the skeleton had wholly disappeared. I took it to Muscat and thence to the Royal College of Surgeons in London. But in my house at Muscat where I unpacked the treasure, my servant Mabruk, a manumitted slave, became aware of his master's queer hobby, and announced next day that he had brought a present for me and produced from a bundle a complete human skull. Another Arab servant emerged sniggering from behind the door to explain that Mabruk had been overnight to his father's. burial-place, and was presenting me with a once vital part of his revered parent. That night Mabruk, unrewarded and rebuked, restored it to its resting-place. Whether Arab feelings would have been hurt on religious grounds in such a case, it is impossible to tell, certainly slaves do not pray in this part of Arabia, and may not normally be regarded as good Muslims.

To return to Dhufar and head-measuring, it was no easy task to find willing subjects. There is always in the minds of rude people the fear of magic or worse, while the religious among them hate to be pawed by infidel hands. In the desert I would not have dared risk putting callipers over the head of a Badu - an uncouth tribesman might have drawn his dagger, for at times Badawin have turned against me for bringing out a camera at the wrong moment - but here in Dhufar I felt I could safely work upon prisoners, warders and old friends behind closed doors, and with these and some enlightened foreign traders I was able during my stay to make forty-five head-measurements, covering a wide geographical range and to take a hundred 'type' portraits.

The work was enlivened by many amusing episodes, but was phys-ically unpleasant, for the specimens were either Badawin with tousled hair full of sandy and other accumulations or sedentary townsmen whose locks were a mass of grease from applications of coco-nut oil. One morning my clients were to be Somalis, a breed which crosses the Red Sea to set up as petty merchants in the bazaar or as middlemen to contract frankincense orchards. Six of them arrived, and averred in answer to my questions that they were *somal khalis*, i.e. Somalis on both sides of the family - a necessary condition, for speci-mens of mixed parentage are useless anthropologically, but on a closer study their squat noses and receding head axes were so obvi-ously negroid that I dismissed them as unsuitable. 'Are you quite sure you are pure-bred?' I asked a Somali member of the police who was next. 'I claim to be,' he replied, 'but God is the knower, and then my mother.'

The wit enjoyed his own lewd joke and disappeared laughing down the roof-steps, promising to appear on the morrow with a number of equally uncontaminated fellow- specimens.

Next came the government *askaris*. These mercenary tribesmen of Hadhramaut or of the Aden hinterland who take service with the Sultan of Muscat, like the Nejdis of old, are labelled as *Hadharim* by the local Omanis. There were forty on duty at Dhufar, so I had little difficulty in finding six of undiluted tribal stock. These - of the Ahl Yazid, Yahar, and Ahl Saad sections of the Yafa confederation, I measured and photographed, but I was soon to discover that they objected to the term *Hadharim* as applied to themselves. '*Hadharim* to us. Sahib, are low- caste inhabitants of Shahar and other non-tribes-men: the genuine tribesman will be content only to be regarded as belonging to one of two rival confederations, Yafaand Hamdan - none other!' they said.

Next day I was measuring a member of another race type, one Ali al Dhaban, a Badawi of the Mashai that roam the desert on the north side of the Hadhramaut. Ali, a very fine shot as Arabs go, had accompanied me on my last year's expedition to Mugshin, and was now my daily companion, and a fount of desert erudition. He knew the southern borderlands well, had shed Rashidi blood and later taken a Rashidi girl to wife to avoid their vengeance. From me he wanted a parting present before going into the Qara Mountains to demand four head of sheep from Al Kathir as part payment of blood-money for his son accidentally killed by one of their number the year before.

What he wanted turned out to be a modest fifty rounds of ammunition - the Badu will unblushingly ask for the moon!

'No,' I said, remembering Ali's record and propensities. 'Certainly not!' Ali was reputed to have taken fifteen lives; the last murder, three years before, immediately followed a visit to my camp at Auhi: he had then shot an 'Amari he met in the wilderness because he coveted the wretch's camel. The camel did not, alas, survive the journey to Dhufar, and Ali had nothing to show for his blood-guiltiness, which he ascribed cheerfully to Allah, and himself felt not at all, but he dare not meet a man of that tribe again. 'I will give you three dollars, Ali,' I added, 'if you will come on a shooting expedition into the mountains next week: but ammunition, no! You want it for some evil purpose. I will be no party to violence.'

'Then tell me how a man shall live?'

'Till the ground or fish.'

He looked at me incredulously. 'That is not a man's work,' he said.

'Then what is a man's work?'

'The rifle and *janbiya* (dagger).'

'Nonsense,' I returned. 'Fighting is all very well when the time for it comes, but how do you think we English became strong if it was not by work? How do you think we get our ships and our rifles?'

'Money!' he said laconically, and I knew it would be idle to argue. A pause.

'O Ali! if every one lived by his rifle and *janbiya* whence would we get food? We owe what we eat to the cultivator and the fisherman.'

'But what *qubaili* (tribesman) would stoop so low? Fishing! it is impossible! Tilling! Yes, I will ask Saiyid Taimur (the Sultan) to give me a plot of land. Then I will get a slave to till it for me.'

'But why not till it yourself?'

'Ah! never fear, I'll pay the slave,' said Ali, missing the point, but adding ingenuously, 'and I shall live on the produce of the garden.'

How Ali was to come by a slave I had every reason to shrink from imagining. Even in Dhufar three hundred dollars would be a moderate price for a slave, and had Ali anything like that sum, the desert would call him and he would invest the money in a she-camel. But Ali's flight of fancy had carried him into the clouds and he now returned to earth.

'Give me fifty rounds. Sahib!' and he slithered the ammunition belt round his body for me to see that it was all but empty. I suppressed a smile at the incongruity of his utter poverty with his opulent optimism.

'Wallahi! I would rather ammunition than a camel,' he said. 'The camel dies on her master's hands, but with ammunition! I can repel my enemies when they come after me, and kill an oryx when I am hungry.'

'No, Ali! Come to-morrow and you shall have three dollars, but mark you! behave yourself in the mountains, or this is the end of our friendship.'

'Let Saiyid Taimur put me on his pay-roll,' said Ali as he went away -he was, maybe, envisaging three dollars a month - 'and I will be a brother to all men.'

It was the Acting-Governor's custom to call on me each morning at the fort. Sa'id bin Saif was yellow-faced, with a long scraggy goatee and a miserable physique even for late middle-age. His conversation centred round the poverty of the *Hukuma* (government), the insufficiency of his pay, and the demands of a large family: and in contrast the vast sums of money the English must have, as shown by official salaries. Said lamented his own miserable portion and attributed both extremes to Allah. Work he regarded as undignified, fit for slaves; his hands were pale and delicate as a woman's and his legs never carried him faster than a slow, dignified walk, attended by a squad of soldiers before and behind him. What he did diligently, albeit with extreme deliberation, was to pray five times a day. For the rest, he sat about aimlessly, his sleepy silences broken only with pious ejaculations, *Al hamdu' l'Illah! al hamdu' l'Illah* ' - a most depressing companion.

There were distant sounds of revelry. A soldier rushed to the roof and came back to report it was the slaves. Drums in growing volume confirmed their approach and we now all went to look down on an interesting spectacle.

The occasion of it was merely a slave's death, but when a negro here dies and is buried, instead of two Muslim angels to share his tomb, an evil spirit enters to molest his slumbers, and so the drums and the devil-dance are invoked to drive away the tormentor.

'God forgive them!' murmured the sanctimonious Omani at my side.

'Drums aren't acceptable to you?' I questioned.

'No, nor pipes; but these are slaves and know no better.'

'Yet the Muqabil tribe in Oman have pipes?' I said.

'Yes! but they are Sunnis. We are Ibadhis, and in Ibadhi Oman we forbid these instruments of the devil.'

Meanwhile the procession was making its brave way to pay me respects inspired by hope of reward — a basket of dates, perhaps, for death with them, as at an Irish wake, is an occasion for feasting. The banner-carrier and drummers moved slowly forward; the main body of negroes about them, with staves held aloft, were dancing and chanting, and a party of negresses came tripping along in rear. As the fort gates were approached some of the men rushed forward threateningly in a mock attempt at forcing the doorway that was already open.

Within the courtyard a halt was cried and the rhythm changed. With the drums and banners for a centre, the men circled round in single file, hopping now on this foot, now on that, and chanting some wild Swahili gibberish while their women moved circumspectly around the outer edge with curious measured step, their mantles lifted suggestively before them. Other negroes detached them- selves for a mock fight, one man who presumably impersonated the evil spirit lying on the ground lashing wildly about him, while would-be vanquishers assailed him from all sides.

So many sightseers pressed into the outer gateway that they made the exit of the Omani at my side impossible, and he remained an involuntary spectator. He stood aghast at this exhibition of paganism, which he would have suppressed if he could, while I felt that I was the object of his inward censure for my levity in taking a cine-picture of the proceedings.

In the afternoon I was to witness more elaborate ritual outside in the gardens, for the Sultan had forbidden the rite within city precincts and thereby won the praises of all True Believers.

'Did not these processions on the *Id of Nayruz* (New Year's Day) with loud gibes enter the harlot's house carrying a kitten - her implied offspring? But,' said my pious informant, 'the Sultan's action in suppressing this may have been precipitate for, alas, since then promiscuity has increased.'

The negro community is almost self-contained, and the biggest single element in the population of the Dhufar capital. Awwadh, a Court slave and most exalted above his fellows, was their *ab* a magistrate to whom negro disputes were usually referred for settlement. Nor was he without an assistant glorying in the high-sounding name of *naqib*, but the rank and file of slaves are *aulad* and *banat*, i.e. 'boys' and 'girls,' euphemistic terms when they are applied to wrinkled negroes and aged negresses.

Slaves may have their taboos. One here, for instance, is that they may not touch dead animals other than those properly slaughtered for food. It is the master and not the slave who would remove a dead cat from the house, and where is the Court slave who would willingly consent to drag away the carcass of a horse? For such and other infringements of their code there is punishment (normally ostracism) by communal sentiment, the decision being cried round the town with a conch - the slaves' alarm: while the offender's readmission is celebrated by the slaughter of a sheep in the blood of which he dips his foot.

Negro slaves in my experience are of a contented mind. They have a cheerful demeanour often lacking in their masters, so that they sing and dance apparently unmindful of their political and social disabilities. It is difficult for a European who has not lived in Muslim countries to form any considered opinion regarding slavery in practice. The lot of the slave must necessarily be compared with that of the freeman in the same environment. Judged by this standard, the life of the slave is not wholly pitiable. The general standard of life is so low - just above the line of bare sufficiency - that the slave-owner, in his own interests, has to feed and clothe the slave nearly as well as himself.

The fundamental difference between them lies in work. In the land of sloth, it is the slave who does the manual labour. He has to produce enough to support both of them, and the freeman sees that he does so. But to suppose that a difference of rewards exists as sharply defined as in the Southern States of the U.S.A. or the West Indian Colonies before the abolition of slavery would be a false assumption. No such difference exists.

Slaves actually enjoy certain fortuitous social advantages. The male, for instance, escapes the perils of the blood-feuds that haunt the 'free' tribesman, and when he is caught in a raid and Arab kills Arab, his life will be spared. It is true he will find himself taken captive and sold to a fresh master, but his lot need not therefore be worsened. As regards females, the slave girl enjoys a social liberty that is in gratifying contrast to the 'free' Arab woman. The latter is probably married at fifteen to a spouse chosen by her father, without being consulted or even seeing him. Thereafter she is destined to close confinement in her house for the rest of her life except for rare excursions out of doors, where she goes closely veiled. The rigidity of the convention increases as her position rises in the social scale, while any sexual lapse -this in contrast to her husband's admitted licence - she will pay for with her life,

The slave girl, on the other hand, is fancy free, and although her marriage will be likewise arranged by her master with an eye only to his own profit, she will walk abroad unveiled throughout her life, and flirt and fraternise where she will.

A group of desert Badawin were interested spectators of the devil-dancing in the afternoon, and though professing Muslims all, none seemed to have any misgivings of conscience about it, in refreshing contrast to the narrow spirit of the semi-sophisticated Omani official. If the pastoral races of the desert have placed their gods in the skies because they were habitually looking upwards for rain, the giver of life, why should not the agricultural races, with their eyes always on the soil, have their earth-spirits? But with such ideas neither party would have had any sympathy.

It was before Hafa village, picturesque in its setting of coco-nut palms, that the *zenug* rites were customarily per- formed three days after a death. The sound of well-played drums drew me to the throng. In the midst was a clearing spacious as a riding-school. At one end sat the drummers, a fire before them for the purpose of tuning their drums. Round about them danced the 'drum boys,' a dozen or so stal-wart negroes of splendid muscular development. They were naked but for their loin-cloths; about their knees was a rattle of dried mangoes. This *khish* swished to the beating of the drums, as the dancers stamped and gyrated.

Across the circle opposite stood the *naqib*. His hands were to his lips as he chanted his incantations – *'Y' Allah ya malengi y' Allah ya malengi* — while a chorus of a dozen companions, standing facing him in a row, took up the responses.

Around the inner edge of the circle Awwadh the *ab*, master of ceremonies, ran hither and thither, slashing with a whip in his hand before the naked feet of spectators, wherever they pressed too closely.

A dozen paces within the ring was the path of the main performers - a stream of young negroes and negresses, who came sweeping round and round the circle in grand parade - young slave girls, singly or in pairs, sturdy, black as ebony, and high of bosom, selected doubtless for their superior graces in the eyes of men. A black muslin veil shrouded each girl's head and drooped about the shoulders, of so flimsy a material that it did not conceal, but rather accentuated the effect of her flashing eyes, her thick scarlet-painted lips, her nose-ring, ear-rings and necklaces of gold. Her dress, new doubtless for the occasion, was a single mantle of starched indigo that glistened in the sun. One end of its long sweeping train she held up fastidiously between finger and thumb, the arm outstretched level with her shoulder, the other arm lay close to her side with the hand poised a span or so from the hip and palm turned back at almost right angles to the wrist. And thus she moves; her head motionless, her face turning neither to right nor left, her body moving by some subtle shuffle-step that has the sinuous slide of a skater. Before her leaps an eager youth, in his hand a drawn sword that quivers with a flick of the wrist; now on this side, now on that, now turning about to face her - spellbound he seems, like the moth to the candle. Other male slaves, threes and fours in line, rifles held above their heads, stalk round in the more deliberate measure of the horse-dance and looking straight to their front regardless of beauty.

The afternoon wears on. More and more candidates enter the drum-throbbing ring. The moment for the climax of the rite approaches. The spirit molesting the corpse must be drawn forth and take possession of a 'drum boy' chosen for his powers, who now draws apart from his- companions. All eyes are turned upon him. The stamping grows wilder; the spirit -possessed puts forth all the frenzy of which his body is capable. His face is hideously contorted, his eyes wildly stare, he rolls himself on the ground and rubs his head in the dust, he slobbers with his lips as though in a fit. He is clearly overcome by exhaustion, and I, sickened by the sight of the orgy, depart as rifles are discharged into the air, to add to the general tumult.

The *muedhdhin's* 'Credo' would put an end to the ceremony if the spirit-possessed slave did not, before then, swoon, symbolising the passing of the spirit that otherwise would have given the corpse no rest. But he has fallen and lies motionless; and now the *aulad* and *banat* gather up his limp body and bear it home, thence they joyfully disperse.

4

IN THE QARA MOUNTAINS – AIN RAZAT

I had already been held up in Dhufar for three weeks with never a sign of the long-awaited camel party from the sands, no word of Sahail, no word of my lately despatched emissaries; only desert news trickled in, disturbing news of wars and rumours of wars.

The curiosity of the market-place concerning my plans [11] was doubtless aroused, and I felt there was no better way to lull it than by an expedition into the Qara Mountains. Here was fresh country, which only Theodore and Mabel Bent had seen forty years before. The land ever surges with tribal unrest, so that only once has the Sultan or his representative, the Governor of Dhufar, seen fit to tour in these mountains, and never at all their predecessors. It was, moreover, the gateway to the great desert. I hoped to make it more than a cloak for my larger plans, for I was eager for the opportunity of living amongst these people, whose heads I had measured; I was curious to discover their customs, their superstitions, their traditions, and for light upon their psychology and way of life. Here would be clues for the anthropologist. Would their languages and culture identify them with the Arabs of the north, or with those of the south-west, or would they challenge any identification to be found within the borders of Arabia?

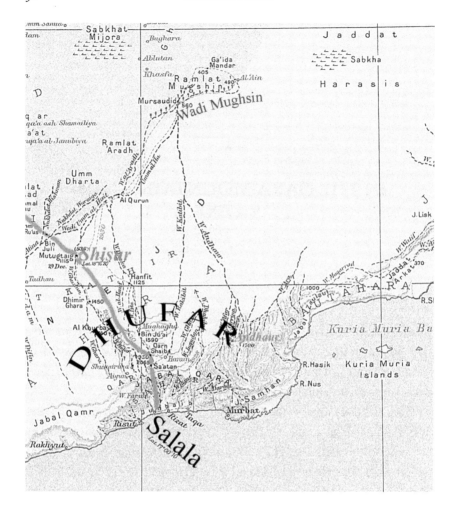

Another attraction these mountains had for me was the hunting they would afford. I had fondly gone over my new Winchester rifle and ammunition, my butterfly net, collecting-boxes and surgical instruments, jars of formalin, packets of arsenical soap, and cotton wool. Arabia, lying on the borders of three of the great zoological provinces into which the world is divided, presents problems of particular interest, and as the museums of the world had almost no specimens of the fauna of this particular central south region, the joys of hunting would be enhanced.

My gun I deliberately left behind, for if I shot birds to prepare them as specimens would demand too much of my time. My Muscat Arab secretary, Ali Muhammad, who had travelled with me on my previous march through these hills in 1929-30 and prepared the birds I shot, had fallen ill in Muscat before we started and had remained behind. As each specimen requires a record of name, locality, altitude, sex and date, besides its preparation, the question I had to solve was how best to divide my waking hours between this and the claims of mapping and note-taking. But experience solved the problem. The preliminary rough skinning of a large mammal — so long as I made the first long incision - could be left to some Badu showing an aptitude, though the finishing touches could not be entrusted to him. The skull, too, could be plunged into hot water and left to clean itself, the snake or other reptile needed only to be gutted before immersion in a jar of formalin; the butterfly and the insect asked for nothing more than loving care; whereas the normal small bird, with a skin as delicate as silk, would make excessive inroads into my time, so I had to neglect the Department at South Kensington of my distinguished friend, Mr. N. B. Kinnear, whose personal interest and encouragement had made me a collector for the Natural History Museum.

We made an afternoon start on 19th October 1930. My companions consisted of two Kathiris and Ali al Dhab'an (three companions of my last year's expedition) and five government slaves. A rendezvous had been arranged with my Qara hosts at a point in the foothills.

Our way lay eastward along the beach past Hafa, through the coco-nut grove that separates it from the ancient ruined city of Balid. Thence we entered the plain behind, strewn with other ancient surface ruins [12] - now called Hasaila, yet a civilisation far in advance of that now existing is evidenced by such ruins and monuments as do exist, while old steyned wells, dry water-ducts and plough-ridges attest the former industry.

Ain Razat

The many shallow quarries in the stony plain point to a bygone time when stone was extensively used as building material. Now cultivators may sow a little in them because of favourable sub-surface moisture, and in remoter places they are refuges when leprosy and smallpox periodically ravage the plain. [13]After a night disturbed by mosquitoes spent in the plain behind Rizat we set out towards Jabal Nashib, the lofty brow of the Qara Mountains. We passed the Sultan's experimental garden at Mahmulah and entered the foot- hills beyond. There we halted in a copse, by a babbling brook, in which a herd of cattle slowly waded in single file or stood lazily blinking in the shade of the thick bushes.

This stream of Rizat rises two miles above the tree- garlanded Milwah al 'Aud, and thence is carried in an old aqueduct, green with moss and maidenhair, to skirt by gentle contours of bare red banks until it is diverted across the plain in two man-made courses, one to the shrine of Hamran, the other through Mahmulah to Rizat, whereby it alternates its bounty.

In the morning I took a butterfly net and went down from my camp to the far side of the dry, rocky torrent bed, to investigate some old stones. These proved to be monster graves - giant ovoids of large flat slabs of rock, the monument a dozen paces long such as I had seen at Khor Ruri and Khor Suli. The Arabs regard them as evidence of man's former giant proportions!

Down the valley came a mountain man, afoot. We hailed him, he paused and after acknowledging our sum- mons by raising his rifle above his head, came over to where we stood.

He was a typical man of these mountains, short of stature, dark of skin, with long gollywog curly hair, almost beard- less, with features that distinguished him immediately from the northern Arab, broad brow, very small ears, nose that was not armenoid, small, round black eyes again not armenoid, a pointed receding chin, shallow square jaws under the ears; well-developed and clean legs, but poor body and arms. His dress was a single indigo skirt reaching only to his knees. His black body, purple in places from the stain of indigo, was bare, as also were his legs and feet, and he was bareheaded except for a narrow *mahfif*, a slender thong of plaited

leather coiled nine times round his head, and worn like an Arab
aqal.

'Het hi Khar?' said a slave who knew the greeting in the Shahari
tongue.

The wild man spoke little, but eyed me wonderingly.

'Hur! Weled an nas' (Free - a son of the free) meaning I was not of
slave stock.

'That's a *kafir* (infidel), is it not?'

'Hashak! he's the Wazir of your Sultan.'

I laughingly asked the man, who said he was of the Qara tribe,
whether he would sell me the beans he carried in his *anit* [14] i.e.
leather satchel, as he appeared to be on his way to Rizat to sell them.

'How much?'

'A dollar.'

He sniffed, as do all these people, to mean yes, and I took the beans
that I did not want, and in so doing distracted attention from religious issues. For the rest of the day he conducted me up the wadi bed
to the source of the brook, where I collected a bountiful harvest of
dragon- flies, butterflies and lizards.

From a cave at the base of a lofty amphitheatre of forested hill-
slopes gushed the stream into a wide pool masked by a fringe of reeds,
man-high. Under the shadow of some giant overhanging trees I sat
down on the edge and watched the tiny fish darting about in shoals,
while one of my slaves paddled up and down vainly trying to catch
them with my butterfly net. My attention was suddenly drawn to
millet and other odd fragments of food lying on the bottom.
'Nughush!' they said. Here men cast bread upon the running waters to
propitiate the *subiro* that brood over them. The word, like our familiar
equivalent, stands for the spirits of the departed, possessed of powers
of good and evil and able to treat man even as they are treated. At
night the natives throw morsels of tobacco and food to them, shouting, 'We are your sons, your daughters; do not harm us; be awake so
that we are not harmed by evil men or malign spirits.'

This spring of Rizat figured in a famous case of magic in Wali
Sulaiman's time. Bait Zaiyan, a section of the Shahara, claimed the

exclusive right to practise *nughush* here. The Qara tribe disputed the exclusive right of the Zaiyan, their vassals, and asked for an equal share in the sacrifice and in the ghostly grace accruing. The Wali, with an eye to his government's own share in the plains, decided that both parties had equal rights, but that government itself would provide the litigants with exact quantities of the sacrifice to ensure against cheating, and thus become a partner. But the time came when Sulaiman was fighting these mountain people, and Bait Zaiyan saw their opportunity; they called upon the spirits of their forefathers, who presently made the stream run uphill. Hence the plains dried up and government lost its share; or so runs the legend.

Many other pagan and animistic cults survive and are practised throughout these mountains. All the natives hold them strongly; whereas elsewhere in Muslim Arabia they would be dubbed ungodly at the least. Another local custom is the blood sacrifice carried out in the Jurbaib just before the harvest, when a cow is led round the crops and slaughtered, the blood drained into the irrigation ducts and scraps of flesh cast amongst the standing corn.

The wooded hills bright with the tropical sun towered above our pool where we sat in the balmy air and listened to the birds' loud singing in the valley. A herd of cows grazed contentedly on the opposite bank. There, too, was a black and almost naked woman surrounded by her friends, and combing her shaggy locks, her reflection dancing in the water, while another woman lay in her midday sleep under a neighbouring tree.

When asked for milk, an African slave girl tripped across to us with a large bowlful, and received a lewd greeting from my mountain guide. She told us that the other women were her mistresses, the wives of a local Saiyid, who owned the cattle and would himself shortly arrive. From her we also learned that my supposed Qarowi was not of the Qara, as he said, but a Shahari.

A Group of Shahara

Such lying is typical of these mountain folk whom the plainsmen accuse, with reason, of inability to tell the truth. 'If there is a thing they do better than lying, it is stealing,' said the Wali to me. They are expert, incorrigible thieves, brother steals from brother, father from son, and a boy that shows no aptitude is suspect -his manliness is despaired of. For the intended victim to report to government a thief caught in the act would be treachery. If the victim catches the robber then they compact a double requital. Judicial disputes may be brought to government, but never a petty theft; this in contrast with the Badawin, to whom petty larceny is abominable. Yet an open raid upon camels is no reproach, not being sneaking theft, but act of war, by men prepared to deal death and to suffer it.

This Shahari, however, was to give proof that he too had his quali-ties. He showed rare courage when he attacked and killed a five-foot four-inch cobra with his two-foot stick. Nor was it a matter of kill where you please. A snake, or any other animal for that matter, must have the head intact to be of use as a scientific specimen, so my rewards were scaled, but a snake with a head intact is usually a live snake, and this Shahari did in fact carry this deadly reptile alive, though with broken back, for many miles on his small stick held out before him. It was dead when laid out on the grass, but for an occasional flick of the tail, with the tip of which the man now anointed his eyelids. He announced that it was medicine for the eyes, but I wondered whether some magical significance originally attached to the end from which life appeared to be ebbing.

And now a large man of the nondescript coastal type, very different from the mountain man, arrived announcing that he was Saiyid Hasan, who owned the women and cows across the stream. Had I enough milk? Let him send for more; and so we fell into a friendly talk about his world, the price of dates in Dhufar and this year's harvest at Basrah and in Oman, which would determine future prices. Now he would tell me of the mountains. Thefts were rife and good men, as well as evil, must lie awake of nights. His rifle was ready loaded. Why was government so weak? Why did not the Sultan cut off an offending hand as aforetime? This system of taking a thief to Muscat and bringing him back whole after a year did no good at all.

But surely, I thought, no tribesman would steal from a Saiyid, else Dhufar is marching with the times. For the Saiyids and Sharifs [15] of Dhufar are its accepted nobility, ranking above the tribes themselves, being the venerated descendants of the Prophet Muhammad. Whoso holds their hands to his nostrils and takes a few hearty sniffs, as does every local tribesman, will acquire virtue thereby.

The Saiyid had turned to the subject of *afarit*, one of a congeries of evil spirits, but I avowed that as we had none in my country I knew not how to pacify them.

'*!* my wife has had seven bellies and she has not delivered one of them,' he said. 'The *afarit* have taken them.'

There are many other evil spirits, *jinns*, *jinniyat* and *zars*. Of these, *zars* are the most accommodating, *jinns* sometimes yield, but *afarit!* they are Allah's worst afflictions.

'Ali al Dhab'an and I had arranged to sit up that night in the hope of shooting a hyena, both hyenas and wolves being common in these foothills. [16]

We had heard on the previous evening the chatter of hyenas from neighbouring hills; our camp-fire seemed to make no difference to them in their caves. To-day while I was away Ali had built a *magbin* shelter in the approved manner, a low half-circle of piled stones capable of accommodating us both and hiding us from an approaching animal, as we lay. The loopholes for our rifles were disguised, as was the whole wall, with small tree-branches. For bait, on the first night, he put the entrails of a sheep eight paces from the wall with a fire, lit just after sunset to carry off the scent. On the second night he used a bait of sardines, and again nothing happened. On the third night I withdrew in favour of a Kathiri Badu. The hyena came. Two rapid shots and a pained howl awoke me just before midnight and I ran to the spot. 'Fled and wounded,' they shouted, pointing to a pool of blood. Confident that the wound was mortal, they followed the trail as well as a bright moon would allow, swearing they would find him dead, but on the morrow I woke to hear that the animal had got clean away, probably to die in some cave.

'Had this been in the open desert,' said my two Badawin, 'we would have tracked him to his lair, but once he made the rocky wadi, it was his sanctuary.'

5

IN THE QARA MOUNTAINS: ANCIENT SURVIVALS AND THE BLOOD SACRIFICE

'Their inward thought is, that their houses shall continue for ever, and their dwelling places to all generations; they call their lands after their own names.' — Ps. xlix. 11.

The mountains of the Qara are still locally called after the original masters of the land, the Shahara, [17] who are by universal consent the most ancient tribe in these parts, and by local tradition derive them from Shaddad son of Ad. To-day they are weak, disunited, disrated, none else giving to them in marriage, a dwindling race now numbering scarcely four hundred men who live in groups among their Qara overlords, hewing their wood and drawing their water; yet men say of the ruins of Robat, that here was once Eriyot, their proud city. If this be so, their decline has changed the face of the mountains, for the Qara who are undisputed masters from Dharbat Ali to Hadhbaram [18] build neither city nor mosque, but live in the open under forest trees or in caves or houses of hay. Their riches are in camels, and innumerable herds of cattle and groves of frankincense. Yet in mastering the Shahara they seem to have assimilated the Shahara culture, for the language of these mountain folk, their dress and manners are popularly held to have come from their dispossessed liegemen.

When this happened, no one knows. Ibn Battuta, the famous Moorish traveller and theologian, writing in the fourteenth century of our era, after twenty-five years of travel through Egypt, Arabia and Mesopotamia, wrote of Dhufar: 'Another thing is that its people closely resemble the people of north-west Africa in their customs ... the outlying portion is not Arab, but of a Sudanic type.'

About and beyond these Qara Mountains from long. 51° 10' to long. 56° 20' range tribes physically different from the typical Arab of the north, and using non-Arabic mother tongues. [19] These are Qara, Shahara, Mahra, Barahama, Bilhaf, Bait ash Shaikh, Bautahara, Harasis, Afar, whom the people of Oman know collectively as Ahl al Hadara, a name possibly identifiable with the Hadoram of Genesis (by the elision of the final 'm' which is a Semitic form of plural and the article in ancient Sabaean) and the Adramitae of Pliny. Hadoram and Hazramaveth (generally equated with Hadhramaut) come together in Genesis and are called brothers, and Dhufar is contiguous to Hadhramaut.

The Qara Mountains, geographically in the centre of this South Arabian ethnological enclave, seem to have afforded a natural asylum for aborigines or early settlers driven south and east before more virile peoples, or attacked from the sea.

(i) Shahari is spoken by Qara, Shahara, Barahama, Bait ash Shaikh.

(ii) Mahri by Mahra and Bilhaf.

(iii) Bautahari by Bautahara.

(iv) Harsusi (Aforit) by Harasis and Afar.

Shahari is normally unintelligible to users of the other languages, who, however, can understand one another with difficulty.

I was unaware that Mahri and Shahari had been written up by the German philologist Dr. Maximilian Bittner, working on material collected in the Hadhramaut and Socotra by Dr. Muller's Arabian Expedition (1902) and by Count Landberg's Expedition (1898-99). My Harsusi and Bautahari, which appear to be variants of Mahri, have never before, I think, been recorded.

What a glorious place! Mountains three thousand feet high basking above a tropical ocean, their seaward slopes velvety with waving jungle, their roofs fragrant with rolling yellow meadows, beyond which the mountains slope northwards to a red sandstone steppe. Two incongruous aspects, but true at any point throughout the strip above the Jurbaib plain. Great was my delight when in 1928 I suddenly came upon it all from out of the arid wastes of the southern borderlands. The red [20] aspect came first. A white pebbly bed (Wadi Dhikur) led up into magnificent gorge of red cliffs, three hundred feet high and more, their faces carved by nature into recesses that threw dark fantastic shadows. The scene brought back old Petra to my mind. Thence we crossed the watershed of the Qutun, thick with *thisgaut* jungle, a libaniferous shrub inferior to frankincense, and so on down through wooded valleys to Adha, a mighty five-hundred-foot precipice, whither the Bents had come and wondered whether Ptolemy's Abyssapolis was not to be found there. But ere we reached it the hazy rim of the distant sea lifted beyond the mountains rolling down to it. Thence we descended to the brink of the Valley of Darbat, an exquisite pictures we looked down through a tangle of tree-tops to the stream, lined with trembling willows, a wall of tropical jungle rising sheer above us on every side. We made our way towards the plashing waters, the snapping of the undergrowth as we went giving alarm to the herons that lived amid these sylvan scenes.

Rizat's wild life, resentful at our prolonged intrusion, was forsaking its haunts, so I decided to leave on the morrow, 5th November, and move up into the mountains. Shaikh Hasan, to forward my wishes, had arrived with five camels, large, fat-humped beasts which favourably impressed me, but when it came to work I was to undergo my usual disillusionment about mountain-bred camels. Unused to any load but sacks of frankincense or sardines, heavier, more compact load bearing on the wrong part of their backs makes them restive. The habitual bellowing and grumbling when loading was now followed by stamping and wild attempts to shed their burdens, so that after two hours' delay in getting on the move we were held up from hour to hour rescuing or adjusting packs.

For two hours we skirted the foothills, moving west towards the entrance of Wadi Thidot, one of the few great intruding wadis that give access to the mountains. [21] The wadi immediately became wooded as our way led along and up a tortuous path thick with over-hanging foliage which brought us to a large pool fed by a tiny stream called Sahalnaut (here, as is commonly the case in these mountains, the water bears a different name from the wadi). We turned out of the right bank to climb more steeply on a general north-westerly bearing. The trees grew thicker as we proceeded, compelling us to dismount, and night fell before we reached our destined halt, so we continued on foot through this dark dense mountain forest. The march was unpleasant, doubly so now from the dread of snakes with which these mountains teem. This was a subject of banter between my compan-ions, whose belief in 'the day' and 'the hour' and a glorious hereafter, makes intolerable positions tolerable for them. I found comfort in the reflection that their jovial attitude and bare legs and feet compared ill with my superior defence, but I was constantly stumbling over boul-ders in the path and my long Arab skirt swung awkwardly round my legs.

Cattle in the Dhufar Mountains

At last the trees gave place to a grassy upland valley lit by the full moon, and here we halted for the night. The lowing of herds followed by shouts of *Rahalat! Rahalat!* [22] denoted that we had halted just short of the village of Midsaib. Delicious bowls of milk were soon brought along, but I was too tired to deal with a snake that a native had caught and brought to me alive, so it was put in a bottle to await the morning light.

The camp was early astir and I found myself in a glorious grassy valley, with cliffs on either side, here and there revealing natural rock caves fronted with stalactites and stalagmites, suggestive of monster jaws. Trusses of straw or thorn thatch edged the accessible ones, which the people in the cold winter and wet summer, when only they require shelter, occupy with their beasts.

A crowd of villagers came along with more milk. This is their staple diet, with honey and beef, the other two luxury items their mountains afford. Another Hasan, an old man suffering from senile decay and almost blind, the father of the village, insisted on leaving his place in the circle to come and sit next to me. I had dates served with the coffee, and he caused mirth by dipping the one into the other. He was clearly unused to these delicacies, if indeed he regarded them as such.

Our Shaikh Hasan excited murmurs of admiration by wearing the new indigo blue mantle that was my gift, and I told the old man that I would like to send him the 'sister of Shaikh Hasan's mantle' as a present.

'*Alaik baidh!*' he cried, a variant of '*Allah baiyidh wijhak*' (God whiten your face), a term of cordiality and gratitude.

'*Wallahi!* I like you. Sahib,' he continued. 'I am old and about to die, but if you will say, "There is no God but God, and Muhammad is the Prophet of God," I will give you two girls to wife, and all my property.'

A titter went round and Shaikh Hasan motioned to him to talk less.

My medicine chest had acquired for me a spurious fame and, as ever, afflicted humanity was brought to me. This time it was a young boy, withered apparently by consumption, who spat blood and was subject to fevers.

'Have you any medicine for this, O Wazir?' asked a suppliant father. 'Men say the infidels have drugs for everything.'

My companions stared at the speaker and let him under- stand that the term *kafir* was distasteful to me, though he really meant no harm, for he used the term to mean merely non-Muslim. 'He is the Sultan's Wazir,' they said.

Loading up was an unpleasant job for the dew had been heavy. Half an hour after starting brought us to a point where we left the wadi by the pass of Sa'arin, to climb five hundred feet into steep stony country. Then followed rolling yellow meadows where hay stood to a man's middle, and occasional clumps of giant fig trees crowned the hills or nestled in the hollows. Behind and below us in the distance was the faint blue sea, and round us undulating down country with the wooded cliffs above Nihaz occasionally edging the western skyline. Here at 1500 feet the bird life so plentiful in the valleys below dwindled to a few sparrow-hawks and many large storks, but butter-flies, grasshoppers and locusts were many and various.

And now we looked down upon a pleasant vale that was our immediate destination, Al 'Ain, a Shahari settlement of Had hi Dhomari, where a spring comes bubbling out of the ground in the belly of a wooded trough. Two wild fig trees, as big and shady as good English walnuts, and bursting with apple-like fruit, made inviting bivouacs, and there I halted. A three hours' climb had made me thirsty, but it is impossible to obtain milk during the noonday, and the curds that were brought me arrived belatedly after I had dealt with the milk of a brimming fresh coco-nut.

From over, the brow of the hill appeared a party of Qara tribesmen of Shaikh Hasan, in extended order, singing their peculiar *danadon* chant [23] of the mountains. Their fellow- tribesmen of 'Ain mustered to meet them, one drawing his sword to dance in honourable welcome. The approaching party halted in a crowd round their leader while he improvised mock heroics for the occasion, and then lined out again chanting new couplets, and so came facing up to their welcomers whose turn it was to improvise a reply in similar manner.

Thus a ding-dong chanting went on for some five minutes on either side.

Of quite a peculiar type are these dark-looking men of the mountains, with their long rough head hair sometimes caught up and tied in a bun on top, but more often left wild and bushy, and practically no growth of hair on the face except a slight chin-tuft, many of them with refined, non-Arab faces. Their dress is the usual indigo mantle, which among the well-to-do is cut to drape half the body, crossing it diagonally and being brought over one shoulder. A leather girdle, looped as a cartridge belt, encircles the waist. Their heads are uncovered, except for a leather thong to keep their bushy curls in place; their black arms and legs below the knees are bare. Most of them wear a single ear-ring in the right ear and a single bracelet above the right elbow like the Mahra and neighbouring cognate tribes.

The reception of these men of Shaikh Hasan's called for the slaying of a cow on my part, and Ali al Dhab'an saw to it that the place of slaughter was within close range of a tree - for to-night's vigil. Ali and I were lying in wait expectantly when at about 10 p.m. an animal came prowling to where the entrails invitingly lay. It was impossible to see even at a dozen yards what the brute was, and quite out of the question to try to use sights in such darkness. All we could do was to wait for it to come close and take a rough alinement, whence the advantage of our both having rifles. As the sniffing creature came on, we both aimed as we thought best. It could not have been more than seven yards away when Ali touched my foot with his, the pre-arranged signal. Two shots rang out and the animal leapt into the air with a snort and fell lifeless in a pool of blood. We both jumped up, Ali with his dagger drawn in case of tricks, but the body showed no response as he kicked it, and our further investigations showed that both shots had told, one through the neck, the other through the body. It was a splendid specimen of a full-grown hyena, the first of five I was to get during the next few weeks.

The 'Dahaq' waterfall Wadi Darbat

I had hoped for a wolf, and the trumpeting earlier in the night of a donkey - alarmed for her foal - was a sign of the wolf's presence. Our bait was sufficient, for though the wolf will attack young domestic animals, goats, lambs and calves - it will also, like the hyena, prey on carrion. The panther on the other hand scorns a cold carcass, and will, like man, eat only what he kills himself. Here he is held to be a menace to man and camel alike, at least to man who has unsuccessfully attacked him in a tight corner, wherefore the natives of these mountains treat a passing panther at more than a hundred yards' range with respectful inactivity. They would only shoot if coming unexpectedly upon him at close range.

'Panthers?' queried Shaikh Hasan in answer to my importunities, 'they are rare, but a wolf you should get to- night. Send Ali to my uncle's. They are slaughtering six cows to-day as the sacrifice to my aunt who died in the middle of last moon. These men of mine are going along for the feast. Surely to-night a wolf must come to the place of slaughter.'

Here was a survival of great interest - the blood sacrifice and the burnt offering. Throughout these mountains it is the inviolable rule that one-half of a man's cows shall be slaughtered as a sacrifice, after his death. Half his wealth must thus be dissipated for the state of his soul - Estate and Legacy Duty with a vengeance, though for a very poor man a single cow or sheep suffices. A limit of twenty cows may be set only for the wealthy man, i.e. one possessing upwards of forty head. With them may be slaughtered a camel and some sheep, but the cow's value in sacrifice seems disproportionate to its actual worth.

On the day of burial, normally the day of death, one or two cows will be slaughtered over the grave to the words: '*Dai bi Huduktos Hadhail ir Hadhail*' (See by this gift M. son of N.)

Two nights are allowed to pass and on the third night another cow is sacrificed. This is called *khutum*. A further period elapses, varying according to the means of the deceased's relatives. It may be as little as a fortnight or as much as three months before the big sacrifice takes place, maybe of ten, fifteen or twenty cows, representing half of the deceased man's herds. This is called *yom el nahaira*. Both *khutum* and *nahaira* are performed at the place where the man lived and not upon his grave. More cows will be sacrificed by relatives, and by friends of the deceased whose bereavements he had honoured in like manner during his lifetime. This vast slaughter attracts the whole neighbour-hood and the section of the tribe to which the dead man belonged divide up the flesh for themselves, and go away under their handsome burdens. Visitors from other tribes have no such rights, but are invited to partake of the feast, for which one cow will have been roasted.

Then takes place the division of the residue of the estate between the relatives. [24]

Among the southern borderland tribes, such as Bait Kathir, and in the Qara Mountains customary, not Islamic law, prevails. Among the Bait Kathir not more than one- third of a man's estate may go to his creditors. Of the remaining two-thirds, one-fourth goes to the wife that has borne children, one-eighth to the wife that has not borne children and the remainder goes to the children in the usual propor-tion of a double share to each son. Where custom differs from Shara' law is that if there is no son and less than three daughters, the deceased's brother is entitled to only a daughter's share, and if there are three or more daughters, they take the whole, and paternal male relations get nothing.

The laws of inheritance of the Qara Mountains are peculiar. They are bound up with the cult of death sacrifice. Their wealth, as already shown, is generally in cows, and at a man's decease half of his cattle are slaughtered as a blood sacrifice. Creditors are allowed to claim up to one-tenth of the estate, and what remains is divided between wives, sons and daughters. The wives take one- tenth in a small estate and generally five cows when large estates are involved. A peculiar feature of this group of tribes is that if a woman has one daughter, or three daughters and no son, no part of the estate passes to the nearest male relative of the deceased husband's family, who would under Muslim Holy Law normally get the largest share. If she has two daughters it does. There thus seems to be some special significance in the numbers 1 and 3. Another point in which the mountain system differs from the usage of the South Arabian tribes, but accords with Shara', is that all wives get the same share irrespective of whether they have borne children or not.

The wife in these tribes may not betray grief on the death of her husband. Mothers, daughters and sisters may weep and raise their voices, and amongst the Qara they let down their hair, beat their heads, and pour dust upon them; but a public show of pain for the man's loss would disgrace a wife. She must hide herself.

6

THE QARA MOUNTAINS- HYENAS, FAITH CURES AND CIRCUMCISION

Hamr al 'ain! Hamr al 'ain! (Red of eye! Red of eye!) Such were the shouts - the usual idiom in praise of manly prowess - that greeted Ali as he returned at dawn from the scene of the sacrifice, for with him was a dead wolf straddled across a donkey.

I could not wait to do more than turn and wave greeting, for I had been called to Adaiqaf, the small village of the Shahari headman Juma'an across the meadow from my camp. In one of its miserable hovels a man lay dying. A straw thatch of beehive shape was not more than a man's length in diameter or height and had only a hole as an entrance to crawl through. The floor was strewn with straw, and there was of course no fire hearth. The only furnishings were a plaited reed basin into which they milk, and a few pots for water, butter or honey and the like- both the products of women's industry. Near by were larger and slightly more ambitious buildings having walls of stone, rough, undressed and uncemented. These were for cattle in the- temperate seasons, but against the summer rain and winter cold both men and cattle take refuge in caves, which are numerous where, in dips and hollows, the lime- stone strata obtrude. The winds of the ages have scooped out natural caverns, which only need thatching in front to provide spacious and effective shelter for man and beast.

And so back across the meadow to Ali and his hyena. The north wind blew chill at this height of 1600 feet, and the sunlit air, fragrant with the scent of hay, made it feel good to be alive.

Three snakes had been brought in to me by Badawin, the smallest a rather beautiful black and white barred *shalthum*, which was found to be a new species of colubrid; the second was very much alive and in consequence did not engage my immediate interest; the third was a *dololat*, a hideous monster only nineteen inches long and as squat as a bun with bold V-shaped markings along his back and an enormous flat head - an African puff-adder. Every day one such was brought in, which suggests it must be the commonest snake in the mountains. It is a sluggish mover and deadly poisonous, so those who walk through the undergrowth here do well to move warily, though to pursue a *charaxes* butterfly (those I got were the only known specimens of this African type to have been found in Arabia), head in air, is to forget perils underfoot.

In disembowelling this adder — its body contained seven- teen tapeworms which deceived me for a time - I suddenly felt a sharp sting on my finger and had an uncomfortable hour or so afterwards lest, despite my precaution in using tongs, some inward part of the snake were poisonous and I had not been sufficiently careful. No ill effects followed, however, and I decided that a spot of formalin had touched a part of my hand where there must already have been a slight abrasion.

The mountaineers will not eat hyena or fox; and eggs, chicken and all manner of birds are also under a strict taboo [25] like frogs and snails in England. What is or is not permissible to eat throughout the southern borderland of Arabia varies from place to place. Except for the sedentary townsfolk and this central group of tribes with non-Arabic languages, the hyena is eaten everywhere from Hadhramaut to Oman; the fox on the other hand is favoured only by the Badawin of Oman and a chance nomad like Ali, the mighty hunter; the wolf is eaten by no one.

The Spring of Khiyunt

Not only the nature of the meat, but the manner of its killing become a subject of lively debate among the faithful. Like the Hebraic Code, the Islamic Law permits only such animals to be eaten as have been slaughtered by a knife drawn across the throat. It is idle to suggest to the Badu that in days when firearms were unknown, the intention was merely to forbid the eating of animals that had died, perhaps from disease. [26] The illiterate Arab prefers down- right guidance and shuns such speculations as *kufr* - heresy. Thus he may not eat of a bird with a hooked beak. The suggestion that a hooked beak implies a carrion eater has for him nothing to do with the religious prohibition. 'Thou shalt not' is the law; its origin, or the underlying reason, is not his concern, nor yours. Thus an Omani townsman *askari* who delighted in fox flesh stood aghast when I asked him whether hawk was lawful food.

'Never!' said he. 'It has a hooked beak. We will not eat even a partridge,' and he narrowly eyed Ali who spent his morning cutting up the hyena into long shreds of meat and hanging them on a tree to dry.

'What's that for, Ali?' he asked.

'I'm taking it as medicine for a sick friend in Salala,' he said (a belief in its curative properties for human affliction, for the back - eat of the back, for the right leg - eat of the right leg, and so on, is wide-spread). Of course every one knew — even the slave cook who took a malicious joy in circulating the story -that Ali, the Hadhramauti, was saving it up for his family.

But the hyena taboo amongst these mountaineers is no ordinary one. Not only will they not eat its flesh, they will 'not kill it or assist in its destruction. They believe that it is a magic animal; it is the riding-camel of the witch, and those who attack it will incur its mistress's avenging hand. Cows will die or other retribution follow. Thus the Qara were much exercised to find a hyena's head boiling (my way of cleaning the skull) in the pot that was usually used for cooking their rice; Shaikh Hasan, under whose protection I was, counselled caution, possibly, I thought, as a sop to his own conscience, for he was an ardent believer and had vowed to me that he had once come upon a dead hyena actually wearing ear-rings. Doubtless some beldame, its mistress and a caster of spells, had pierced its ears and put them in. The same story was vouched for by the Kathir Shaikh of Dhufar, who called God to witness that he spoke the truth.

'What is there more succulent than hyena flesh.?' said Ali to me. 'These men are not like us Arabs, for we of the Karab and Sa'ar call it *kabsh an nabi* — the Prophet's ram. The Prophet himself made it lawful for us to eat,' and he proceeded to tell me how it came about.

Once upon a time a hyena claimed the young of a gazelle as its own offspring. Hyena and gazelle appeared before the Prophet, where each pleaded, 'The young gazelle is mine.' The Prophet sent them away and told them to appear before him again the next morning.

And lo! before dawn broke the gazelle came prancing up to the Prophet's tent.

'How have you spent the night, O gazelle?' asked the Prophet.

'I spent the night watch by watch standing like Cassiopaeia always in my place.'

Well after sunrise the hyena came leisurely ambling along.

'And how have you spent the night, O hyena?' asked the Prophet.

'I spent the night, O Prophet, asleep in the protection of Allah until the rising of his great star, the sun.'

The Prophet (upon him and you be peace), turned to the gazelle. 'Take the kid,' he said, 'it is thine.'

Up leapt the hyena shouting, 'God curse the Prophet and his father!'

Whereupon the Prophet seized the pestle from where it stood in the coffee mortar and struck the hyena as it turned to run away, so that its hindquarters withered to their present miserable proportions, and the hyena became food for man.

Verily the *kabsh an nabi!*

The ape is found in the Hadhramaut, but not in these Qara Mountains. There is a folk story that apes spring from a human being who stole Muhammad's sandals, for which offence the Prophet forbade him to enter the mosque, whereupon he went out into the fields like Nebuchadnezzar and ate grass, and became a *rubah* ape.

My hunting at 'Ain prospered, but I had the greatest difficulty and sometimes failed in persuading my collectors to slaughter in a manner that would not spoil the skin as a scientific specimen. The main difficulty was the religious requirement of a lateral gash across the throat, but Ali and I devised a compromise whereby he should first make a longitudinal slit of the skin down the throat (as required for my purposes), fold it back and then perform his orthodoxies under the skin.

I had been adamant in refusing any reward for a spoilt skin, and in the light of our new-found formula, Ali now declared how much he lamented a fox he had killed in the old way, and was unlawful for eating. I admired such piety in the acknowledged slayer of fifteen sons of men!

Yet the Omani soldier looked at Ali disdainfully as much as to say, 'That slaughtering is not orthodox - I would not touch it!'

But to them both, such is custom, a beast could be shot dead, and all would be well so long as there was a prompt lateral cutting of the throat made with the pious expression as the blood gushed forth, 'Bismillah ar rahman ar rahim' (In the name of God the merciful, the compassionate). But without the lateral gash God would not be pleased.

The scent of cooking food, or was it the hungry sense of an approaching meal hour, brought natives from all directions about us. And now one of these, an old Mahri who had not come empty-handed, stood by watching me despatch his chameleon.

'Wallah! By God!' he burst out, 'it is treachery. I found it innocent in a bush and it came along with me trusting, and this is what I consent to happen to it!'

A dear old man! I thought, you shall have a dollar. He took his place in the circle of interested onlookers who sat around.

'Have you any medicine for a barren woman?' he said.

'A strong man,' interjected a youth, and a titter went round.

'There may be medicine,' I said, 'but I have none with me. Is she young? Twenty?'

'Older,' he rejoined. 'She has had four husbands and I'm the fifth, and she has never borne a child yet.'

'Then there is no medicine probably,' I said.

'She is as a *bint* (virgin) still!' he returned.

'All the better!' said the youth unhelpfully, amid more tittering.

As the party broke up the old man remained behind, and I saw that he was not despairing.

'I want a writing [27] from you!' he said.

'What for?'

'A woman who is not yielding to her husband.'

'I don't hold with writings for that,' I said, by way of escaping an impossible request.

'But do you understand what I mean?' he returned.

'Yes, perfectly,' and I repeated his story.

'But she is my wife. I would like a letter from the Sultan ordering her to surrender herself.'

'That, I fear, is impossible. Take your case to the Wali.'

He clicked his tongue, which is the mountain negative, then put it into words:

'Lob! Lob!' he said. 'It would be shameful for me; promise you will not tell.'

'I promise,' said I, and the old man trudged back, I suppose, to his two unsatisfactory women.

The Qara Shaikh was slaughtering a cow the next day in my honour - let the unwary Arabian traveller be warned that this is the most expensive way of buying one - and a Shahari vassal of his brought it along. I looked at the Shahari and wondered whether or not it was his 'ewe lamb'; it probably was. The neighbourhood came to the feast, which was followed by the usual *haydanadon* chanting, though I gathered that heroic verses are often rendered in the Mahri tongue, as opposed to the love ditties of the mountains which are chanted in Shahari. 'Abdullah, the poet, did the improvising - a friendly garrulous individual from whom I was soon to hear a tale of woes.

'Have you medicine for this?' he asked, calling attention to one of his legs, abnormally swollen. It was little good my protesting that I was no doctor, for there was a pitiful predisposition among the sufferers to believe in my powers.

'How long has it been like that?'

'Three years,' said 'Abdullah. 'It does not trouble me when I rest, but when I run it swells and gives pain. And the blood of the sheep has not availed.'

For human sickness these tribes sacrifice a cow or a sheep, and sprinkle its blood over the patient's shoulders and breasts when the sun is high. The animal must be female, a sex distinction not observed at the death sacrifice.

'What is that mark?' and I pointed to a scar over a bunch of the varicose veins from which he clearly suffered.

'The cautery!' he said (the hot iron is a universal medicine throughout these parts), 'but it did no good. Have you no medicine, Sahib? *Wallahi!* I have no son, but if I were offered cure of my leg or a son, *Wallahi!* I would choose a whole leg.'

His friends looked at him incredulously.

'I know naught for it but a surgeon's knife, and that means a visit to Aden or Muscat,' I said.

To 'Abdullah, a wild man of the mountains, Aden and Muscat were remote as Mars, and a journey thither, entailing an unprecedented absence from his females, about as feasible.

'*Tawakkul al Allah!*' he said resignedly, 'Rely on God,' from whom, such was the implication, affliction and cure alike come.

'Abdullah's geniality was exceptional. The mass of these tribesmen are a dour breed, sly, suspicious, unamiable. They do not invite personal contacts, but the exceptional spirit among them can be cultivated. None thinks it necessary on arrival to bid one the respectful salutation universal throughout Arabia, none says a word of farewell on leaving the circle, but abruptly rises on an impulse, slopes his rifle, and turns silently away. Among themselves they are engaged in constant bickerings and brawlings, and I went among them apprehensive of trouble which might prejudice my own activities. Cow-thieving seemed to be the main cause of the troubles, for adjustment came not by restitution, but by revenge. Shaikh Hasan himself had, he told me, suffered the loss of a hundred head, much of it from the malice of enemies, for the animals were cut down and left where they profited no one. Other men told me that Hasan had despoiled his neighbours of far more, and that much of the repute he now enjoyed derived from the ethically questionable exploits of his youth.

To-day there was an alarm!

'Ya wulaid! Ya farha! Ya wulaid! Ya farha! call throughout the country-side, and all looked at the distant figure on the northern skyline who was raising the *taguwid* - the war alarm! Were the Badawin of the steppe coming, for the Sa'ar have, in times past, raided the Qutun.

Labkhit, the Shaikh's son, whom I was on the point of sending to Dhufar to purchase stores and bring me news, seized his rifle and ran off loading it, with the others, leaving me standing with just a few Shahara who took no action. The Shahara are a spineless people who will meekly consent to be pillaged or allow one of their number to be killed, without raising a finger in defence of themselves.

'Bahaim taht Allah!' No better than cattle under God,' said Shaikh Hasan, speaking of them afterwards to me. 'They are afraid to shed blood!'

This indeed is the crux of the matter, the dividing line between prestige and discredit, between tribesman and non- tribesman, between Qara, Mahra, Kathir on the one hand, and Shahara, Bara-hama, Bait ash Shaikh on the other: namely the power and will to fight; it springs from a corporate consciousness on the part of the tribesman by which the acts done by or to any member of his tribe are virtually acts done by or to himself, with all the consequences that that involves.

'The Shahara! they are no better than slaves!' says the tribesman, for whom marriage with a slave would be un- thinkable. It is dishon-ourable; let the nobility - the Saiyids and the merchants of the coast - use their slave girls as concubines at their pleasure!

The treatment of the Shahara by the Qara leaves the traveller in no doubt which is which, though the typical Shahari (who from the inter-diction of marriage outside his people, must be racially pure) is distin-

guishable by having a much broader face than his neighbours or the
northern Arab. His weapons help also to distinguish him, for very
seldom will you meet him carrying a rifle.

Not only the dress, but the arms of these mountains are unique
throughout Arabia - a bare double-bladed sword, a buckler (of the
circular kind found amongst Hamitic tribes) and also and chiefly an
aget - a heavy straight stick of *mitain* [28] wood, pointed at both ends
and thrown with great skill. This is the regular weapon of the mountains. The well-to-do, chiefly those of the Qara, will carry a rifle, in
which case he will not carry the double-bladed sword, but a single-
bladed one, and instead of the *aget*, an ordinary stick. 'And whence
came these Shahara?' I asked.

'They are the people who killed the Prophet Salih's camel, and are
suffering to-day for their wickedness, for they are no longer tribesmen, that is, men of honour,' was the answer.

'And had Salih bin Hut a camel?' I queried, simulating ignorance of
their story.

My informant, pitying my ignorance in his branch of learning,
continued. 'Not heard of Salih's camel, the most famous was she of all
God's creatures ever!' His stick traced the sun's course in heaven as he
went on. 'She journeyed from east to west, and from west to east, and
she yielded to all peoples honey, milk and wine. That was in the time
of Talmud and Ad, but an ignorant man of the Shahara killed the
camel and God sent on the Shahara a pestilence of ants, which
crawled up their legs and over their bodies and devoured them, so
that few have survived to this day!'

The next time I heard this story, an old man told it to me, embell-
ished with a sequel. 'Tempted by a woman this same wicked Shahari
pursued the dead camel's calf, hoping to slay that too. But God set a
cave in the way, and Nabi Salih's camel calf [29] entered into it and the
entrance was closed up like a wall of mountain and prevented the
man from coming after it any more.' A pause. '*Shuf! Sabhan Allah!*' -
'Do you call that nothing?'

'And what of the origin of you Qara?'

'The Arabs call us Qara but we call ourselves Hakalai, and we came here from Hadhramaut, and to Hadhramaut we came from across the sea.'

I had heard this many times, and Shaikh Hasan held that the tribe migrated westwards with the Mahra, and that they had lingered together over Habarut. This seems improbable to me because they, like the Shahara and Barahama, have no camel *wasm*, and for a tribe that was at one time nomadic and still breeds camels not to have had, or to have lost, the camel mark which is the tribal coat of arms, is inconceivable. Its absence suggests that they came in by way of the sea.

'Hakalai was our ancestor, and the Qara sprang from the Guraish. He and the Baliyoz [30] sprang from one race: but we crossed the sea.'

A Saiyid pointed out that this was not the Guraish from which his revered ancestor the Prophet sprang, but from another, only remembered in Qara traditions.

It was interesting to me as implying a consciousness of racial distinction from the typical Arab; it also suggested that the Qara are not improbably a survival - an eddy of that Abyssinian stream of Christian conquerors that invaded and proselytised South-west Arabia before Islam.

But of this my informants had no knowledge; for them the world is divided into believers and unbelievers, though of the text of the Qur'an they know nothing. Scarcely a man in these mountains can read and write except a few itinerant Saiyids. Writing indeed has a magical significance as the Mahri episode, and many like it showed, and whenever applicants for my medicines were about, they were eager that I should look into my book (it was a star-chart) to see the cause of their affliction.

'I have heard men say that the Qara sprang from Himyar,' I continued.

'Do you mean Hamyar or Himyar?' said the learned Saiyid, 'for there are two.'

'Allahu 'Alim' returned the Qarawi. 'I am not the son of yesterday - 1 was not living then, how should I know.'

It had seemed to me that 'Mahra' and 'Himyar' are not improbably

anagrammatic forms of the same word, though here again the word
Mahra is used only by the Arabs, but they are called in the language of
the mountains Inharo (with a nasal *n*). As between Mahra and Qara
there are both physical and linguistic differences, and neither will
agree that they had a common origin.

It was their turn. 'And you Inglaiz!' they said. 'Not less honourable
than you,' I claimed. 'Then you are *qubaili?*

This was a poser, for it is difficult within the limits of strict
veracity to make plausible an English tribal system in which people do
not carry rifles, nor defend their honour with their own right hand;
where women are unveiled and men's equals. But I dare not lose caste
in the eyes of my companions.

'We *Nasara'* (it does equally well for English) 'are a very powerful
tribe,' I told them.

'And who do you say is your forbear?'

'Adam!' I said, somewhat evasively, 'so that we were all very closely
related at first and only fell away afterwards.'

'That's a fact,' they said, looking at one another as much as to say -
'he speaks a divine truth. '

'And do you practise cleanliness? (i.e. circumcision).'

'It is not compulsory,' I hedged.

'Then there are men and women uncircumcised among you?' 'Yes,'
I confessed.

'God forgive you,' he replied.

With these tribes circumcision is a rite of great importance, and is
so different from the practices of the rest of Arabia as to suggest an
independent origin. The male is circumcised on reaching adolescence;
the girl on the day of her birth. This system of adult male and infant
female circumcision is the reverse of that found elsewhere in Arabia,'
[31] notably in Oman where the practice is infant male circumcision
(about six years old) and circumcision of the girl when approaching
the age of ten. In both regions, with the male the whole of the foreskin
is removed, but as regards the female, while the Arabs of Oman
merely incise the top of the clitoris, these tribes of the central south
perform clitoridectomy. This adult male circumcision conforms to

the ancient Egyptian practice, for male mummies dug up at Thebes show that this rite was even then observed. Here in these mountains there are elaborate ceremonies attending male circumcisions, and batches of youths undergo what is a severe public test of their fortitude on the same day. Large numbers of men and women assemble round a large open space. On a rock in the centre sits the boy of fifteen, a sword in hand. This sword, which has been blunted for the occasion, he throws into the air to catch it again in its descent, his palm clasping the naked blade. Before him sits the circumciser, [32] an old man; behind him stands an unveiled virgin, usually a cousin or a sister, also sword in hand.

She raises and lowers her sword vertically, and at the bottom of the stroke strikes it quiveringly with the palm of her left hand. The stage is now set. The boy sits, his left hand outstretched palm upwards, in suppliant manner, waiting for the actual operation. This done, he has promptly to rise bleeding and run round the assembly raising and lowering his sword as if oblivious of pain, and by his performance his manliness will be judged. [33] The rite is attended by brave songs and drumming and the firing of rifles, the women opening their upper garments as a gesture of baring their breasts. But no such manifestations of joy, indeed no manifestations at all, accompany the clitoridectomy of the infant female, which is done in secret.

Hair customs seem to be connected with the sexual life. A conspicuous feature is the central lock worn by boys, connected perhaps with the ancient Egyptian *Horus* lock, giving the effect of a metropolitan policeman's helmet, or recalling a certain Hindu caste. This is cut off only at circumcision, after which time the hair is allowed to grow normally.

Not less strange are the hair customs of the women. The young girl's head is shaven in alternate stripes rather after the manner of a poodle, a brow fringe being left; the back of the head is shaven like a tonsure, except for three or four narrow plaits. When she is betrothed, customarily at the age of thirteen or fourteen, the hair is everywhere allowed to grow freely. Within a month after marriage has taken place, as a sign that she is maiden no longer, a long strip of skin about three-eighths of an inch wide is removed with a razor, like a parting through the centre of the head, so that hair never grows there again [34] -a scalping operation extremely painful and sometimes fatal.

Women paint their faces on ordinary occasions with a curious pattern of striped black markings, on festive occasions with red, black and green paint. The common face paint pattern produces a rather elaborate clownish effect. A continuous black stripe borders the brow hair, cheeks, jaw and chin. Another black line circles the nostrils and runs straight across the cheek on each side to the ear-hole. Straight bars for the eyelashes are at each extremity carried slightly up towards the temple; there are two short vertical lines under the eyes. Broad black stripes encircle the throat. There may be a spot of vermilion in the centre of the forehead, Hindu fashion, and the lips will be painted red. A married woman will have the scalp parting - *munserot* - painted with a central black line. It is a universal practice amongst the women of these tribes to have one tattoo mark on their chins, a stroke between two dots, thus - a practice noted in Egypt by Lane.

Jewels are elaborate. The edge of her ears, pierced in infancy at equal intervals in six or seven places, are adorned all round with a large light ear-ring, or alternatively a little silver chain. As puberty approaches she will have a nose ring introduced, pointing forward from the left nostril. Her many finger rings have no marital significance; she has elaborate tawdry necklace bands, but wears no anklets, as do the coastal women.

An old Mahra lady, unveiled like all her kin, her face smeared indiscriminately with the greenish yellow dye (of a local tree) came to see me. The same pigment coated her arms from the elbows downwards, the legs from the knees downwards, and the upper part of the breasts to the neck. Her dress was the normal single loose black garment, low in the neck and reaching to the ground, with a black muslin head -wrap that fell about the shoulders, but her clothes were green and fretted with age - which gave her a monkish look.

She had brought me a present, and on opening the reed basket in which she carried her knick-knacks she exposed other feminine customs. Snuff was there; a most ladylike habit, but not found with men. Men smoke but not women, though both sexes chew - a mixture of tobacco and lime is held between the gum and the cheek; it is said to have a narcotic effect.

The present which the old Mahri now offered me to gladden the heart of some hypothetical European lady was an article of toilet - a small piece of local pottery quite beautifully shaped and recalling a Roman lamp - a nose irrigator, in common use throughout these mountains. It is filled with a kind of clarified butter, and the woman, lying recumbent, applies the spout to her nostril and empties a little of the contents into her head. 'A cure for headaches,' said the donor, 'which will make the eyes bright and the complexion clear.'

A Badu youth who had brought me a badger, a precious specimen because very hard to catch, kissed the old lady a fivefold kiss -left cheek, right cheek, left cheek, right temple and top of head - thereby showing a close relation- ship.

'This is Halairan bin Mir'ai, my nephew,' she said. 'Don't you know him He was in Muscat.'

'Yes, *billah*,' laughed the rogue, 'you measured my head in Jalali prison, but I told no one, for they would say, "Why did you let him do it?" '

I enquired the offence that had taken him there. He had squeezed a girl's hand, it seems, and the girl's family petitioned the Governor, and so he was deported for a year: but it had done him no harm, he assured me, for he had found *rizk* - God's bounty - in Muscat, and held up the rifle he had acquired there for me to see.

The salutations among these tribes are peculiar. Hand touching, universal among Arabs, is reserved for meeting the woman, and becomes only a smart tap of the fingers, the lady withdrawing her hand sharply. For a man to squeeze a girl's hand, or clasp it as in a European handshake, is to make an improper overture, for which the girl's relations may take blood. Men salute on meeting with a recip-rocal kiss on the left cheek, the right arm of each resting on the other's left shoulder, but they are so uncouth that if one party is sitting he often does not bother to get up - un- thinkable boorishness judged by any Arabian standard; for a shaikh or old man the cheek kiss is sometimes followed by kissing his brow; if shaikhs or persons of quality meet they will kiss, then withdraw and stand facing one another for a few seconds in dignified silence, before sitting.

I now rewarded the two Mahris who deserved well at my hands, and they withdrew with the usual remarks of the satisfied, 'God whiten your face,' and 'God preserve you.'

Sounds of girls' voices came floating up from the spring in the valley where a party of Qarawiya had gone off with their water-pitchers. Their song was said to be one of joy, but the love-fraught lyrics needed a bilingual native to turn them into Arabic for me, and none was present, so I must be content to record in our musical notation the curious wail of its melody. Where else in tribal Arabia would an honourable woman dare sing in public, if indeed at all? In puritanical Oman she would be beaten for a hussy, but here in these mountains and valleys I often heard the distant chanting of girls, and very pleasing it was to my ears.

Khiyunt

7

THE QARA MOUNTAINS-
EXORCISING THE EVIL EYE, AND
ORDEAL BY FIRE

Ain. The second week of November. A big moon sailed in and out of low-driving clouds, and I remembered the last full moon that had shone on my unobtrusive departure from Muscat harbour, but how different the scenes I had then envisaged for this moon, and their realities. Yet, though the sands seemed unattainable, and therefore in prospect very sweet, there was solace in these mountains.

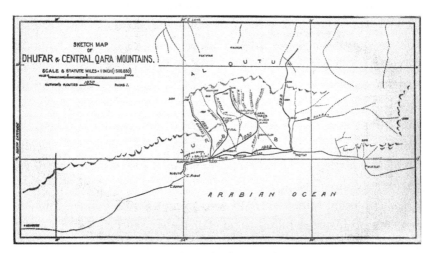

Bertram Thomas sketch map of Dhufar

Against the night the twisted branches of the fig tree that was my roof made an exquisite picture; loud and continuous were the hissings of crickets, and eerie the darting of large black bats from tree to tree; a rush of air betrayed the vulture that glided swiftly overhead; white and brown storks gathered in their accustomed tree-tops for the night, but took to flight at early dawn, for they seemed to resent our intrusion, and no longer gladdened the sunlit fields of 'Ain with their grotesque but decorative presence.

The dawn was heralded by the curious *glissando* note of a bee-eater calling to his mate. A joyous dawn? No, for the baby coney we had caught two nights before and had kept alive with cow's milk, was found rolled up in a cold s tiff ball. It needed us no more, and Sa'id, a young *askari* whose practice it was to come and fondle it, could not bring himself to watch it skinned, but walked away with bowed head - a display of sentiment unusual in these barbarous places!

We were leaving to-day for another camp four miles to the westward. My old camels that brought us here I had dismissed at the instance of their owners, who considered that they would be safer in their own district, and because I found that I could raise local ones. The problem when carrying precious specimens is to avoid having them dashed to the earth and ruined by restive pack animals, consequently the selection of new beasts demanded infinite care.

Our route climbed westwards from the basin of 'Ain through rolling stony meadows; it was nowhere so steep as to make us dismount, yet here and there it crossed high ground commanding magnificent views of the whole mountain chain. To the northward spacious downs, gentle and undulating, rose to the skyline. Behind us they swept downwards till they merged into the forested ridges and valleys that tumbled to the plain of Jurbaib. I halted to take bearings on known points on the coast seventeen miles below, while one of my party raced down the grassy slope to a clump of trees that marked the spring of Isam, famous for its wild-growing, bitter limes, soon to return with his skirt full of them. Thence we reached the brink of a wooded vale, one of the upper sources of the Wadi Arbot, and moved down to camp in it at 1650 feet.

There I was soon to grow familiar with the cry of herdsmen - *whop - whop — whop r-r-r-r*, and the swish of moving cattle herds, for the pool of Khiyunt was only a little way up the valley, and the hills about my camp swarmed each morning, at intervals of half an hour or so, with droves on their way to or from watering.

The cattle wealth of these mountains must be prodigious by Arabian standards. Every man and woman possesses some head of kine. A few individuals of the Qara and Shahara may have upwards of a hundred, though the line of prosperity starts at about twenty, and the owner of forty is passing rich. Only the cow calf is reared - for her milk and butter. One or two bulls will suffice a herd, so that the bull calf is slaughtered and eaten. His stuffed skin is placed before the mother at milking time that she may lick it and yield more freely -a universal Arabian practice recalling the camel *bau* of Oman.

The camel is bred in the wooded valleys below on a fairly extensive scale, but by limited groups, for its rewards to man are less and its care makes greater demands; even the sexual act necessitates man's assistance.

Milch camels normally never know a saddle, and miserable mounts they make, as I know by costly experience. Their breeding is only for the production of he-camels, the stronger sex, to serve the transport needs of the province, and carry frankincense from the mountains to the coast, and to return with sardines to the mountains for cattle fodder.

Flocks are raised to a small extent on the Qutun, the grassy roof of these mountains, and also in the plain of Jurbaib, very largely also in the Zaulaul below Jabal Samhan. The flocks are of goats, not sheep, for mountain men think ill of mutton, and refuse to eat of it when they find themselves at a feast in Dhufar. Yet to be served with it is not a personal affront, as eggs or chicken would be. There are no dogs in these mountains and few donkeys. The latter are bred by Shahara and kept by them and Al Kathir.

Sardines Dhufar

As for cultivation, the Qara may sow a few beans in the western mountains or elsewhere, where there are no meadows to yield grass; eastward in Jabal Samhan under the same conditions they collect frankincense, or get the Mahra to harvest their groves for them. But the predominant means of life is cattle raising; for these mountaineers are essentially a race of non-nomadic herdsmen. Only males may milk cattle. No woman dares to touch the udder of cow, camel or sheep. It would be the greatest offence. [35]

Illness, such as failure of milk in their animals, is readily ascribed to the Evil Eye - *Ain Balis* - which in consequence has terrors for them. Exorcism is by a frankincense rite, performed usually at sunrise or sunset, of which I was on more than one occasion an interested witness. The practitioner, the cow owner, brought an incense burner containing smouldering wood. He broke a fragment of incense into three pieces, and spitting upon them three times introduced them into the burner. The animal was held by two other tribesmen, one seizing it by the lower jaw, the other making it doubly secure by twisting its tail and lifting its near hind-leg off the ground.

And now the first tribesman circled the burning incense over the animal's head, chanting a rhymed sacrificial chant in the Shahari tongue:

'Look at this your sacrifice; frankincense and fire: from eye of the evil spirit: of mankind: from afar: of kindred: near by: and from afar: be redeemed if from me: be redeemed if from another: from the evil spirit: from mankind: I am a man: bringing expiation: for the Evil Eye: of man: of woman: look at this your sacrifice: frankincense and fire.'

His companions now released their hold and the animal bounded off, swishing its tail merrily and doubtless no worse for the experience, [36] to join its kindred that had passed on up the valley.

'But you Badawin have no such practices?' I said, turning to a Bait Kathiri of the steppes.

'Tawakkul al Allah' uttered with upturned eyes, was the pious response of this man - 'but after cauterising a camel for lameness we sometimes break a twig to throw after her and say, *"Kesert cud: wa sher ma'aud"* — a twig (incense?) is broken; evil return not.'

Next morning I went over to witness the practice of *nafakh* or vaginal blowing, which is universal amongst these tribes, as a stimulant to milk production. The animal stood, its hind legs firmly bound, while a boy coaxed it with food to be still. The owner took a deep breath, and holding the cow's tail to the side, applied his lips to the vagina and emptied his lungs: he drew back for a moment, holding her with his other hand, so as to prevent the escape of air, then took another deep breath and repeated the performance, running his hand along the udder at the same time to see whether she was responding to his action. This practice is said sometimes to be undertaken by the practitioner with his mouth full of salt, but I have not seen this done, though I have often witnessed *nafakh* operations.

The Qara at Khiyunt seemed in a bad temper. At first I fancied I might be the cause of their dispute, and wondered if they meant to hold me to ransom - a thing never yet done, to my knowledge, in Arabia. There was a real risk of bloodshed, however, and of my being unluckily involved. The disputants would settle by my tree, a ring of gollywog mountaineers, half-kneeling, with one hand resting on the muzzles of their upright rifles. They would begin peaceably enough, though with no sign of laughter, and with a running babble of voices, unlike the typical Arab gathering, with its major intervals of silence. Suddenly the tone would change, one man rising in his place and gesticulating wildly, to be met by another who would get up and harangue his adversary with an intensity that surely presaged trouble. Everybody now seemed to start shouting and nobody to listen. On this occasion a small boy tugged at his father, one of the most excited disputants, to come away. The others shouted gibes at the man as he went. Suddenly he turned round and walked back towards them.

'Zir-r-r-r-r-r-han alaik,' he snarled, drawing his forefinger across his teeth, a challenge to someone to come and fight it out, presumably with sticks or rifles, and the challenged one jumped up excitedly and fingered the bolt of his rifle, but wiser counsels among those present prevailed, and the parties were separated.

As in most tribal societies in Arabia, hukm al hauz or system of precedents and ancient sanctions is the law. [37]

This varies regionally, but is generally based upon the eye-for-eye principle, that the punishment may fit the crime. A recent example was told me by the Governor of Dhufar. A certain man was going on a journey and took a rabia [38] from another tribe into whose country he was going. On arriving there the sacred law of protection was transgressed and the traveller found himself wounded with a bullet through the fleshy part of his thigh. A hauz heard the case and decided that he who had furnished the rabia, an innocent party but a member of the offending tribe, must submit to the infliction of a wound similar to that which the traveller had sustained. For this purpose a piece of stick was brought and sharpened skewer-fashion. This was thrust into the defendant's leg and a bullet was threaded and drawn in its path. By local canons the plaintiff's grievance was removed.

In Oman abuse of the rabia would be followed by war between the two tribes unless the offended party agreed to the ruling of the hauz, when he would receive from the offenders, laum-al-wijh (blame of the face), which is usually assessed at four hundred dollars. Murder, which in Arab tribal societies is almost invariably settled by blood-money varying between four hundred and a thousand dollars (or the equivalent in kind) in these Qara mountains is assessed prodigiously high, in theory something like five thousand dollars, which may take a lifetime to pay off, but settlement is usually complicated by a vendetta. The murdered man may be poor, so that his close relatives will in any case be impoverished, but collections are made from all members of the tribe who, as a point of honour or from immemorial custom, must bear the burden. A Shahari or a slave may be murdered almost with impunity, for he is not a tribesman, that is, an equal, and has no clan to avenge him.

The tribes of the central south have a poor reputation as regards the *radud-as-salam* [39] - response to salutations. In other parts of Arabia it is commonly accepted that when two men meet, between whose tribes there is 'blood,' and one says to the other, 'Peace be upon you' and the other replies, 'And upon you be peace,' they have put aside their enmity for the nonce. For one now to take advantage of the other and slay him in his sleep, for instance, would be the deepest treachery, and would be punished by expulsion from the tribe with name besmirched. Not so amongst this lawless brood of the central south, who also neglect to observe the *thamn-al-batn* or 'stomach price.' This seems to be an extension of the law of three days' hospitality. If a South Arabian Badu has 'eaten the salt' of a man, that man and his goods are safe for a period of four days and four nights, the time for the last vestige of food to have passed from the Badu's body. Should the latter's tribe unwittingly raid the man during these four days they must and will return the loot. This *thamn-al-batn* is sacred with the other tribes of the southern fringe, but not with the mountain group.

Another peculiarity of these tribes is their addiction to oaths upon shrines (many of pre-Islamic origin) and the ordeal by fire. In cases of offences against their code, the oath or the ordeal will be adjudged necessary by the *hauz*.

Swearing on the Qur'an or in the name of God, as practised

throughout Arabia, is nothing to them. They will do it and lie cheer-fully. Sometimes, indeed, the accuser will not accept such an oath, but insist on the accused swearing by a sacred shrine. Powers of vengeance in varying degree are attributed to these shrines. [40] The foremost of the hierarchy appears as ferocious to local minds as Hazrat Abbas the hothead is to the Shiahs of Kerbela. The petitioner in a dispute will often demand an oath on one of the higher order, while the defendant will be prepared only to swear on a lower one. Public opinion in the tribe, which is formed from the degree of suspi-cion attaching to the accused, will then usually decide which shrine it must be. Oftentimes the accused will confess rather than face the consequences of false swearing.

A Group of Shahara & Kathir Girls

Ali, a well-known Kathiri of Dhufar, once stole a camel and killed and ate it. He was suspected and accused, and thought he would take the risk of swearing a denial on the shrine of Bin Othman. He swore; that night he was stung by a snake in the foot and his foot withered.

He promptly betook himself to the man he had robbed, confessed his guilt and paid him the price of his camel, lest worse befall. Ali lives to this day, and if asked what caused his foot to wither will reply, 'Bin Othman.'

But swearing on a shrine is not always sufficient. A suspected murderer may be called upon to undergo the ordeal by fire - *tamrit* or *besha*, and my Qara host. Shaikh Hasan, had as a young man been sent to the Hadhramaut to undergo the ordeal before the *mabesha*, had emerged vindicated, and lived, as he assured me, to believe in its efficacy.

Not every man, however endowed with these powers and with the requisite learning, will dare to practise for fear of the assassin's dagger, for so suffered Baihan, a blacksmith of the Yaham tribe, a famous *mabesha* or master of ordeals in Wadi Irma. 'But,' said my informant, 'who is there who will not accept the decisions of Ali bin 'Abdullah bin 'Abdul Wadud, whether he be *dheheb* or *hadid*, gold or iron, innocent or guilty.'

The ceremony takes place between the dawn and noon prayers. The parties assemble before the fire. The inquisitor inserts a knife blade into the fire, and after some time has elapsed the accused opens his mouth and puts his tongue out. The inquisitor then takes the tip of the accused man's tongue in his kerchief between finger and thumb with one hand; with the other he withdraws the red-hot blade, holds it to his own lips in benediction and then gives two smart raps, first with one flat side, then the other, laterally across the outstretched tongue. The accused should be able to spit at once if the portents are propitious, but two hours are allowed to elapse before the tongue is examined. If there are signs of swelling or undue burning, or gland affection in the neck, he is declared guilty and must pay with his life or as his accusers may require, but if there be none of these symp-toms, he is adjudged innocent.

'But what of its justice?' I asked.

'It is true *wallahi*, by God, the fire is powerless to harm the inno-cent,' Said replied, and I thought of Nebuchadnezzar and his burning fiery furnace, and 'the furnace of affliction' of Isaiah. Sa'id's sophistication dated from journeys to the pearl fisheries of Oman and was increased by his being able to read a little. 'Does not the *mabesha*,' he continued, 'invoke God to witness by kissing the blade and saying:

' "In the name of God, the Compassionate, the Merciful, O fire, O fire, be cold and at peace. As it was to the Prophet Abraham (upon him be prayer and peace!)." '

'What, O Sa'id, is this you say concerning the Prophet Abraham?'

'Surely you have an account in the Old Testament?' he asked.

'No,' I returned.

'Don't you know,' he said, 'that the *Nasara* - Nazarenes — Christians, your forefathers, wishing to kill the Prophet Abraham, hurled him into a burning wadi, and God sent the Angel Gabriel and quenched the fire's appetite so that it did no hurt to the Prophet, and he was delivered?' [41]

I have already dwelt at length upon their pagan cults, but the account would be incomplete without a word about witchcraft, in which there is widespread belief. Old men are particularly liable to suspicion, and are sometimes killed on the grounds that they could never have attained so ripe an age except by communion with supernatural powers. Death is often attributed to the spell of some suspected witch, who is forthwith persecuted. A tribesman of Bait ash Shaikh, who incidentally fired on us when we approached his camels in Wadi Afar, had as a young man killed his widowed cousin for a witch - an act which received public approbation, if indeed it was not actuated by public opinion; and a case occurred within a month of my arrival, where an alleged witch had been done to death by unknown hands. It appeared that she had long been accused, but had proclaimed her innocence and had submitted herself to the ordeal of fire. She emerged from the test vindicated, but even this failed to convince her tribe. It was a case of lynch-law in its most elementary form.

Murder in these mountains, is, however, a common occurrence. Life appears to have a low value. Blood feuds actually divide the Qara one from another, and exist between sections of them and sections of Al Kathir and Al Mahra. None of these tribes acknowledge one paramount shaikh, and their relations one with the other vary from time, to time. They seem to regard government as a superior tribal section.

At my camel side one day ran a Qara tribesman. The quality of his rifle and full bandolier, to say nothing of his self-complacency, showed him to be a man of standing, a *qubaili*. Salim was his name.

As I was riding on ahead of my party he took my camel rope from time to time to lead me along the path in the jungle least obstructed with overhanging branches, that I might not have to dismount.

'Are all infidels like you?' he presently asked. 'Big red men, with red beards and blue eyes?'

'Yes,' I told him.

'And how many cows have you got?'

'None, alas!'

He eyed me critically, wondering where my dollars could have come from.

'And is it true you *kuffar* find your money in the rocks of mountains?'

'Quite true.'

'God pardon you,' he returned, as though to ask forgive- ness for the possessors of this black magic.

'Is there money in our mountains here?'

'I don't know, Salim.'

'Then why do you come here?'

'Because I like to travel, and meet the sons of men, and study all God's creatures.'

'But do you get money for it?'

'No, it costs me money,' I said. 'These specimens that I pay you a dollar each for, nobody in my tribe will give me a dollar for the whole lot.'

He looked at me strangely. 'And these mountains, are you not afraid to come into them?'

'No! Why should I be?'

'*Ya hamr al ain*' — O red of eye - he said flatteringly, 'Taimur the Sultan has been here only once.'

'But I love your country, Salim. It reminds me of my own,' I added.

Murder was the subject which seemed to obsess my questioner, however, for he kept returning to it. Did I know, he went on, 'that a man of his tribe had recently killed a government *askeri*?

'Why did he do it?' I asked.

'Well, don't you know that in Wali Sulaiman's time government had murdered a Qarowi?'

'But that was fifty years ago' I said, 'and this *askari* lately murdered wasn't born then.'

'True,' said Salim, 'but he came and mocked a Qarowi who was the nephew of the man Sulaiman had murdered. *Wallahi!* he cursed the memory of the man's uncle, so that the man was blinded by fury and shot the government slave.'

'Well, Salim!' I said, 'in our country we have one remedy and a good remedy it is. If one man kills another, we kill the murderer. His tribe dare not protect him, and government will not accept any requital but the life of the culprit.'

'Indeed,' said Salim, 'but with us, a life from the man's tribe will do; and did not government privily send out another slave who killed one of our men last year, so that now we are on level terms. But why did they kill Hamdan ibn Jasim (a stalwart of the tribe)? *Wallahi!* he was a good man, and I had rather that they had murdered thirty others and spared him. But *ham katib* — it is written.'

I enquired for Salim the next day as I had taken a liking to the man, and thought of taking him to Dhufar and giving him a small present. But there was no sign of him. He had fled, and for good reason, for I discovered afterwards that he was the actual murderer of the government *askari* and conceived himself as having a blood feud with the Sultan's government, which had indeed at the time of the soldier's murder wished to take Salim's life.

I thought of our hour together through the lonely forest yesterday, and breathed a sigh of relief.

8

THE QARA MOUNTAINS- FAREWELL

Dawn brought with it the hour of prayer. The figures of my companions sleeping everywhere on the grass now began to show signs of life. Individuals, Qara and Shahara, roused themselves to pray where they stood, using dry earth for the prescribed ablutions, and I wondered how their Shafi' tenets permitted this laxness; while my three Omanis of the more punctilious Ibadhi sect went off with their rifles - in these mountains no one would move a yard without rifle in hand - up the valley to the pool for the ablutions without which their prayers would be null and void.

The Muslim prayer duly offered five times a day by these wild men seemed more like an incantation in magic than any stirring of the spirit. Even with the orthodox, more importance attaches to correct ablution, the exact hour and posture than to the very words, or so it would seem to a disinterested onlooker; while these mountain men just gabble the lines aloud with impious haste, looking irreverently this way and that throughout.

As to women and prayer, about half the mountain women are said to pray; probably a liberal estimate, for I have never seen one in the act of prayer in public view, and here as elsewhere in Arabia it would be as unthinkable for men and women together to pray in public as to eat. Yet if report be true everybody, man and woman alike, observes the Fast of Ramadhan which again would seem of less spiritual than ritual significance - something that if neglected might bring down God's wrath.

Later came along five travelling Badawin of the steppe, easily distinguishable, for environment and calling have left their mark. Legs not required to climb mountains are less muscular, and tend to handiness with much riding; while feet that turn inwards are an unmistakable sign, when accentuated, of the man of the desert steppe. Their dress was typical too, *musur* and long-sleeved *dish-dasheh* reaching below the knees. Their names added confirmation, Bir [42] Annekid, Bir 'Uwaiga, Bir Annegim, on the pattern of son of Kate, son of Jane, etc., for the nomad practice is that a man as often as not is named after his mother instead of his father, a custom nowhere to be found among town dwellers, or these mountain tribes. These five Mahra had come by ship to Sudh, a frankincense port under Ras Nus, to collect dues of debtors (their slaves?) who were 'serving the frank-incense' this season, and now they were returning to their place, the mighty Wadi Rama (sometimes Arma).

Next came another Mahri, but obviously a native of these mountains, bringing, a snake which he held by the back of the neck between finger and thumb, while it coiled itself menacingly about his wrist. 'It has stung me,' he said, and holding up his other hand showed a pinpoint of blood on his second finger, which was much swollen from being tied tightly round the bottom to prevent the poison from spreading. He now put the snake on the ground and it showed itself still full of life. As I edged away I saw him dart his hand out to secure it once more, but it was too quick for him, so that he caught only the tail. The monster immediately veered round and, with a sharp strike, stung his hand again, and I turned away sickened, for the bystanders declared it to be poisonous. Holding it out by the tail at arm's length, so that its head hung earthwards, he slid the other hand gently from the tail downwards to its middle, and then with a lightning movement grasped it again by the back of the head, and so squeezed out its life. I handed him over the customary dollar, but without the customary joke, for I was much exercised lest the man should die and the tragedy put an end to further hunting in these mountains, and even prejudice my larger schemes.

Yet another party of local Mahra, Bait Shaitana - the Devil's Family - suitably named, for they are of evil repute, headed by their crippled Shaikh Labkhit, came to see me. One of them wanted a drug against shortness of breath dating from a bullet wound received in a raid. He showed me where the bullet had entered and left his body, clearly to the hurt of both lungs.

'Then have you any medicine for a useless leg? The man isn't here, he can't walk.'

'Since when?' I asked.

'Since getting a bullet through the head.'

'There isn't any remedy in the world that will help,' I said, scenting paralysis.

'*Al hamdu lillah rabb al alimin*' (Glory to God, Lord of the Two Worlds), said one, in a spirit of resignation, and the four men looked disconsolately at one another, but I felt myself being judged. Either I was too niggardly to help them, or I lacked the magic or skill which they had believed me to possess. I gave them some dates and sent them away with promises of reward if they could bring me a badger, most difficult of all specimens to collect.

After dark the shaikh and his four sons came over to my tree and entertained me with their mountain songs in Shahari, while the carcass of a coney I had shot that day was left out where I hoped its scent would attract a wolf or a fox. The big red Arabian fox - the local ones seem to have an abnormally dark ventral surface - is very common in these mountains, and whenever I swept a torch round my camp bed, I could be certain of lighting up a pair of bright and brazen eyes. My Arabs were supposed to keep watch by turns, but to-night I walked across to their tree to find them all fast asleep, the Kathiri whose watch it was having first hauled the coney up into the branches, so that there should be no gnawed remains in the morning to show his lapse. I touched him with my foot, whereupon he leapt up with a startled shout and grasped his rifle, as every Arab in such circumstances does, for there is no tribe without its hereditary blood-feud that makes each man of it fair game for some enemy. Sa'id now kept his vigil and was rewarded almost immediately by a fox that prowled in his way, but this scarcely made up for a panther which had been shot at and missed in the Wadi Nihaz.

These mountain tribes being sedentary, have a sense of proprietary right not found in the Badawin. While in theory trees and grazing belong to no man, sections of tribes hold squatters' rights. Caves, too, are privately owned. They pass from father to son, but are not entailed, so that a present owner could at any time dispose of his, within the limits of his tribal section.

'But what of your caves bordering the steppe?' I asked a Bait Kathiri.

'As free as the air and the desert,' he said. 'To-day I occupy one and move on, to-morrow it is occupied by another. They belong to no man, but are of God's creation.'

In the villages of the coastal plain, where man makes a house to shelter himself, the first thing he does on staking it out is to hammer four long nails into the corners to keep out the Evil Eye. When the house is completed he slaughters a lamb on the threshold as a sacrifice to his walls enduring - a ceremony such as we perform in a degenerate fashion when ships are launched with a bottle of wine. In some parts of Oman when a new house is finished the prospective occupant will first slay a sheep, dabble his hand in the pool of blood and smear the door-posts. A similar custom is also observed in the plain of Dhufar, but during building operations. The meat is eaten by the builders themselves and the blood is smeared indiscriminately over the walls. On the completion of the house the incomer dashes two hen's eggs on the threshold, two on the stairway, and two on the upstairs doorway.

Fifteen is the customary age for both sexes to marry, but a boy is sometimes married before that age to prevent his acquiring bad habits. A girl too may be given in marriage before attaining puberty if her father is alive and gives his consent. If one party is of age, immaturity in the other is not held to be a hindrance to sexual relationship.

'But are these marriages common? What of your own?' I asked Shaikh Hasan.

'I was grown up, sixteen, perhaps,' he said, 'when my father found me a woman, but Labkhit here,' and he pointed to his eldest son, who appeared to be on the brink of manhood, 'I married him to his bint am (paternal cousin) two years ago. Now he has grown up he loves another, and when you dismiss him at Dhufar, he will, of your bounty, return and marry her.'

'And what of his cousin wife?'

'*Wallahi*, she is the fairest girl in the mountains, and has property as well, but he does not love her, but the other.'

'Is she young?'

'No, old!'

'Twenty,' I suggested.

'God forbid,' he replied, 'eighteen perhaps. He will divorce her and she also will marry another.'

It is scarcely surprising that marriage in these mountains is embarked upon in a spirit of levity. The bride is a marketable chattel. The most expensive costs about twenty cows (four hundred dollars), the cheapest one cow or even ten dollars -this marriage price is termed *gailap*. The bridegroom and bride's male representative, generally father or brother, descend to the plain where a *Qadhi* legalises the marriage, and on returning, the womenfolk of the tribe, preceded by men of her locality, conduct her to the cave of her spouse, where the only furniture will be a small carpet bought for the occasion. The man will have slaughtered a cow or perhaps two, if he is well off, as a feast, but beyond the *rabot* chanting of the men [43]there is no wild dancing and merry-making such as mark the rite of male circumcision.

Divorce is supremely easy for the man, as throughout all Arabia. He has only to tire of his wife and say so in the usual formula and she must go home to her father, with a parting gift of half a cow. Divorce by the woman is also easy, though financially more onerous, for she must return to him half the marriage price, which may amount to ten cows. Both are immediately free to marry again. Divorce does not require a *Qadhi*'s sanction, so marriages and divorces are frequent. A man may by religious law have four wives at any one time, but the general rule is one, or at most two. If a woman has borne her husband children he is usually unwilling to divorce her, but when he marries again, inevitably a young girl, it is customary for him to pacify the older woman with a gift equivalent to the new bride's marriage price. Thus women acquire wealth, indeed the independent possession of property by man and wife is regarded in a favourable light.

'How many children have you got, Instahail?' I asked of one of my Qara escort.

'Three,' he said, 'a girl and two boys.'

'From the same wife?'

'No, the girl is old and is the woman of Fadhlallah here. Her mother I divorced.'

'Why?' I said.

'She bore me nothing (that is, no sons). But it was she who asked for the divorce.' 'And did you claim half your *gailap* back?'

'More. I gave six cows for her, and demanded and got eight for her divorce.' 'And what *gailap* did you get for your daughter's marriage?'

'Four cows. She was worth more, but Fadhlallah is her cousin, and could afford no more, so I let him have her.'

'So you were six cows to the good. Two from your wife, and four from your daughter?'

He laughed. 'I was a fool, for she married Zaidi and bore him four sons.'

'And your second wife?' I enquired.

'She bore me three sons and six daughters, but only two of my sons live.'

'And supposing you meet the first wife who is the wife of another, what are your relations?'

'I may not salute her cheek or hand, but only ask "*het bi khar?*" — Are you well?' - (the usual greeting of the mountains).

A woman works under two extraordinary interdictions. She may not milk the animals; she may not cook the food. These are men's prerogatives. Her occupations will be grazing and tending cattle, collecting firewood and water, making pottery, cutting hay for the bed. But her main object in life is to bear children, preferably males. Contraception is unknown, and the idea abhorrent. Child-bearing is easy to her. She works up to one day before the birth and bears under a tree in the open or in a cave, in the standing position of a quadruped with the assistance possibly but not always of one other tribal woman, who may be her mother or sister. She is fit for work the next day.

Illegitimacy is almost unknown throughout these mountains, despite the greater freedom enjoyed by women. This is due to easy marriage, divorce, and re-marriage, not to drastic penal measures such as are resorted to elsewhere in the peninsula. In Oman, for instance, a girl, unmarried or married, who had willingly transgressed and was with child, would be killed by her father, brother or paternal cousin, but not by her husband. Here she would be turned out of the tribe and permitted to go off to the coast to fend for herself. In Oman the man who had seduced her would, if the act was by her consent, escape penalty and be free to come and go. In the Qara Mountains he would be pursued by her male relations. If they could wound him with a sword so much the better, but if he fled, they would hunt his wife, or sister, or mother and make the punishment fit the crime.

The girl of the mountains having been affianced while she is yet unfledged in body and mind is safe from irregular overtures. For a girl's first marriage it is the inviolable rule for her father to provide a husband without consulting her. This rule in Ibadhi. Oman is so rigorous among the elect that it would be shameful for a father to consult the wishes of his daughter or tell her of his visit to the *Qadhi* concerning the nuptials, so that she knows very little until the night she is conducted to her new home.

Here, on the other hand, the boy's father may speak to the betrothed girl herself, and will certainly speak to her mother, praising the qualities of his son. Once the mountain girl has been divorced and is considered a woman, her wishes concerning a future husband will be consulted, and cases occur of her marrying the man of her choice if he have the approval of her father. The right of *bin am*, the paternal cousin, elsewhere in Arabia universally accepted, [44] is not insisted upon in these mountains, except by the Mahra, where the sole right of disposal vests in the father.

We left Khiyunt. Our way climbed by a wooded bank out of the valley on its south-west side to a point 1850 feet above sea-level, where I was able to check my position by compass bearings on known coastal points. Thence we proceeded for the rest of the day on a course a little to the east of south, through rolling meadows of wild oats. The country became very stony and wooded and the valleys deeper as we went; so I dismounted and proceeded on foot with a butterfly net and killing-bottle, sending the camels by an easier but longer way round.

I was thus separated from the rest of my party when a Kathiri Badu came running up behind, shouting in alarm.

'Stop, Sahib, stop! You have no *rabia* with you, and Bait Qutun have held up our camels.'

Bait Qutun, a section of the Qara, were in evil odour with government at Dhufar; one of their headmen I had left in prison at Salala; they had refused to pay the year's taxes and were raiding.

However, I was in no mood for halting.

'*Wallahi!* he shouted excitedly. 'Bait Qutun are capable of any evil. Did they not kill a government *askari* last year?'

I had no Qarawi at hand and in fact could do no good if I went back; so I decided to press on with the single slave that was with me in the hope that we would meet no evil in our way. The road of Hamirir led along a ridge that sloped on either hand into thickly wooded wadis, Arbot on our left hand, Nihaz, of Bait Qutun, on our right. And thus early in the afternoon, after a three hours' unprotected tramp, we arrived weary and footsore at the water-hole of Fuzah, overlooking the Arbot; my aneroid read 1350 feet.

For our camp at Fuzah I chose a tree at the top of a field of waving grass that looked out across a scene of much grandeur. The yawning valley of Arbot below us went sweeping round to where it debouches in the Jurbaib, the plain on its far side framed with a ribbon of silver sea. Here edging the plain the seaward slopes of the mountains stretched away in diminishing perspective to hog-backed Nashib, the great wadi entrances marked by spurs were discernible at this distance only by the shadow that each cast upon its neighbour.

Wadi Arbot from Fuzah

Here at Fuzah was no lurking enemy, but only a young shepherdess passing, and from her I bought a goat to take down into the wadi that night and tie up over the water as decoy for a possible panther.

Two hours later my delayed camels arrived, the Qara being reluctant to talk of what untoward events had befallen them upon the road. Their day had been exhausting, nevertheless they cheerfully took their water-skins and descended to the Arbot to bring water from the pool of 'In, Fuzah being merely a dirty trickle.

Magnificent climbers are these men, with clean muscular legs, and the eight hundred feet of steep descent followed by a climb with full water-skins across their backs was as nothing to them, nor did they find terrors in the undergrowth after nightfall, though it proved to be a veritable snakepit and I collected four snakes (two of them puff-adders) within the first twenty-four hours of arriving.

Two nights had passed. I lay awake at 3.30 a.m., a dark, raw, damp night, under low clouds and a dwindling moon, when suddenly a distant rifle shot rang out, and a little later came the faint sound of men chanting. My first impulse was to rejoice at the thought that my panther party sitting up over a sheep in the valley below were celebrating a kill. But it was a kill of a different kind.

A young Qara shaikh tripped against my bed in the darkness, startling me, for I had heard no footsteps; off he went in the direction of the chanting to investigate it, and on a hill but two miles away found the corpse of a Mahri tribesman, hot still with lately ebbed life, and bloody from a shot wound in the heart.

Early in the morning he and Shaikh Hasan came to me to suggest that we could not safely remain longer. We must move, and in this the Kathiris, a lazy pair, agreed. The memory of their own blood-feud with the Mahra rendered them unusually alert. They feared that the deed was that of some hothead of their tribe, so that their own lives would be exposed to peril.

'And who do you suppose did it. Shaikh Hasan?' I asked.

'God knows. Bait Jabob (a Qara section), I fear. Did you not hear a fusillade after the chanting? That came from their direction and sounded to me like a tribal celebration of the murder,' which indeed it proved to be. 'The Mahra killed a Jabobi last year in a raid. Bait Jabob have now had their revenge.'

'But the Mahri must have known. Why did he travel in Qara country? Was there not a truce between them?' I said.

'Yes, the Sultan made a truce for one year. That expired two months ago, and the two tribes between them then made another truce for another year.'

'So this was treachery?'

'Ham katib' said the shaikh. 'It is written.'

A truce had indeed been signed. The signatory of that truce was none other than the murderer himself. He had sworn that his whole tribe would avoid shedding Mahri blood for a year. After two months he had himself dogged a Mahri's footsteps and slain him while he slept.

I knew the murdered man, Sahail. He was one of those four of the Bait Shaitana who had come to see me at Khiyunt but three days before, and had told me a folk story. A young man and a splendid specimen of his kind. That indeed is the way of the blood-feud. It is not always the murderer who is pursued; some outstanding man in the tribe, particularly if he be the culprit's cousin, is usually marked down and ambushed, as on this occasion.

'But why, O Hasan, did it take place here dose to my camp? Whose territory is it? Bait Jabob's?'

'No, my own!' replied Shaikh Hasan, 'but by our sanctions I am not to blame, for he had no *rabia* from me. If a *rabia* had been with him, then would our faces have been blackened by an abominable crime. If Bakhit (pointing to his son) were *rabia* to anyone killed by the Qara, we could not rest until it were revenged. I would rather Bakhit were killed than that the man under my protection should die and my son live.'

The speech was according to the book, but I thought how much more suitably it would have come from a noble Arab tribe.

Shaikh Hasan and the perpetrators of last night's murder were sworn enemies, for the Qara are much divided among themselves, yet one detected in his faint damning a certain gratification that a Qara life had been avenged.

I turned to the Kathiri. 'You must be relieved it was by no Kathiri's hand.'

'God pardon them, we Badus respect a truce, but in these mountains there is treachery. The Qara and Mahra think naught of outraging conditions to which they have called God to witness. *Wallahi!* even the *rabia* is not sacred with them. Do you know - but you will not believe it - Sahail who was murdered last night drank the milk of his murderer overnight. God forgive them!'

I decided to decend to Dhufar on the following morning and bring to an end my sojourn in these mountains. The hyenas, at least, would not regret my going. But, in spite of recent sinister events the thought of going was an unhappy one, for I was leaving what surely must be a unique land in all Arabia, a land of perpetual feasts for the artist, of endless surprises for the anthropologist, a naturalist's paradise, and to me, the wayfarer, a source of much interest and delight. On this last journey my party did not retire with the sun as was their wont, and the camp was alive until far into the night with brisk noises as they went about roping up my trophies [45] and preparing packs against an early start.

I slept fitfully, and awoke to look down in farewell upon the valley of Arbot, softly alluring as it came to life from its still slumbers. The crickets seemed to be silenced by the false dawn. From the top of the hill where my Arabs were worshipping, came an indistinct drone, like a mumbled prayer heard distantly in some vast cathedral. The stars grew dim in a salty sky that already turned amber over the sea whence a great golden disc came blazing up.

The long grass rustled, stirred by morning airs, and in the trees birds twittered with the joy of a new-found warmth. The hill crests lit up while the soft: valley between them still lay hushed under a purple mantle.

But now the sun is risen, radiant, all-pervading. Only mighty Jabal Nashib with its back to him dare still resist, its dark mass gaunt beside the shimmering sea. The passing minutes paint the scene in brighter colours—the clouds like mass of thistle-down have changed from green to salmon pink, and the sky is an intenser blue, the deep valley has at last awakened, and thence the bare-bosomed foothills beyond are delicately tinted pinks and mauves, and above them, meadows edging the sky bask in a golden light.

9

DHUFAR—THE ELEVENTH HOUR

Dhufar fort. It was 6th December. I was recovering from an attack of dysentery that had kept me to my bed for three days since I returned from the mountains.

Two months had passed since I had set out from Muscat; six weeks and more since my emissaries had disappeared into the sands. But those sands seemed to me to be even more pitiless than their own evil repute and I despaired of receiving news. Perhaps my envoys had been intercepted by their enemies and put to death, wasting all my years of preparation and the largess I had so carefully designed and cunningly dispensed.

To-morrow the Muscat State gunboat *Al Sa'idi* was arriving. I must return in her. Surely there would be official instructions brought by the Commander's hand to-do so. Some situation might have arisen in Oman, a war perhaps, a riot, or even lesser mischief to require my presence. In any event, I was due back.

A messenger ran through the streets below the fort keep. The crowd kept barring his way to hear his news, for had galloped from Murbat after hearing a ship's salute, and seeing the red flag of Muscat flying at her forepeak, and to be first into the market-place with these wares always brought rewards. From the housetops around rang out a

fusillade to spread the good news, while within the fort I sat rumi-
nating upon the failure of my designs. Last year a caravan had taken
me some two hundred miles northward to the very edge of the sands
—to be driven back, it is true—but this year I had not even gazed
beyond the Qara Range. Half an hour may have passed in such
gloomy reflections and the sun was near to setting when my servant
Muhammad came bounding up the steps.

'News! Sahib! Two Badawin have just arrived in the bazaar from
the desert, and they say they are an advance party of some forty
others with camels, and of them are Ma'yuf and Khuwaitim whom
you sent. To-night they halt over the water-hole of Forum; to-
morrow, insha'llah, they will be coming down to the Jurbaib.'

Joyous news indeed if true; but the gunboat would also arrive for
me to-morrow. Had my desert party - if such it was -come a day too
late? Was I to be cheated at the eleventh hour?

I looked down into the fort courtyard upon forty dainty riding
camels and as many ragged Badawin, that had come two hundred
miles at my secret bidding out of the sands of Rub Al Khali. I looked
out seawards where Al Sa'idi rode at anchor. And now her gallant
commander. Captain Salih al Mandhari, came ashore cheerful as
always, and expecting to take me back to Muscat. I eagerly ran
through the sheaf of letters that he brought. The first bore the Sultan's
crest. It was dated from India and was in that intimate and friendly
hand I knew so well. I read it a second time, a third time, and in the
strength of the confidence which marked our relations for six years, I
made a decision. I would send the gunboat back without me to
Muscat. I would attempt the return by another way. I would join
fortune with those attractive ruffians below, strangers all, and take the
plunge with them into the uncharted wilderness.

Khuwaitim and Ma'yuf brought Shaikh Salih to see me, and all
were at pains to enlarge upon the difficulties they had had in getting
the party together, and persuading it to come, the dangers of encoun-
tering their enemies, the hunger of the road (to which the condition of
their camels bore witness), and lastly and inevitably the rich reward
they expected at my hands.

I took an immediate liking to Shaikh Salih. He bore the magic name of Bin Kalut - Kalut, the most famous lady in all the sands, daughter of a famous warrior, and mother of three warrior sons, for to have kindred who destroy their enemies (and cleave to their friends) is of the very essence of nobility in this environment. Salih was a short man, big of bone, with a rather large head, bald - unusual for a Badu, even of Salih's sixty years, and a heavy jowl. His brow was big, perhaps from his baldness, and his eyes large, his countenance open and frank, his voice slow and measured; he inspired confidence.

I swore him to secrecy and unfolded my plans. I wanted no less than to cross the desert from sea to sea.

'But at what place do you want to come out?'

'Wherever it is possible,' I said. 'Riyadh, Bahrain, Abu Dhabi.'

'Impossible, Sahib!' he said emphatically.

'What is possible then?'

'We can take you into our country, the Rashidi *dira* of the southern sands, and bring you back, and God deliver us from the Sa'ar, but we cannot take you into the grazing grounds of another tribe. '

I was, adamant. Either I must cross the desert or never start at all. It would profit me nothing to do as he suggested.

'But,' returned Salih, 'the Fast of Ramadhan falls a month hence. Who will travel at such a time, when he should be fasting in the bosom of his family?'

Naturally Salih was in no mood to travel in Ramadhan or to undertake a longer journey than was necessary. But a Badu cannot be browbeaten. An inflammable person himself, he will not stand bully-ing, but be understands resolution, though it is well to give him a day or two to accommodate his mind to any idea that at first is unpalat-able to him.

The next day Salih came to see me again, and I once more set forth my irreducible requirements, for which I was prepared to pay gener-ously. I importuned him, lest I be driven to embark in the gunboat for Abu Dhabi and enlist 'Awamir help for my designs from that side. I hoped he would come with me in that event; this with my tongue in my cheek. Salih was impressed by this hint that I had the means of achieving my ends without Rashidi assistance (though I had not, despite the 'Awamir being old friends), and he became more amenable.

'But, Sahib, you don't understand. What you are asking is not in my power to do. Within Rashidi country I can and will take you as you wish, God sparing us from the enemy, but where you want to go is Murra territory. I am no *rabia* for the Murra, and dare not enter their marches myself without their consent and protection. I do not know whether they will have you in their place. I cannot give you the undertaking you want.'

It was a fortunate occurrence that *Al Sa'idi* was here. If the Badawin were in earnest about the difficulties, then it would be idle to start on a journey with them; their resistance would harden as we went along, an experience that befell me the previous year when I started without a clear understanding. To start and fail meant returning to Dhufar a month hence defeated in my major aim and proceeding thence to Muscat by dhow, a forbidding prospect. So I must for the moment keep *Al Sa'idi* standing by.

A third day passed and the Badawin from the desert were reported to be getting restless, for they had expected money and I had given them only food and camel rations. Salih came again protesting that he was in an awkward position, with myself and his men equally unreasonable. There were murmurs about my objectives, and the most improbable motive would be accepted by these simple and gullible folk. It was essential to win their confidence and to disabuse their minds of ulterior motives, such, for instance, as spying out the number of their camels for the ear of Bin Sa'ud or the Sultan Taimur or some other hypothetical collector of dues, so I deemed it wise to dissociate myself from any external authority, and avow, what was indeed the truth, that I made my journeys first because I liked travelling, and secondly to serve the cause of Him (science), which my tribe considered honourable.

'Well, Shaikh Salih, and what is the position now?'

'As I told you. Sahib, I want to help you, but cannot promise what you want.' I was indeed aware of the genuineness of Salih's argument, but it would never have done to accept the position that it implied. Obviously Salih was not in a position to guarantee the protection of another tribe, especially for a foreigner and an avowed non-Muslim.

'But you know well. Shaikh Salih, that the Murra are your friends; if I pay them well and they see that I have your goodwill they will make a way.'

'I believe they will. Sahib, if there is pasture and water, but only they know the way into their sands.'

This was my real object; to obtain the sworn support of Salih that he himself would come the whole way with me, and work to ensure Murra co-operation, and their marching through the fasting month of Ramadhan. If he did these things he should have at my hands a camel, a rifle and a robe. In our bargainings I induced Saiyid Sa'ud the Wali, who had just returned, to arbitrate between us, for he was a man of good standing and much respected, and I was deeply grateful for his kindness. As a pious Muslim too he bore witness to Salih's oath to me that I would be under his protection, and that no treachery should befall me subject to two provisos, which were beyond his control - the *gom,* i.e. enemy raiding party - and the will of God.

I felt, knowing Salih's fatalistic standards, that the latter proviso would render the oath nugatory, but I was careful not to press for a precise definition, lest it raise a delicate religious issue, which would have been most inopportune. It was the spirit and not the word that I valued.

So I had Salih's sworn promise that he would co-operate in my design in good faith: 'But none of these Badawin with me must know,' he added. 'They have come expecting you to visit Dakaka, our present camp, as you arranged with Sahail the Rashidi last year. They heard of your bounty to him, and that is what has brought them to you – *toma!* - greed. Avarice. That is the Badu's burning passion. But it is well. When we come to the water of Dhahiya their camels will be exhausted. You shall dismiss them while I ride ahead and arrange that others come there to carry us on.'

'But what of the way. Shaikh Salih?'

'War, Sahib, war, the Ghafariya of the Ma'arab [46] there is blood betwixt them and us; they are strong. We shall not *insha'llah* meet them upon the road. But the Murra, them you must meet else you cannot go on,'

We had to compute our precise number and rations most carefully. It was clear that with one set of camels or even two, I could not possibly carry loads across these hungry sands in the quick marches I desired; the beasts would lose condition. 'Four relays,' said Shaikh Salih, 'do not count on less than four relays.' He thought that their numbers could be reduced as we went along, but in the first march across the steppe, exposed to the Sa'ar, it would not be safe to move with less than forty. For financial reasons I would have preferred a smaller party, but my counsellor was right. Indeed, forty might be inadequate, remembering that raiding parties of two hundred and three hundred are not unknown in these southern borderlands where the shedding of blood, and the robbing of camels and rifles are among the normal activities of life.

'And if we meet a party larger than ourselves, Salih?'

'There is no might and no power except in God the Almighty.'

Rations were to consist of butter, rice, dates and flour. The quantities would determine the numbers of pack animals required to carry them on each successive stage of the journey. Too much food would be a great source of expense, not so much on account of its value, as because of camel hire, for these desert camels are small and light, and cannot carry a big load; too few rations would effectively destroy all chance of fulfilling my aims. I must budget for four separate relays of men: forty, thirty, twenty, fifteen. The first party would have their rations issued to them individually before starting; the pack animals would be carrying rations of the next three parties. The process would be repeated at each stage. By this progressive reduction I estimated I should require fifteen pack camels at the outset.

Accurate and careful organisation was essential to success, but could not itself ensure it. We might meet a larger party of Sa'ar upon the road (news of the three thousand silver dollars I carried would bring upon me a thousand raiders), while we would reach the desert only to face three more in- calculable factors, the first being the

Murra attitude towards my passage through their country, the second whether the pastures and water-holes were good enough this year, and the third the possibility of finding Arabs prepared to risk their camels and themselves and travel during the fasting month of Ramadhan. The Murra attitude was at present indeterminable. No stranger had ever been into this territory, certainly no white man and Christian. Would they co-operate? Shaikh Salih thought the chances were even. It was in this uncertain mood, after being held up for two months, that I marched from Dhufar on 10th December 1930.

10

OVER THE HILLS AND FAR AWAY!

A stream of camels issued from the town gate of the Husn quarter, where an interested crowd of black gollywog humanity had assembled to see our departure and to commit us *fi aman Illah* — to God's protection.

The departure of the Badu is ever sluggish; his thoughts are with his camel under its strange and heavy load; then he himself has forgotten something he wanted from the bazaar which he sees but once in many moons, and he hands his camel over to a neighbour's charge and goes back to dally there for an hour or more.

Khuwaitim came riding up with three giant iron nails in his hand. 'Did you remember these?' he says as he hands them up to my servant. 'You will require them for a hob in the sands, where you will find no stones for your fire.' So we halted at Salala while the blacksmith was made to produce a dollar's worth, to complete the deficiencies of the entire party.

'Drink, Sahib!' and two Badawin handed me up a bowl of water drawn from the mosque well, and after I had had my fill, themselves squatted down, for it is *aib* - shameful - for a son of the desert to drink standing, and drank after me - a display of tolerance gratifying to me after residence in 'Iraq, where close contact with the priesthood of the

Holy Places of the Shi'ah persuasion has had its effect on tribal custom in such matters.

We had scarcely gone five miles, my party struggling out across the plain in aimless formation, when as we approached some camel thorn, shouts came from the rear, 'Let the camels eat,' 'Let the camels eat,' and the tribesmen, upon overtaking us, counselled our dismounting, their excuse being that Shaikh Salih was still behind. No sooner had I dismounted than they off-saddled; the animals were knee- hobbled by the two forelegs, and so sent off to feed at the bushes near by. We were there for the night. The rations were heaped up into a single pile, as precaution against arch-thieves of the district, for whom the sight of such plenty must have been a sore temptation. Shaikh Salih knew their kind too, for when he came along a little later he stood amidst the baggage, loudly exhorting his party.

'Ya Jumaa! Ya Gom' — O Assembly! O braves!

'Zad al Wazir' - The stores of the Wazir!

'Fi aman Illah' - are in God's keeping.

'Wa fi amankum' — and in your keeping.

'Tam tam' came an acquiescent chorus from my Badawin, distributed and busied upon a multitude of activities. Some were cutting riding-canes from thickets; some oiling their water-skins to make them tight against the long marches ahead; the owners of pack animals sat sewing up sacks of hay as improvised pack saddles, for the ready-to-wear article does not exist in this remote corner of Arabia, and I had to buy a supply of sacks at Dhufar; others were looking over their bazaar purchases, including a large aluminium kettle, while one fine youth romantically fondled a golden coloured mirror, probably destined to call a sparkle to the wondering eyes of some frail and cherished being in the sands. 'Come and see *ahfat an naga*,' shouted Shaikh Salih, who sat on the ground with a large sail-maker's needle in his hand, bending over a camel that was held down on her side by a few Arabs in the customary way; one held the head turned back along the body; another had a twitch on her upper lip, a third held one leg stretched out behind.

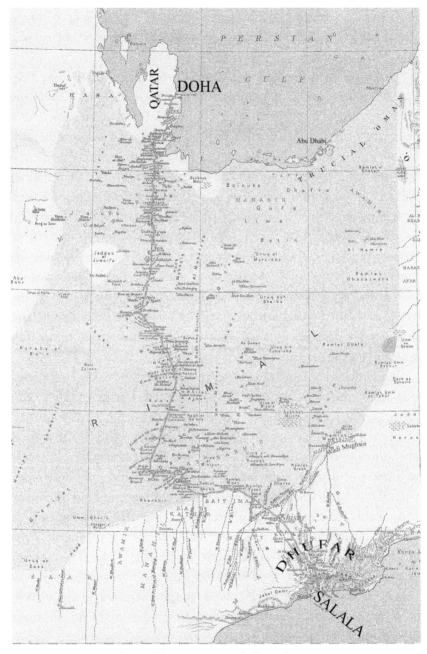

Bertram Thomas route across the Empty Quarter

The operation was to sew a small leather patch on the side of the foot over an abrasion which had been caused by the unaccustomed stony tracks of the mountains; it would be a protection on the morrow's journey.

No sooner did the Badawin come to the end of their tasks than they fell to arguing, as they inevitably do, about the inequality of the loads, each Badu being jealous for a light task for his own camels: as a result the loads were reshuffled and I found myself a sufferer thereby, for the mount I had ridden was taken from me on the pretext that she was not good enough, and on the morrow I found myself riding an animal much less to my liking. A day never passed without some such wrangling about loads, for the camel is her master's dearest dear, and he will cease fighting her battles only with his latest breath.

Two parties lined up for sunset prayer, one led by Shaikh Salih, the other by my Karabi *rabia*. According to my servant, their performance was in pleasing contrast to that of my Bait Kathir party of the previous year, men who prayed not in a line but individually, and though they declaimed aloud were woefully ignorant of the words, which to instructed ears became a sorry jumble.

We were mounted by seven next morning, and after two hours' ride across the plain towards Wadi Nihaz made Ghaur Fazl, a hole in the grassy foothills. So far as I could ascertain from local enquiries, this is the only place answering to Bent's description of a natural phenomenon he identified with Ptolemy's Diana Oraculum. I confess to a sense of disappointment. It was unusually large, certainly some twenty feet across, and round its top is a circular mound which may conceivably conceal a wall as described by Bent, but appears to contain excavated material as well. The sides of the gaping hole are of bright red clay and show signs of having, at one time, been bricked or stone-lined. A pebble dropped into it took approximately two seconds to reach the dry bottom. It may therefore be assumed to be a hundred feet deep. The Qara attributed it to Minguwi, most famous of their mediaeval rulers, as they do every old relic, and to me also, Ghaur Fazl was the work of man's hands. Scattered around it, indeed throughout these foot- hills, were beehive-shaped mounds the height of a camel. They are not archaeological remains, as Bent suggests, but ant-heaps [47] — in the language of the mountains, *izdirit*.

Cave of Sahaur

A mile beyond, within the entrance to the Nihaz valley and on the west side of it, was the famous cave of Sahaur, a black, gaping hole two hundred and fifty feet above, amidst a dense forest of trees. Thither I had climbed with Sahail, a Bait Qutuni, and grandson of that Sahail with whom the Bents came to see this cave, though they did not enter. Its mouth proved to be a yawning alcove a hundred feet wide and some forty feet to its roof of stumpy weathered stalactites whence rock pigeons fluttered at our approach. Legend has it that *jinns* share a dark existence here with snakes and scorpions, but when I pointed to a tiny low hole on the left side of the caverned mouth which alone gave entrance to the interior and asked for volunteers, my party of five men, *jinn*-believers to a man, said that they were ready. So we cheerfully said *tawakkul al Allah* and one by one slithered feet fore-most into the dark sloping hole. It was so small that we could enter only lying flat, but a wriggle of ten feet brought us into a large inner chamber of irregular shape with comfortable head room, and utterly dark. My torch showed its formation to be a pure dazzling white crystalline rock. There was a slow hut continuous drip of water from innumerable stalactites of slightly darker hue, and small stalagmites sprang up in places from the floor. A giant pillar had a basin-like annexe some three feet in diameter on an almost perfect hollow hemisphere of the same formation. This chamber led to others, their entrances often very narrow, the one we explored being only accessible on all fours. The natives say (though few, if any, have dared its hazards) that the cave continues as a series of connected chambers for miles back into the mountains, and at one point is so spacious that a stone thrown by a man will not reach its roof. It was so stiflingly hot and sweaty inside that I stayed only for half an hour to collect some geological specimens and a bat (one chamber proved to be a veritable cage of bats) before leading the way out with my torch. One by one we emerged into the refreshing air and light of day.

We now climbed the Aqabet al Hamra on the opposite side of the valley through thickly wooded slopes, reaching the top an hour and a half later, where just short of our old camp of Fuzah my aneroid read 1300 feet. Thence onward through undulating meadow country on a northerly course to halt at half-past two at Lehez (2370 feet), just below the Qutun.

Khuwaitim came to me. 'The water of Aduwiz,' he said, 'lies a mile to the west. It is like honey. To-morrow we Badawin will water our camels and fill our own water-skins at Hanun, but the water of Hanun is not like the water of Aduwiz. It is better that we halt here for your water-skin to be filled with this sweet water.'

'Why, oh why dissemble, Ya Khuwaitim,' I thought, for the real reason, and a very good one too, was that here were some *ghaf* acacias, a most unusual tree in these latitudes at this height, and incomparable food for our camels. I readily commended the halt, for the best way to win esteem was to show not indifference but solicitude for the camels' welfare.

The party straggled uphill into camp and turned to replacing the old straw stuffing of their pack-saddles with the new standing hay.

Shaikh Salih, like Shaikh Hasan on my mountain expedition, was the most active of all his tribesmen in collecting firewood, for tribal shaikhs lead their followers in war and work alike.

The inescapable crowd of natives surged round our camp- fires, and my Badawin showed their previous anxiety for our rations and kit, gathering them into a heap upon which some of them would sleep and the others lie round it, for they ascribe to the mountain men almost supernatural powers of thieving.

'There is only one medicine. Would you like to see a "cure," Sahib; an old patient is in the camp,' and they brought along a man of the Qara. After some persuasion he allowed his indigo mantle [48] to be drawn back, and there appeared a withered arm. The offending hand had been cut off in accordance with the 'Law of God' - Shara' law - by order of the Sultan when on his first visit to Dhufar. The man had been caught red-handed thieving, and the appointed slave at the fort had made a good job of it with one fall of the axe. Good people saw in it a religious act, but as a deterrent its effect was short-lived.

The southerly wind veered round to the south-west and blew cold at this altitude. The sky was veiled with low dark clouds, and the heavy dew vexed me, for I was carrying no tent with me into the sands. Previous journeys made me fear that the Murra or other Badawin would so resent the camels having to bear the intolerable burden of my tent as to prejudice them against the trip. So I left it behind, and regretted it during these two December nights in the hills. The wet and dry bulb thermometers registered almost alike, my upper blanket was wringing wet and the pillow so damp that it had to be turned over during the night. I wore my Arab head-dress as a shawl to sleep in, but woke up with eyes sticky from external moisture.

The camels couched around the fires sat all night contentedly chewing the cud. They were astir with their masters' dawn prayer, and stood like so many statuesque sentinels, waiting till a little more light and warmth should sharpen their appetites. Then their masters came to drive them off to crop the nearest thickets until we set out on the day's march.

Our north-westerly course led up into the Qutun, the roof of the

Qara Mountains, and I turned in my saddle to take a last glimpse of the Indian Ocean three thousand feet below. Here the meadows ceased and gave place to stretches of *gudelat*, a large gum-yielding shrub. Children, in the hope of *bakhshish*, ran at my side to hand up plants that they hoped would excite my favour, now *halgum*, a tomato-like fruit used to clean hides, now *subur*, a cactus whose bitter sap is medicine for the belly and balm for the eye, whilst the skin yields a greenish-yellow dye beloved of local ladies. Bare bleak hills about us, with rough going, drew out the party into single file. The divide passed, we began to descend the far side of the Qara Mountains by the torrent beds of Qabliya (2500 feet). Our route lay at the bottom of its bleak gorge, sculped on both sides with deep cavities - one of these Reddit, a shelter for flocks - while the boulders lying in the valley were speckled with a white efflorescence.

'*Rahman ar Rahim* muttered Shaikh Salih, riding immediately behind me, as we passed some graves.

'We bare our heads in the presence of a corpse,' I said.

'And how do you bury your dead? Is it true the *kuffar* burn them?'

To burn a body destined for physical resurrection would be sacrilege indeed, and I deemed it wise to pass over the growing practice of cremation.

'We take our dead into the masjid,' I said, 'and pray over them to Allah, and then we wrap them in a white shroud (this very important!) and so bury them in the ground.'

'*Wallahi Muslimin!* said one of the Rashidis approvingly.

But later in the day I found my view of religion not so widely shared. A Bait Kathiri youth ran at the side of my camel and seemed very friendly disposed. By and by he dropped a little behind and I heard myself being discussed.

'They are a truthful people,' said Shaikh Salih.

'You don't say so,' said the youth.

'And success is theirs in this world!'

'*Rubi y hassabhum.*' 'My Lord will hold them to reckoning (in the next),' came the youthful response.

'*Istaghfirullah.*' May God forgive them,' said the shaikh, as if apologising for acting as my guardian.

The aneroid fell gradually as we moved along the gorge and after four miles we came to the soft sand of the wadi bed of Sa'atan. Before us was a panorama of pale sandstone hills, characteristic in their conical and pyramidal shapes. Amongst those that bore names the most conspicuous were the Horn of Fahad, which lay due west, and soon before us, bearing north-west, the Horn of Shaiba, below which we proposed to camp for the night. Beyond these nearer hills we could see a vast waste of red rolling country, its ruddy wastes in pointed contrast to the hills and their wooded meadows behind us.

Hidden in these desolate wadi beds, which drain north across the steppe, flourishes the wild *mughur*, frankincense tree. In appearance it is a young sapling, having almost no central trunk, but from near the ground there springs out a clump of branches which grow to a camel's height and more, with ash-coloured bark and tiny crumpled leaves. One of my men leapt off his camel to bring a specimen of the sap in the raw condition on his dagger blade for me to see; it resembled green transparent lard and was very fragrant. The tree begins to bear in its third or fourth year. The collectors, women as well as men, come to make slight incisions here and there in the low and stout branches with a special knife. A gum exudes at these points and hardens into large lozenge-shaped tears of resinous substance which is known as frankincense (*liban*). After ten days the drops are large enough for collection, and the tree will continue to yield from these old incisions deepened as necessary at intervals of ten days for a further period of five months. After this the tree dries up and is left to recover, the period varying from six months to two years according to its condition. Collection of the *liban* is made chiefly during the summer months. It is stored in the mountain caves till the winter, when it is sent down to the ports for export, for no country craft put to sea during the gales of the summer south-west monsoon. This delay enables the product to dry well, though normally it is ready for export in from ten to twenty days after collection.

Frankincense Tree

From Bombay it finds its way to the temples of the East, a little being kept in Dhufar where the good housewife may put an incense burner under the bed at sunset to keep away evil. Frankincense has from the earliest times been a precious spice and the most acceptable of offerings. It was used by the Egyptians to preserve the bodies they held sacred, Pharaohs and others of royal blood, and crocodiles; it was burned before the tabernacle of the Israelites in the days of Moses, the hill of frankincense is mentioned in the Song of Solomon, and it was brought as a gift, with gold and myrrh, to our Infant Lord.

It is found growing, as a commercial crop, only in central South Arabia between two thousand and two thousand five hundred feet in a region [49] which happens to be identical with the territorial limits of the Qara tribe, from long. 53°00 to long. 55°21'. Its occurrence on the edge of the unique summer rain belt of Dhufar suggests that climatic conditions favourable to its growth exist nowhere else in the peninsula. If so, this region is not improbably the famous frankincense region of historic Arabia. In any case, the famed groves of the Yemen and Hadhramaut have become insignificant; the tribes of Dhufar remember them not.

For an hour we passed through a grove of young frankincense trees scarred with the marks of recent milking. Its Qara owners, herdsmen and not pickers, are content to rent it to Kathiri and Mashaiyikh for half the produce. This point, but a bare twenty miles from the sea, marks the northward limit of the settled tribes - the Qara, Shahara, and mountain elements of Al Kathir and Mahra; it also roughly approximates to a geological division. Behind us were the limestone mountains. Upper Cretaceous to Eocene; before us was a great wilderness of sandstone steppe sloping down a six days' march to the edge of the sands, the scene of a sparse and sporadic nomad life of Bait Kathir, Mahra and Bait ash Shaikh Badawin.

It was a joy to be in the saddle again, and a joy to have left the busy humdrum world of Dhufar behind for these wide clean spaces. My companions were as yet songless on the march, as indeed were the other South Arabians of my last journey, and I missed the rousing camel chanties of the march in Oman; only Sahail [50] occasionally broke into song. Still, they were merry enough conversationalists, even if their subjects were limited to camels, rifles and women. The conspiracy of silence of European convention is completely absent, with it the element of conscious in- decency. It was like schoolboys

ridiculing a bad bowler, or deriding one of their number who persis-
tently failed to 'convert' a 'try,' for they see no shame in joking about
each other's impotence with women, and Sahail, the most persistent
of them, wondered whether in my medicine box of magic I carried no
aphrodisiac. But one thing was even more important. Could I divine
water?

Qarn Shaiba, under which we halted for the night, is a conical hill
lying on the north side of the shallow wadi bed of Sa'atan.

Salih and I being mounted were with a few other favoured spirits
first into the jungle of *samr* acacia where we were to camp, while the
rest of the party, afoot and leading their unused camels down the
rough mountain gorge behind us, came trickling in, and soon a dozen
camp fires sprang up along the valley. Shisur lay four days ahead, and
there was no water, except the neighbouring water-hole of Hanun,
until we reached it, so we must water camels here to-morrow and
leave with full water-skins for ourselves.

Dawn prayers over, the Badawin scattered in all directions to
round up their camels, and soon they came riding in bare-backed, and
so off to Hanun. Two hours due east, in and out amongst desolate hills
surfaced in places with black flint, brought us to the high conical hill
of Qarn Hanun on the one hand and a triple-horned system called
Ardaf on the other.

Just beyond the earth suddenly opened to form a V- shaped fissure
of crystalline rock, which descended in terraces of sparkling whiteness to a green wadi floor one hundred and fifty feet below. The
uppermost stratum was often overhanging; the lowest also had been
eroded here and there into long shallow caves. This was Ghabartan, a
tiny winding wadi which joins the Rakibit within view, and is thus a
source of the Katibit, a big trunk wadi running north to the sands.
Here at its tapering source we looked down upon the green pond of
Hanun in its bed. The water-hole occasioned the usual disillusionment when I recalled the Badu stories in its praise - intelligible
enough in a very thirsty land.

The little wadi leading down into Ghabartan is called Ba
Musgaiyif, 'the place of tombstones,' and I was anxious to explore it as

its name promised more archaeological remains of a kind I had discovered throughout this frankincense belt, and for some miles eastward of it. This was a crude ground monument sometimes bearing pre-Arabic, possibly early Ethiopic inscriptions, thereby suggesting that the central south tribes speaking tongues having Ethiopic affinities may be of considerable local antiquity. Ba Musgaiyif proved a disappointment in that there was no inscribed material among the numerous but badly weathered monuments.

The more elaborate kind I had met with elsewhere consisted of a system of triliths, three elongated blocks of undressed stone (or sometimes round boulders with a naturally smooth surface), about eighteen inches high, standing on end and leaning inwards with their tops touching to ensure stability. These triliths were set up in series along one alinement, each pile standing at about one and a half paces from its neighbour. Sometimes the trilith had a fourth and smaller capping boulder, and occasionally a series of triliths was enclosed by an elliptical line of small pebbles.

Triliths

The series varied in number. I found them of five, seven, nine, fourteen and fifteen triliths. Running parallel to each series at about three paces distant was a smaller series of large conical rubble heaps, such as I have seen elsewhere used for *mashuwa* cooking, a method of grilling flesh on heated stones. These, I suggest, had some sacrificial significance. Some of the smaller series of triliths, e.g. the runs of five, were without them; the longer lines had a stone pile to three or four triliths. Between triliths and sacrificial piles were sometimes small square boulders which might have been used as seats.

These monuments had no common orientation; wherever I found them they lay in wadi beds and were in line with their courses. Most of them lacked inscriptions, which may in part be accounted for by weathering of the soft local limestone. Inscribed boulders were first met lying near the monuments in Wadi Andhaur, but in Wadi Dhikur I found them as the headstone of one of the terminal triliths. The inscriptions were generally separate characters an inch and half high, rudely done, and having a dotted superficial impression which suggested that the implement used was a pointed flint. On account of the weathering of the stone many of the inscriptions were so blurred as to be unrecognisable, except for a character here and there. For the same reason the squeeze and the photographs I took were unsatisfactory, but I copied the better preserved inscriptions in full. Transport limitations prevented my bringing back more than one specimen of this work. It appeared to represent a camel; this I presented to the British Museum. I found the monuments in the following wadi beds: Sarab, Ainain, Banat ar Raghaif, Haradha, Andhaur (below Khungari Pass), Dhaghaub, Dhikur, Ba Musgaiyif, and near Aiyun water-hole. The majority (and most of the inscriptions) occur in Wadi Dhaghaub and Wadi Dhikur where there are long lines of them in parallel groups. It is, I think, probable that they are graves. This is suggested not merely by their appearance, but by their abundance in Wadi Dhikur, which preserves a continuous burial tradition, having a large recent Muslim cemetery, as well as two other cemeteries of pre-Islamic or at least non-oriented types of grave, namely, rock burial and the mammoth grave, while its name could be taken to mean 'Vale of Remembrance.'

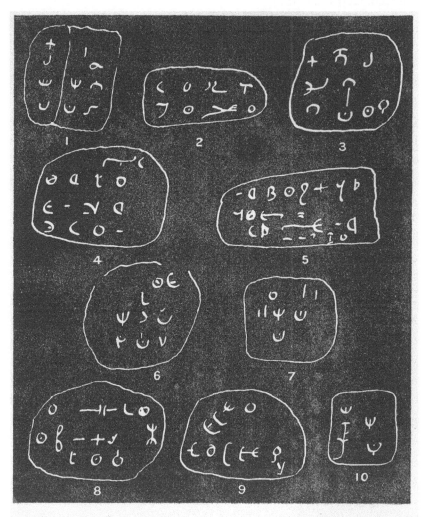

INSCRIPTIONS ON LARGE ROUNDED BLOCKS OF STONE OF TRILITH
MONUMENTS

NOS. 1–3. IN WADI ANDHAUR.   4. IN WADI DHAGHAUB.   5–10. IN WADI DHIKUR.   (NO. 5 IS
BROKEN AT BOTH ENDS, AND PROBABLY FORMS PART OF A LONGER INSCRIPTION)

Inscriptions on Triliths

The natives were unaware that the scrollings were 'writing,' nor

had they any precise knowledge of the origin of the monument,
though they vaguely associated it with the Prophet's daughter (Salih
bin Hud. Hud's camel?).

In Bait Kathir country to the west they call the monuments Bit
Aba Ghassan, which name would appear to preserve the Ghassanitae
of Ptolemy. There was, of course, a post-Islamic Ghassanid dynasty of
Dhufar, but the distribution of triliths is beyond Dhufar limits, and
the monuments themselves, judging from their pre- Arabic inscriptions, where inscribed, their non-Islamic orientation, and local tradition, belong to 'The Days of Ignorance.' The religion of ancient South-
west Arabia was the star worship of the Sabaeans, and it is not impossible that the triliths were in origin symbolic of the ancient South
Arabian Trinity of Sun God, Moon God and Zahra, the Venus of the
Arabs.

The sun was getting high, and I was anxious to be on the move,
so as I returned past Hanun where my men were watering, I called
to them urging haste, and they cheerfully shouted back 'Yes'; but I
knew well as I rode on that it would not make them hurry. Their
love of dallying over a water-hole, especially if the next one be
remote, I knew from long experience to be an incurable tendency to
which I must resign myself. Shaikh Salih was not watering here, he
and one other were leaving me to-day to go ahead for another relay
of camels and to spy out the land. They hoped, too, for a Murri
guide from Dakaka, to meet me on arrival at the water-hole of
Dhahiya where I planned to be for Christmas: to-day was the 13th,
but Salih would not ride our way via Shisur, but north-westwards
across the barren steppe by a route possible only to fast camels
carrying no loads. They were watering at Umm as Shadid, an unusually deep hole in Ghudun. The descent is by stages totalling thirty-
six fathoms. Umm as Shadid was made by a falling star, not by the
Sons of Adam at all, God bless you. Whether or not this tradition is
a relic of some ancient star worship, I know not, but I have met it
elsewhere in these southern borderlands. Thus in the sands of
Ghanim and in the Jaddat Harasis are water-holes bearing the tell-
tale name of Khasfa, [51] and the tank-like depression of Lahit in

Bautahara country was ascribed, perhaps with more reason, to a similar cause.

So Salih left us, with a stock of flour and dates for the road, and a robe as a gift for the Murri shaikh, whose importance loomed large. Then, as the noon prayer ended, our camels came back from watering and by two o'clock we were on the move. We turned out of Sa'atan almost immediately and marched on a north-westerly course that took us diagonally between the two trunk wadis of Ghudun and Dauka, first across some low hills which, like other small systems to east and west, were of the characteristic flat-topped ridges and pyramids of sandstone. In our path lay Istah, a tributary of Dauka where samr acacias and palmy *asaf* or *ghadaf* delayed my men. Afterwards we crossed another small transverse ridge which marked Hughugit, a twin tributary, and there we halted for the night. The camels came trudging along with long palms dangling from their saddles. The Badawin were carrying these into the sands for their women to weave into milk basins; some of it perhaps they would themselves use to make rope and sacking - work meet for men, and in fact one of the night watch addressed himself to making a hobble for my camel so that she set out on the morrow with a new green fibrous rope about her neck.

A strong southerly wind that night proved unfavourable to my star observations, for it raised waves in my mercury bath (artificial horizon) and turned the desired pin-point of a reflected star into a nebulous shimmer. To fix one's position by sextant is no easy matter in these low latitudes, where Polaris is so near the northern skyline that to get a reflected image of it means sitting at a great distance from one's artificial horizon. Sand too was for ever getting into my instruments in the darkness. So I took with me a camp-table, on which my instruments were set up at night. Not my sextant and artificial horizon, however, for it was necessary to keep secret my star work lest I be suspected of magic or worse, so these were kept in their padded box and brought out for an hour each night. Polaris observations, and meridian altitudes of Achernar and Canopus, gave me my latitude to check my position from day to day. To serve the ends of secrecy I contrived from the first, in opposition to my men who raised the usual bugbear of dangers and lurking enemies, always to take up my position on the edge of the camp at some thirty or forty yards' distance, and not among my Arabs. There, on reaching camp, my servant would dump my bedding and boxes while I joined the squatting circle of my companions and shared their conversation and food till after dark. I would then retire for the night, and my servant allowed it to be known that no one who wished to see me after that would be welcome. My three chronometers, two aneroid barometers and a wet and dry bulb thermometer were set out on the table by routine on arrival in camp and were packed again in the morning just before leaving. It was necessary after each day's march to compare and record the time of all the chronometers and this was done again the first thing in the morning to ascertain the performance of each, and deduce daily rates and Greenwich Mean Time. Height readings and temperatures as registered by the other instruments were recorded at intervals as time afforded, at sunset and sunrise always, and probably twice or thrice during the night as well. Some of my companions had never seen a watch. All of them were greatly excited when allowed to place their ears against the face of the biggest chronometer to hear the ticking. As they heard the marvel, their faces would light up with a smile and one would look at the other in wonderment before suddenly bursting out, *'La Illah il' Allah'* - 'There is no god, but God.'

Sa'a that is, a watch, became the generic name for each and every instrument. It did for my prismatic compass which I must hold to my eye every ten minutes of the march for recording our direction against the time (wrist watch), and cross-bearings on topographical points - necessary data for a route traverse of my journey. But the 'tick tick' was unquestionably *the* watch. Once when we halted to change camels, I found one Arab who had travelled with me holding a thermometer to the ear of a friend that he had brought as a recruit. He was showing off, but his friend was not impressed, so he set the aneroid to his own ear and was chagrined; somewhere, he felt, there had been cheating.

Our march the next day only lasted for three hours. The Badawin straggled out from the first and spoke of companions in the rear who had not caught up with us from yesterday. The reason was obvious. Here we were back in the Istah where there was good pasture while the way before us to Shisur - and a bare palm was held before me to indicate its barrenness - was hungry going. Impatient to get on to the sands, I had hoped to make a good day's march, but that suggestion found small favour. The traveller in the great desert soon discovers that the welfare of the camel is the supreme consideration. Starts and halts are normally determined by the quality of the grazing. Fodder is almost more important than water, for the camel can carry a load for a week and more without water, but food is a daily want. The European accustomed to a programme, a time to start, a time to halt, a time to eat and an expectation of a certain average daily mileage, gets a rude shock. The son of these barren marches subordinates every-thing to the efficiency of his transport — the health of his camel. Camp over good pasture with water at hand and he will not leave it; come upon a few verdant bushes at noonday, and, though the hot sun is striking down, he will dally for an hour; arrive at sunset after a gruelling day in the saddle and if the pasture does not please him he will insist on riding on, indifferent to fatigue.

And so, to-day, it was with a sad heart I had to couch my camel at a miserable seven or eight miles from last night's camping ground. I went off at once with my rifle into the wadi jungle. There were traces of a wolf, and marks of fox, hare and gazelle, but the afternoon proved barren. In Wadi Ghudun, a few miles to the west at 1200 feet, where *samr* acacias gave place to the willowy tamarisk, I had got my first antelope, *Oryx leucoryx*, a full-sized cow. I took great precautions to secure her skin whole as a scientific specimen, for the Badu normally esteems her face skin as a trophy, like a fox-hunter the brush, and makes from it a rifle-butt cover. Indeed there was scarcely a man in my party whose rifle-butt was not adorned with the face skin of an antelope or a gazelle: scarcely less solicitous were they for the paunch, the gastric juices of which they carefully drained and drank with relish before administering the solid contents in handfuls to their bellowing, protesting camels. The benefit to the stomachs alike of man and mount is said to be equalled by nothing else in- the desert. These are but two of the antelope's seven virtues. [52]

Out of the antelope's horn is made a pipe upon which the girls of South Arabia play. There is no drum, no stringed instrument or other manner of music to be found through- out these marches, but only the antelope horn, and if the shepherdess may not sing to her flock she may soothe them with the pipe and find consolation in it for herself. There may be here some remote connection with our medi- aeval legend of the maiden and the unicorn, for it is commonly supposed that the antelope is the prototype of that mythical beast. Certain it is that he runs with his head down so that his sloping horns appear almost vertical, and in profile seem to be one, whence the one-horned oryx of Aristotle, and in the Hebrew text of Deuteronomy xxxiii. 17: 'His horns are like the horns of unicorns. [53] The unicorn of tradition was a symbol of strength. and a guardian of chastity, a terror to men, whom he devoured at sight, but according to mediaeval legend a ready victim to a pure young virgin. On seeing her his ferocity abated, and he would meekly come and lay his head in her lap, and submit to the caresses that made him her willing captive.

Abu Qursh (Uromastyx thomasi)

We made an early start, and left the last slight ridges behind to move across an utterly flat and featureless plain, now a hard sandy floor where in places we came upon nests of fossilised oysters, lying on the surface as they might have on an ocean bed barely covered by the fine sand, now fields of flint or rubble and at rare intervals an outcrop of laminated red sandstone. There was no animal life and all I collected was a beetle, a snake (*colubrid*) and a lizard, the last named, however, of great interest to the Natural History Museum, for it was new to science - *abu qursh*, 'the father of the dollar,' the Badawin called it, on account of its round tail.

And so a dreary ride for seven hours, when I judged we had made twenty-one and a half miles. The next two days, which brought us to Shisur, were alike -a vast expanse of featureless wilderness. The only movement came from sand devils, which raised their spinning columns, bringing with them a refreshing gust of wind. Not a vestige of vegetation, and our camels seemed to know that here it was they must step out. We pressed on towards a white expanse of shimmering mirage that obscured the skyline and practised its habitual deceit as it receded before our thirsty column.

11

NEJD-LIFE IN THE SOUTHERN STEPPE

Shisur to-morrow. No wonder it looms so large in the Arab mind, for it is the first water-hole we meet for five days, and after leaving it there will be none for a further seven or eight. To-day a long anxious march across the barren plain, sun-baked and filmy with mirage, brought us just before nightfall to a copse where it bears due east. Approach to a water-hole is made with much caution, for if an enemy is already in possession, there is a choice between hasty retreat tormented by thirst and fear of pursuit, or a fight for possession. As always we arrived with empty water-skins. The Badawin no sooner off-saddled and hobbled their camels than they wandered off on all sides with their eyes to the earth for sign of an enemy, or fresh tracks of a raiding party, while three chosen men went in a wide cast round the water-hole to see if all were safe to dig it out for to-morrow's watering. Shisur's loneliness makes it an inevitable place of call for raiders, and it is a proper practice to fill in a water-hole when leaving to delay possible pursuers. Here Nature does the work, sand filtering in and filling it up after a day or two.

Next day we went off there by relays of six to eight camels, for the thirsty brutes take hours to water out of the small leathern buckets and the spring is a mere trickle. The way lies across a spacious stone-less plain (an excellent landing ground) to a rocky eminence crowned by conspicuous ruins of a rude fort. Undercutting the knoll lies a cave some fifty feet deep, and in the base of its sloping floor is a fissure which barely admits a human arm to the water beneath. According to legend, one Badr bin Tuwairij was the builder of the fort of Shisur in some distant past, and I have heard that in the surrounding desert plain are still to be seen shadowed furrowings as though once it had known the plough; astonishing if true, for so limited is the water of Shisur and so arid the place that a fair-sized raiding party could not last out there for more than a week. 'The sword of God has been upon the *dira*,' said one Badu to me in allusion to the, drought of recent years. [54]

Beyond to the eastwards in the otherwise naked plain lay Hailat ash Shisur, another tiny copse, the scene only three years before of a bloody affray between rival raiders, amongst whom were members of my escorting Arabs. Their story was of particular interest to me because I had myself barely escaped colliding with one of these parties a hundred miles to the eastwards. It comprised twenty-five men of the Sa'ar and Karab tribes who had come by this way to fall upon a small Mahra encampment at the water- hole of Andhaur. There they killed seven men for the loss of one, but he a shaikh, and departed with booty of forty camels. Four or five days later my exhausted little party reached Andhaur from the east after a six hundred miles' march to hear of the disaster from a terror-stricken member of the Bait ash Shaikh; and I remember well taking part in a discussion upon the unhealthiness of camp-fires by night; we discontinued them forthwith in spite of bitter cold.

Now I heard that this particular raiding party, which had been a nightmare to me in that winter of 1927-28, was intercepted by a chance raiding party of forty Mahra and Kathir, amongst whom were two of my present escort. Nukhaiyir took me over the ground and reconstructed the attack. 'This is where we came up with them; this is where I lay. We had followed their tracks all day and judged them to be returning raiders who must halt here at Shisur, for westwards there is no water until Sanau. There under that skyline we halted and waited till after the sunset prayers. Leaving our camels with a few men we crept on, under cover of darkness, towards their camp-fires. It was nearly midnight and they had mostly fallen asleep, for we could see their sprawling bodies in the dying glow. We crept till within fifty paces and then suddenly opened fire. They leapt up wildly in the darkness shouting, but in utter confusion, and we drawing our daggers fell upon them and God gave us the victory. Praise God from whom all blessings flow. Four of them fell, and all the booty that they had taken at Andhaur was restored to our hands, and we took five of their own camels, too, so that many of those that escaped in the darkness must have left riding two to a camel.'

A Badu at Nukhaiyir's side now interjected, 'Next day as I was grazing my camels in Wadi Ghudun one of those Sa'ar who had been in hiding all night emerged, and coming up to me implored sanctuary, and I call God to witness that he had no arms and I spared his life.'

Shisur

'Then supposing they had made no fight for it,' I asked, 'and all had thrown down their rifles, would you have shown them mercy?'

'No,' said Nukhaiyir, 'in time of declared war between tribes, it is shameful, amongst Arabs.'

Shisur lay ninety miles from the south coast, 935 feet above sea-level, near the foot of the steppe where it verges on the sands - from which indeed we were now only a day's march.

We had crossed the Nejd, this wide southern borderland of steppe between ocean escarpments and sands, that stretches west-south-westwards to the confines of Najran and east-north-eastwards to merge into the Jaddat Harasis. Last year I had explored the sand border in the latter direction for a distance of one hundred miles to the famous oasis of Mugshin. [55] This year I was turning westwards and would explore its southern edge. But before continuing the narrative of my journey it may be well to turn aside to consider briefly the geography of the southern steppe that lay behind me.

Reference to my map will show between longitudes 51° 40' and 54° 40' a continuous coastal mountain chain that is known sectionally from west to east by the names Fatk-Shaghuwat, Jabal Qamr, Jabal Qara and Jabal Samhan. From its intra-montane side falls away a series of dry old torrent courses which form a large single wadi system, and must have constituted from remote times the drainage of the great steppe. This system consists of seven main tributary wadis running in more or less parallel courses northwards from the coastal range to the verge of the sands where they join a trunk wadi, and the trunk wadi marches with the sands in a general north-easterly direction to a point where it turns and is lost in them in lat. 19° 35', long. 54° 50', a point marked by the bountiful oasis of Mugshin. The seven wadis all rise in the neighbourhood of the divide, averaging three thousand feet at a two days' march from the coast, so that their sources are the region of the frankincense groves. From east to west they are called Katibit, Dauka, Ghudun, Aidam, Hagulun, Shihin and Hat, [56] and their lengths, diminishing, broadly speaking, in the same order, vary from an eight days' march in Katibit to a four days' march in Hat. The main trunk wadi has six sectional names. Hat, Shihin,

Atina, Umm al Hait, Al 'Aradh and Mugshin, in its course from south-west to north-east, but the whole system may conveniently be termed by the generic name Umm al Hait (mother of life), which name has also the sectional connotation referred to.

To the northward and westward of the trunk wadi, the Great Sands stretch continuously westward to the confines of Dawasir and Najran. Actually the southern edge of the sands overlaps the trunk wadi in Mugshin and Al 'Aradh, hugs it in Umm al Hait, and falls away to a day's march north of Shihin and two days' north of Hat. Thence its trend is west-south-west towards the Hadhramaut, where only a day's march is said to separate the mountains from the sands. The intra-montane steppe of the southern borderlands would therefore appear to be wedge-shaped, narrowing to the west, and sloping very gently upwards as far as long. 51° 30' and by rumour further.

West of the Umm al Hait system the steppe is crossed by individual parallel wadis rising in the mountains of Hadhramaut and running north to disappear at the edge of the sands. The names of these, proceeding westward from Hat, are Mitan, Khuwat, Shu' ait, Arkhaut, Urba, Thumurat, Dhahiya, Thuf, Rama, Aiwat al Manahil, Jinab, Khadhra, Hazar, Aiwat as Sa'ar and Hudhi.

There are only very rare water-holes, namely, Sanau in Wadi Dhahiya, Thamut in Wadi Rama, Shagham in Wadi Hizar and Minwakh in Wadi Aiwat as Sa'ar, so the route of raiders east and west of Minwakh is precariously circumscribed. In the mountain sources of the wadis there is in places running water, e.g. Andhaur and Habarut, but their lower courses are all cruelly dry. They follow a uniform formation. Steep and narrow gorges with pebble beds form their upper courses; thence they grow wider and shallower and sandy as they run north, until they lose their trough character in the plain approaching the sands and become perceptible only by a line of parched scrub. They are the arteries of life in the steppe, the path of Badawin movement, the habitat of animals, by reason of the vegetation - scant though it is - which flourishes in their beds alone. Elsewhere the steppe is arid and desolate and hence these borderlands are capable of supporting only nomad Badawin. The summer drought drives them back into the mountain courses around the perennial water-holes - Andhaur, Hanun, Shuwairima, Aiyun and Habarut (these in Umm al Hait longitudes). But immediately after rain they sally out again and in winter they may remain for a month or two in favoured localities, their movements often being guided by their pillar of fire, the direction of lightning. It is a hungry and thirsty life and those whose habitat is the hinterland of Dhufar are drawn back to the settled comfort of the frankincense orchard, especially during the summer, when its comparatively rich rewards are the means of acquiring rifle, ammunition, clothes, coffee, and sometimes rice. But the true Badawin despise any but their spartan existence. They live mainly on camel's milk and hold life cheap. Raiding to them is the spice of life, and there was never a man in any of my escorts who had not raided into the Hadhramaut, nor one who had not been raided in his own grazing grounds, and some bore honourable scars of bullet or dagger wounds. Arms and ammunition and the health of the camel are thus the primary necessities of life; where hereditary blood-feuds divide the tribes, might is right, and man ever walks in fear for his life and possessions.

The tribes of importance occupying these southern borderlands are, from east to west. Bait Kathir, Mahra, Manahil, 'Awamir, Sa'ar, Nahad and Karab. [57] The Mahra are the largest, and number many thousands; the Nahad and Karab, the smallest tribes, only a hundred or two each.

The life of the steppe is primitive in the extreme. I have already observed that drought and the fear of raiders drive these tribes back on to their water in the mountains. But at heart they are wedded to their nomadic existence, and whenever rain comes they launch out with their flocks and herds into the desert, where every little rock hollow capable of holding rain-water has a name and a memory. Here they remain for a space till once more drought threatens and hunger drives. There is not sufficient water to support the horse or the dog. Tents or houses are unknown. In the steppe their place is taken by the shade of an acacia, and in the mountains by a cave. The people are wholly illiterate. Few know anything of the Qur'an, though they pray zealously. They have a reverence for shrines, and are of the Shafi' rite. Alcohol is unknown, but tobacco much esteemed.

The usual Arab practices of polygamous marriage and facile divorce obtain, but it is rare for a Badu to have more than one wife or at most two, at any one time, though a quiver full of sons is a much-desired blessing. The woman looks after the flocks, [58] - which she is here allowed to milk.

Disputes within the tribe are settled, as is general in tribal Arabia, by the *hukm al hauz*, a code of local sanctions, not the holy or Shara' law. Petty theft is rare and looked on as immoral: but robbery with violence a manly act, and the raid, with murder and looting, as unquestionably honourable as military prowess in Europe.

Bodily illness is dealt with by certain herbs, by the branding iron, by exorcism, by the gastric juices of animals slaughtered in the chase, and by the urine of the young cow camel. The cautery comes first, and few, if any, are the dwellers of these steppe lands who do not bear scars of the hot iron. One process I met with seemed to me to have some magical significance. My party was held up by the sickness of one of its number; he had been suffering for several days from stoppage of the bowels, which had not responded to all my explosive medicines. His companions now resorted to a measure they called *ghuwaira*. A rifle-bolt striker was introduced into the fire, and when it became red-hot was applied to seven prescribed places on the man's body: left heel, right heel, behind right ear, behind left ear, centre of forehead - where it joins the hair - top of the head, and immediately above the navel. The cure was instantaneous, and we moved the next morning.

For the Evil Eye, I have often witnessed a rite of exorcism called *hamra raaba* [59] which is held equally efficacious for the recurrent three days' fever from which they suffer, and for snake-bite. The patient is laid amidst the circle of his sitting friends and the affected part of his body laid bare. They then commence bowing low over it and chanting one of two formulae; slow at first, the imprecations growing quicker and louder and the body bowing more energetically as the rite proceeds. A leader chants the lines in a vigorous voice and the rest of the party excitedly shout their responses, often just *hamra raaba*.' Now and again one bowing head lingers, with lips to the patient's abdomen in the region of his liver, to draw up a mouthful of flesh and let it flick back as he raises his head; others from time to time bark, and spit upon the body. And so a climax is reached. A rifle is sometimes fired at the termination of proceedings, but that bravery is only used for the 'Evil Eye.'

I once observed a different rite after *hamra raaba* had failed to achieve results. It is a kind of divination and propitiation called *habile* i.e. the rope, and perhaps may not be unconnected with the Quranic reference to 'blowing on knots.' The practitioner, rope in hand, sat about three paces from his patient. A third party was called to hold the end of the rope. Taking an arbitrary length of it with the thumb and forefinger of one hand, the practitioner measured the outstretched length of it with his disengaged arm by means of fore-arm's length, hand span and finger breadth. The operation he repeated three times, each occasion preceded by a pause to bend his head low over the rope and shake his head, making a curious burbling noise with his lips, and to take a handful of sand which he sprinkled up and down the rope. In conclusion he looked up at his patient and gave him the following remedy; 'At sunset take so many dates and so much butter and go and cast it away upon the sands,'

So much for man and his ways.

The animal life of the southern steppe is limited. A point of interest is that from the nature of their almost rainless environment animals here must be able to do without water and to content themselves with the moisture contained in herbage, or collected in rocks from dews. Zoologically they belong to the Palaearctic group.

Arabian Oryx (Oryx leucoryx)

Among the mammals that I shot were the antelope (*Oryx leucoryx*) - a comparatively rare kind, gazelle and fox. I saw marks of wolf, wild cat and badger, but did not get the steppe varieties of these. The rim or pure white gazelle is said to be almost extinct, though I picked up a pair of its horns, lyre-shaped, and with a characteristic tuft of white hair still attaching to it; in reality this animal, unlike the red gazelle, belongs to the sands rather than the steppe. Two hedgehogs which I caught were of a sandy colour and small in comparison with the larger black type of Oman. Here they are said to attack and kill snakes, but to go in craven fear of the vulture, on whose approach they weakly unbend and, abandoning their natural protection, become ready victims.

Of birds, I saw no vulture in the steppe, though I had expected to meet it, but came upon the lifeless body of a large black eagle. The presence of either vulture or eagle in the sky is regarded as a sign that an encampment may be near. The black raven was common, and I shot an interesting example with a neck ringed with white feathers. A

Badu asked for the heart of another pure black specimen which he proposed to eat raw because of some virtue it possessed: its bile is also used by them for the eyes in the same way as kohl (antimony) by the sedentary Arab. A bird which I did not see but heard night after night at Mugshin was the owl. Ostriches had been shot in this steppe by members of my escort in past years, but they are now extinct (except for a few in the Sa'ar habitat to the west), though I picked up many fragments of petrified ostrich shell. The extinction of the ostrich in the southern steppe dates from its pursuit by Badawin armed with modern rifles. Of the smaller birds I shot, a finch lark was the rarest and most interesting scientific specimen; the bulbul, Senegal sand-grouse, and a brown babbler were indigenous creatures one expected to find, and a Kashmir redstart, white wag- tail and Tibetan desert chat were all migrants either passing to winter in Africa, or possibly cold weather visitors to the Hadhramaut. I also collected butterflies, wasps, ants and spiders.

My Badawin toyed bare-handed with a large scorpion, picking it up, scatheless, by the tail just below its sting. Of reptiles there were three different snakes — the inevitable horned viper amongst them - very few compared with lizards, of which I met ten different kinds. These included three new species and also the three largest edible varieties - regarded by the Arabs as a most succulent dish, and more nourishing even than the larger mammals of the chase. One of these gave us an exciting hunt. I saw it disappear down its hole, and soon had three Badawin in chase prodding the roof with their sticks. Suddenly the tip of a tail appeared and one of the diggers was just able to get hold of it between finger and thumb, and although cautioned by his companions to beware lest it should be a snake, he held on while they continued digging. Able in time to get a better grip of its tail, he now, as he knelt over the hole, pulled it out with a vigorous tug and held it in the air head downwards, its eyes rolling wildly and its jaws gaping menacingly. The Badu now slipped his other hand down its back and catching hold behind the head held it the other way up, but the creature finding its tail free lashed back with it and caught another Badu on the knee, drawing blood. This man later came to me for *duwa* for his knee, and I for once diagnosing correctly the complaint gave him a dollar and he went away cured.

Another interesting reptile, an inedible lizard, was the *shuwaira ash shams*, so called because it delights to sit on the most glaring eminences in the face of the tropical sun towards which it nods its head - a large creature with a tail red and smooth and ratlike, and a heavy pouch of royal blue under the chin which changes at death to silver. This creature alone of all the steppe life that I met scorns refuge from the sun.

12

MARCHING ALONG THE SOUTHERN FRINGE OF THE SANDS

We bade farewell to the little copse of Mutugtaig in the bed of the Ghudun, where two days had been spent resting and grazing our camels and watering them at neighbouring Shisur. Under an eastern sky crayoned with crimson and gold we turned our backs upon it this cold December morning and marched out into the plain - a wilderness that recalled to me the Land of the Two Rivers. Scarcely had we been on the move an hour when my companions started shouting excitedly, *'ar raml! ar raml!* sweeping their canes as they did so along our right front, where in the far distance a sunlit yellow ribbon now edged the skyline; and I gazed eagerly towards this southern bulwark of the sands of my desire.

Between the sands and us stretched a dreary plain unrelieved except by low whitish outcrops, forming low, rocky ridges -Dhim Himla, Thuwairib, Lahaga, Qarun Kelba - places honourably known to the Arabs, for here water collects after rain.

Before us stretched a hundred miles of perilous incalculable marches. The open state of war existing between the tribe I travelled with and their powerful neighbours made this stage of my journey very dangerous. Many had been (and will be) the bloody conflicts upon this road along the southern borderlands, for waterless no-man 's-lands as they are, yet they are the fairway between water-holes which are used only and inevitably by raiders on murder and plunder bent. Any party we met would be a potential enemy. The stronger or warier party would announce itself with a volley of rifle fire, prelude to fight or, alternatively, to flight. My party betrayed by word, look and act that they were on tenterhooks, and whenever my camel bore me ahead of them or lagged behind, someone was soon beside me to remind me that we were in dangerous country; yet on making camp never were there dispositions made so far as I could see for meeting an attack or escaping from one. The desert holds a philosophy of the inevitability of events. 'Reliance is in God,' 'What is written must come to pass,' 'God be praised, the Lord of the Worlds' — these expressions are always on Badawin lips, to meet death or adversity or the expectation of them. In the acceptance of destiny is comfort; the doctrine of Free Will a disturbing heresy. Unless the beast became his by the will of God, a man could not enjoy killing the master and riding away upon her. War would become wicked, blood -feuds impious, and the practice of religion impossible.

Before us the conspicuous large white dune of Bin Juli marked where Umm al Hait, the great trunk drainage system of the steppe, changes its name to Atina. To the northwards the great sands reappeared in the distance as a pale wall backed by ridges of rosier hue. Before them ran the verdant line of Umm al Hait. When nearer we found the sands of the valley gathered in hummocks like the roofs of multitudinous mosques with their thousand cupolas. The thick tamarisk looked inviting to our fasting camels, and the poor brutes that had shuffled sluggishly across the plain trotted eagerly up to the scanty diet before them.

Umm al Hait is a precious name to the steppe dweller, though if no rain falls for two or three years together, as sometimes happens, the wadi becomes hungry, bleak and deserted. The meagrest winter rain will, however, quicken it into fertility and life - though the blessedness actually before us was the result of the unusually heavy rains I had experienced in the eastern marches last year.

How well I remembered members of my party pointing out to my unaccustomed eyes the evidences of some shower, here the pitted surface of sandy elephant masks [60] about some tree-roots, there the swept path of some tiny freshet! How joyously they talked of rain! That night low heavy clouds raced northwards and forked lightning lit up the black heavens, while we and our beasts sought refuge from a howling sand-blast behind the solid hummocks that grew about the *selem* bushes. But no one was unhappy. Rain was about and rain to the Badu is as gold to the prospector; the morning was welcomed with rousing chanties on the march. The low, rumbling thunder was like music to our ears. A drenching would have been glorious. As we went on the sky grew dark, the lightning nearer, and the thunder-claps more violent; our camels shared the excitement, sniffing with their monstrous noses in the air, to the delight of their masters. We split up into three parties and spread fan-wise to scout the plain for rain-pools, rather against my judgment, for I felt they would be insufficient, and I would have preferred to press on towards the certainty of our next water-hole. Some twenty minutes later a rifle shot rang out. Ordinarily it would have been interpreted as an alarm or as a promise of gazelle flesh for dinner. 'Water!' exclaimed Nukhaiyir excitedly. 'The Arabs ' (Badawin in conversation always thus refer to themselves in the third person) 'have found water.'

'True,' said another jubilantly; we wheeled about and proceeded in that direction. For some time I had felt my curiously resembles the own camel edging that way, never imagining that she smelt water, but supposing that she fretted after a particular companion in one of the other parties, for camels that have been reared together, whether or not of the same sex, find separation irksome.

'Are you quite sure it is water?' I had said a little testily, for we had already been six hours in the saddle and our halting place was said to be three hours ahead.

'*Isqut,*' replied Nukhaiyir, which in other parts of Arabia is an imperative order to 'shut up,' but here has the idiomatic meaning of 'without doubt.' We soon breasted a rise in the plain to see our party beneath us upon a stony outcrop with the camels' long necks stretched down, and themselves frantically scooping handfuls of water into their water-skins. My thirst soon had me on my hands and knees beside them, with my parched lips in the saucers of the rocky floor; and very sweet the collected rain-drops tasted, after the water of our march, which had been sand-coloured or pestiferously green to begin with, and had acquired the taste of rank meat from its churning day after day in goat skins 'cured' in crude Badawin fashion. There were times when I elected to go thirsty, though the stuff was whole-some enough, and I have never suffered any serious ill- effects from drinking it, despite my never having taken measures to doctor my water on any desert journey; there is neither time nor opportunity for such refinements.

And now Tha'ailib, a Bait Kathiri, in a high, reedy voice raised again the lyric that had cheered the morning's march while his companions showed they knew and loved it by joining in, either one by one, in a duet, or together, making some last phrase of a line into a chorus.

I translated it at the time to run:
'Behold lightning in the far distance,
May its bounty fall in Umm al Hait,
Continuous and flowing rain
Flowing along between sand and stream course
Until it pass from Bu Warid onwards.
Thence shall a beautiful woman live and enjoy.
She, who standing up unveiled.
Her lover falleth at her feet
And is healed of the wounds of his heart-veins.'

Our march that day was cut short abruptly by the over- mastering need to rejoice. These few spots of falling rain were reason enough for my vanguard to halt and graze their camels.

Sahail, a Rashidi, announced that he would smoke, and a circle soon squatted about him, for a pipe in the desert invites all to share. His hand disappeared down the opening of his shirt front (Badu clothes have no pockets) towards the region of his dagger belt, and drew forth his smoking outfit - the typical tobacco pouch of cowhide, flapped over and roughly sewn, carrying a leather thong with wooden

toggle. It was one of Sahail's few possessions, but clearly had a senti-
mental value of its own. As ever, it must be lovingly unrolled with all
eyes upon it. It had two partitions, one for tobacco, the other for pipe,
flint and steel striker, for matches in the desert if not quite unknown
are a rare luxury, and fires invariably lighted with a flint. The pipe,
also typical, was an empty -303 cartridge case, the mouthpiece being
the flat-rimmed end with the cap removed. He proceeded to fill it
with the green local leaf of Oman or Dhufar, holding the end well up
to avoid spilling the precious stuff. A scrap of rag which probably
belonged to his last shirt was next ignited by a spark from the flint,
then placed on the ground, and a little dry camel dung sprinkled over
and blown upon to make it smoulder; to this little fire a twig was
added, till it charred red. The glowing cinder was then placed over the
mouth of his pipe, as for a *narghileh* or hubble-bubble. It was filling
the pipe that took up the time so pleasantly; smoking was to be a
matter of a few crowded seconds. Sahail took six or eight quick, deep
inhalations, holding on to the last one until his eyes rolled and his
body swayed; meanwhile he had passed the pipe to his neighbour,
who similarly intoxicated himself and so it went round the circle. This
pipe was smoked clarinet fashion, others of the same type I have seen
smoked flute-wise. The experience did not tempt me, so I refrained
from asking my almost speechless company which was the better
mode; nor could I find heart to mock Sahail, whose pipe was one of
his rare indulgences.

We camped in Umm al Hait at a point where Nukhdat Waraiga, a
distributary, takes off on a north-easterly bearing. A twin Nukhdat
Hishman lying to the north-west has a more northerly course, both
penetrating into these southern sands for a distance of a day and a
half's march to embrace a region called Umm Dharta.

The temperature fell to 47° F. that night, and we felt the cold
bitterly as we were sleeping in the open after a hot day in the saddle,
and on waking my hands were too numbed with cold to do much
note-taking. For the next six nights the temperature fell about as low.
My two blankets made it endurable for me, wearing all my clothes as
well, but for my companions it meant wretchedness. The Badawin

sleep on the sands, which are very hot by day and very cold by night; they have no other clothes than the cotton rags they wear by day; no bedding, which would be a nuisance, anyhow, and be thought effeminate. They collect a night's store of brushwood for the camp-fire, and curl up before it, naked but for a loin-cloth, for their other garment, a shirt, is doffed and used as a sheet. So also the women folk, though they have 'tents of hair' in the sands for a shelter, and a rug to sleep upon, wear only their trousers by night, their outer garment - except in case of the well-to-do - serving again as sheet. By day nearly all go barefoot; but if the sands are very hot, both sexes may use a roughly knitted sock. Excessive indulgence is, however, deprecated.

Our course for the next five days skirted this southern fringe of the great sands, first west-north-west, then gradually veering to west. The altitude remained fairly constant at about 950 feet, though the fall of wadi courses made me think that higher ground lay to the west. The afternoon march was unpleasant, as we were marching into the sun's eye. I had experienced this in former journeys, when long marches into the sun turned my face first lobster colour, then blistering raw; but now I had learnt the secret of swathing my head in the full wraps of an Arab head-dress and so saved all but my nose and lips. A more lasting disadvantage of a westerly course was that map-making became a difficult task, as I was equipped only with chronometers as a means of obtaining Greenwich Mean Time. I could obtain latitudes with fair accuracy and thus check daily my dead-reckoning by watch and compass when marches were from south to north (and fortunately nearly the whole of my journey lay in this direction); but longitudes which check traverses east and west are untrustworthy when obtained with chronometers carried on camel back, even with three chronometers checked one against another and recorded before and after every march. A wireless set would have given perfect accuracy, but I feared to excite the suspicions of my company with such an apparatus, whose bulk and weight would in any case have been too much for my limited transport.

Three and a half hours through hummocky sand after leaving Hishman brought us to the bordering plain, which we crossed at a good pace, scarcely checked by groups of small white sand-drifts that ran out at intervals of a mile and a half or so. Beyond Umm al Ru'us these grew to be transverse ridges so that we were slowed down, losing a half-hour in crossing the first one, into a long corridor flanked on our left hand by a single sand ridge at about a mile's distance, and on the right by the Great Sands. *Kharaiyim*, as the skirting corridor is called, became the characteristic feature of the next few days' marches. Hungry marches they were, for the only verdure was sparse willowy *abala* or *markh* on the sides of the dunes. These formed part of a system which lay athwart our path, and ran south into the plain on the flank of a wadi, shrinking steadily to disappear, it was said, at no great distance.

Such were our halting-places. The camp in Nukhdat Fasad - a distributary of the Atina that gives its name to the local sands - lay below three mighty dunes of Umm al Jau, Umm al Laisa and Umm al Dhalua (mother of ribs). So wretched was the grazing that we were obliged to split up into three parties and distribute our animals over an area of a mile or more. The party with which I found myself consisted of Karab, 'Awamir and Bait Kathir *rabias* and they immedi- ately clambered up into the tall spiky bushes of *markh* to snap off the youngest and most succulent fodder for their particular mounts, so that my own beast and the baggage animals came off second-best. This greed for their camels aroused my interest because of its strange conflict with the generosity of their personal relationships. Where water or food was shorty no one of them would think of not sharing it equally with his companions, and if any one was away, perhaps tending his camels, all would wait his return, to eat together. But over camel fodder or camel loads each Badu will take any unscrupulous advantage to best his fellows in his camel's interests; her welfare he seems to set above every other consideration.

On the march no halt was cried for the midday prayer; the five daily observances are reduced to three when men are marching, midday and afternoon prayers being said together, so also the sunset and evening prayers. This is an orthodox expedient and does not reflect upon desert piety. The assertion sometimes made by preju-

diced townsmen, that the Badawin neither pray nor fast, is not borne
out by my experience. My companions always prayed diligently; ever
mindful of the many perils through which they have to go, they call
upon God morning, noon and night. Hunger and thirst are never far
distant phantoms, the hosts of Midian are ever prowling around; the
knowledge of such present dangers has implanted in them, as in our
soldiers and sailors of a past generation, a combination of resignation
and of trust in the supernatural that is childlike in its simplicity. Nor
is simplicity its only virtue; it is a rule of life that is pragmatically
justified by the fact that it forms a working basis for daily life in a
harsh environment. It is an attitude of mind which is closely paral-
leled in its essentials by the accepted conventions of the West.

In the name of God the Compassionate, the Merciful,' was shouted
as we moved off each morning. Suddenly at my side after long
silences a Badu would burst out like our Puritan forefathers with,
'Deliver me from mine enemies, O God,' 'Deliver me, O Lord, from
evil.' The last note of the Credo calling them to prayer at dawn would
be greeted with long-drawn-out supplications to Allah, as the shivering wretches struggled to their feet to worship as their first act of
the day. Even a devout Christian travelling in their company, his mind
obsessed with worldly affairs, might well learn something from their
complete acceptance of and trust in the Unseen but Ever Present God.
As we sat in circle the silence would be broken by a mumbled, 'There
is no God but God,' while twice a hysterical Murri exploded with,
'Hide not your faith, O Muslimin!' Yet these outbursts I knew affected
not their relations with me at all, and I felt among these wild men a
tolerance rare amongst townsmen, whose smattering of the Qur'an
gives them an intolerable religious conceit, because they feel themselves in exclusive possession of divine truth.

In contrast let me recall my encounter with Shaikh Salih at the
outset of this journey.

'Bear witness!' one of his men had begun, inviting me to repeat the
Islamic creed, in affirmation of my avowed belief in God, and prayer,
and fasting. So I took hold of my beard — which I had let grow, as

must any European who would travel here; for by his beard a man must swear. I said in Arabic after him, 'God is great.'

'There is no god but God,' said he, and I repeated it.

'And Muhummad is the Prophet of God,' came his third and last tenet.

'Let me explain,' said I. 'He is your prophet, a great and good man of your race of Arabs; but we are of another race, also creatures of God, and we say and believe that Jesus is our prophet.'

'Jesus, son of whom?' they asked, for they are universally illiterate, and have no acquaintance with the Qur'an, which records that Jesus was the Spirit of God.

'True,' intervened Shaikh Salih to close the breach, 'to every people their prophet. But, God be praised, this man is no unbeliever, but a confessor of Allah, the One and Indivisible.'

My companions were at pains to discover whether we burned our dead, whether our marriages were 'knotted' (sacred from free-love), whether we fasted and prayed. My replies assured them and corrected another illusion which I had met with on my earlier journeys and is, indeed, wide- spread throughout the Muslim East; they pointed to the skies, saying that unbelievers hide their faces from God. This I suspect originated in the sun helmet of modern use, [61] which for obvious reasons comes well down over the eyes. It is interesting to note too in this connection that prayer according to Islamic practice necessitates the brow touching the earth. Clearly a hat with a brim will not allow of this, and therefore the outcry amongst conservative men of religion in Persia, Iraq, Afghanistan and other Muslim countries against the adoption by their armies of a head-dress based on European models.

On my journeys I wore the Arab kerchief, and hidden beneath it a shallow flying helmet with the brim removed, an antiquity inscribed 'Southey, Royal Air Force.' My dress and beard and food and talk must be as like those of my insular companions as possible to soften the differences between us. For the same reason I did not wear glare glasses or other obtrusive sun-protection, as the suspicions of my desert friends to sun helmets showed that these might have hindered the successful prosecution of my plans, nor have I ever found them necessary.

Beyond Fasad the edging plain which yesterday had been stone-less, to-day became stony and undulating. Gravelly outcrops (*hazm*) some twenty feet high were followed by others of putty colour, red-veined and highly glazed. Through my telescope the bases of the distant sand dunes here also appeared from a distance, similar solid rock. On the surface I found oyster and other fossils, *Ostrea*, *Lucina* and *Rostallaria* all much weathered but with sufficient ornament to date them geologically.

Mitan was another hungry camp, and our poor camels standing silent, idle and hobbled were more than ready for the onward move. Unlovely beast the camel may be, but what patience in adversity she shows. All her delight is in fodder, and if she find it in sufficiency you may put upon her a heavy daily load, permit her to drink but once a week, and manacle her at every halt, lest she stray.

Our morning start from Mitan was sluggish. We straggled because of the cold and the hunger and the many transverse sand ridges, and straggling camels mean a slow caravan. An hour's march brought us to a wide depression, whose high western bank, Tof Mitan, marked the miserable end of the wadi of that name, so mighty and fruitful at its source in Shaghuwat, six days' march south. Beyond it was the hard steppe again and better going. Suddenly the Arabs, who were always childishly anxious to draw attention to anything they thought would interest me, pointed to the ground. 'Look, Sahib,' they cried. 'There is the road to Ubar.'

'Ubar I wondered.

'It was a great city, our fathers have told us, that existed of old; a city rich in treasure, with date gardens and a fort of red silver. [Gold.?] It now lies buried beneath the sands in the Ramlat Shu'ait, some few days to the north.'

Other Arabs on my previous journeys had told me of Ubar, [62] the Atlantis of the sands, but none could say where it lay. All thought of it had been banished from my mind when my companions cried their news and pointed to the well-worn tracks, about a hundred yards in cross section, graven in the plain. They bore 325°, approximately lat. 18° 45' N., long. 52° 30' E. on the verge of the sands.

Some days later Mayuf, the most intelligent Rashidi in my party, volunteered the information that as a boy while grazing his father's herds after rain, between Mitan and Fasad (he had long ago forgotten the precise site, but thought it within two days' march of the sand border) he had come upon a complete earthenware pot, with broken potsherds of red and yellow, a part of a grindstone, two coffee pestles (?) of black polished stone, and two large white rounded blocks of stone, notched at the edge and both alike, but each so big as to require two men to lift it (drums of a column?): he had turned the sand over to look for more, only to come upon black ashes. But these humble things he had never associated with a mighty city; though it had surprised him to find pottery in the sands, for no true nomad of the desert carries earthenware pots on his camels, but only vessels of woven reeds and an occasional iron one.

It would have been suicidal for me (even if I could have carried my companions - an unlikely event in their present nervous temper) to have turned aside into that arid pasture- less waste: moreover our water was scarcely sufficient to carry us along to the next water-hole. According to Badawin report, the tracks are lost in the plain to the southwards. This is probably due partly to wind erosion in the soft sandy floors there, and partly to the fact that the ancient road must have followed a pebbly wadi course, the natural avenue of approach to the mountains, where there never would have been tracks. That the sands are encroaching southwards is in accordance with Arab tradition and supported by the prevailing northerly winds all along these southern borderlands which account for the orientation of the sand-drifts' steep and gentle slopes. These deep tracks in the steppe are explicable if climatic conditions have changed within historic times. Just to the south lay the ancient and famous frankincense groves, which were probably connected by an overland route with Gerrha, the old port of the Persian Gulf, or with Petra of the Nabataeans, and Ubar may well have lain upon it. Can there be any connection between the words Ophir and Ubar by the change - a philological commonplace – of *f* for *b*.

This tradition of ancient trade routes across what is now an almost prohibitive barrier of sands should not be lightly dismissed as impossible. South Arabia is held never to have had an Ice Age, so that when the higher latitudes of the northern hemisphere lay beneath an ice cap, Arabia was enjoying a pluvial period, from which epoch date the great gorges draining the coastal mountains, and the limestone fossils washed down to the edge of the sands. This very different climate may have long persisted in modified form and made possible a very early civilisation in this region.

Another interesting link in the chain of evidence has been established by zoologists from the distribution of animal life in South Arabia. The animals I collected in the Qara Mountains have proved to be mainly African or Ethiopic in affinity; they form an enclave there, for those I collected to north, east and west have been found to be exclusively Palaearctic. This enclave may well be a relic of the former animal population of the entire southern part of the peninsula when India, South Arabia and Africa had a common climate and fauna. Later, desiccation may have confined this primitive fauna to the Dhufar province, which alone in Arabia has continued to enjoy a tropical rainfall and flora, thanks to an adventitious south-west monsoon, while the denuded spaces round about have come to be repopulated by another group of animals from the north.

13

ACROSS THE MOUNTAINOUS SANDS OF URUQ-ADH-DHAHIYA

The bordering sands of Shu'ait now veered to south of west and our course lay facing them. Here and there we seemed to have bid adieu to steppe only once more to emerge upon it, now it was obscured by a single high ridge, now reported to have receded to half a day's march to the south. The light colour that distinguished the southern aspect of the bordering fringe gave place to red interior ridges that as we proceeded grew into vast squat hills mounting up in billowing masses. Gentle valleys and saddles marked our way except when we saw scant herbage upon some slope, which we climbed, there to stop and graze.

My attention was suddenly arrested by the phenomenon of silver patches in the low troughs, looking from a distance like sheets of ice or the salt residues of dried-up lakes. Such *ghadhera* - they proved to be gypsum - appeared with growing frequency throughout these dunes of Yibaila and Yadila [63] and two days later in the sand mountains of Uruq- adh-Dhahiya.

Hungry marches of nine and ten hours a day had told in varying degree on our camels, so that we had been obliged to make a redistribution of loads.

Rub Al Khali

The two sixty-pound baskets of dates that had been a normal camel load were now found excessive, each basket was halved and spread among such camels as were in better fettle for the rugged way before us. Their masters grumbled and I must needs requisition animals of unattached Badawin with us at added expense. At last we agreed that the riding camels of my party would carry a small load every second or third day, though it meant much argument and the promise of reward, and there were moments of apparent deadlock when I sorely felt the absence of Shaikh Salih.Rougher marching and tired camels stretched out the column interminably at times, so that parts of it were lost to sight in the folds and turnings of the sands. This was by no means satisfactory in the face of possible ambush, for we were daily growing more exhausted and less mobile, and must be easy prey for a larger raiding party, operating light and fresh from one of the three water-holes now within a two days' radius. As we neared each high hill one of my Arabs whose turn that day it was to be free of a load, went ahead, as our custom was, and clambered to the top, there to spy out the country before us for sign of raiders, keeping his head below the ridge to avoid detection, and there he lay motionless but ever watchful while we came pounding along to pass beneath. An hour later another would repeat the performance, and so a look-out was kept during the long day while we below scanned the ridges of distant hills for any sign of similar activity on the part of an enemy.

The straggling meant a long-drawn-out arrival, and made the daily choice of a halting-place increasingly difficult. The spot must be determined according to what pasture availed in this barren country, having regard to the time it took for the last animals to make camp in daylight. The procedure was for two or three leading men to scout ahead some two hours before sunset and for us to follow to the best of any pastures that were reported. An unusually happy find on one occasion was signalled from afar by the scout waving his head-dress and shouting madly from the highest ridge, so drunk with the sight of good grazing as to forget the possibility of any enemies.

The camels dribbled in to be couched, off-loaded, knee-hobbled and driven off to the nearest scrub. But in a hungry camp the Badawin would scour the neighbouring hills for armfuls of fodder with which to feed their couched animals by hand, as a mother her child. After the camels had been provided for, the party lined up for evening prayer before they broke their own fast. Stacks of kindling rose by the side of the four or five camp-fires against the cold of the night. Round these the little self-chosen parties habitually ranged themselves and it was my daily custom to go and sit with one or other in turn.

This night I was interested in their manner of making unleavened bread. Ma'yuf, who was the cook of our particular party, squatted amid the circle of hungry and expectant watchers, while he filled his cooking-pot with flour, poured water upon it, punched and kneaded it into an excessively soft and slimy dough. He divided it into fistful shares, one for each of those present, rolling the lumps into balls to prove their size. He balanced them in his hands in the manner of scales, one eye upon the dough and the other upon his neighbours. Then any ball that had had an unfair start in life grew at the expense of another, until all were equal and laid out at his feet. Next he took up the first ball, sprinkled more water on it, flattened it with his palm into a bun some four inches in diameter and an inch thick, and laid it sagging across the glowing embers. A scorching smell was the signal that it needed turning, and so both sides came to be baked. Afterwards he made a hole in the hot sands under the fire, tumbled it into this and covered it again, and so with the rest of the batch. After a term of burial deemed meet, the loaves were one by one disinterred, and the caked sand partly brushed off by hand, partly blown away with a deep breath, but most of it left on to give the customary flavour. My companions favoured this delicacy piping hot; a little sufficed me - it was very heavy, perhaps two or three times the weight of English bread, and though baked to a cinder on the outside was doughy within. This may be one of its attractions, and yet be the main source of the stomach trouble which they all complained of. They were unused to solid food, so that the rations I provided of dates every day and bread and rice on alternate days were luxuries such as may have come their way once a year, for the Feast of Ramadhan perhaps:

Ma'yuf, however, had a side-dish to-night: a hare pulled out of its two-foot hole as we came along was simmering in the pot. But the amateur cook of the sands is a stranger to the use of butter, camel's milk being so poor in fat content that it will make neither butter nor cheese (though the hump of a young camel on the rare occasions of slaughter affords excellent fat), so that I found hare boiled in brackish water unattractive fare and, with little virtue, left my share to my companions.

Did I prefer the flesh of the gazelle? The question led on to the tale of the gazelle and the hare - one of those animal stories, beloved of Badawin, which are indeed attractive as told in the simple rhythm of their vigorous dialect, for Badu narrative speech tends to fall into the measure of blank verse.

A gazelle came grazing to a juicy tuft of *thamama*, not noticing that beneath it lay a hare asleep. The hare startled, leapt up and fled, the gazelle jumping back at the same time, even more frightened, so that it forgot itself. But now, coming to its senses, and feeling annoyed, it shouted in mock heroics after the hare:

'*Hubi!* whose flesh is of small account.
Whose skin gives no pleasure
O joy -giver but to children,
O vexer of neighbours!'
(i.e. there is so little meat on you that it will not suffice the guest).

And the hare, turning, sat up on its hindquarters and shouted back to the gazelle:

'*Hubi!* O father of forgetfulness,
O rimmed horned one,
If thou seest the wadi green
Thou becomest partner of it with the jinns!'
(*i.e.* the sight of pastures makes you mad).

And they parted ways.

The camp-fires would have been replenished if firewood had been available, for the poor Badawin were numbed with cold and the night was cruel. As the fires flickered out beneath them, they one by one lay down with their rifles, only the night watch alert against surprise by an enemy, while I went off to do my 'star taking.'

22nd December had been a long, uneventful day, marching through the sands of Yadila, and whenever we had to turn south in avoiding obstacles, the full blaze of the sun burnt my face.

We were floundering through heavy dunes when the silence was suddenly broken by a loud droning on a musical note. I was startled for the moment, not knowing the cause.

'Hanaina! Hanaina!' [64] shouted my companions. 'Listen to that cliff bellowing. Sahib!' and a man at my side pointed to a sand cliff, a hundred feet or so high, and perhaps a hundred yards or more away on our right hand. I was too much absorbed to reply. The hour was 4.15 p.m., and a slight north wind blew from the rear of the cliff.

Before this, in similar winds, we had passed many such cliffs, but they had emitted no sound, only the light surface sand being carried up the gentle windward slope to spill like smoke over its top. The leeward face of the cliff was a fairly steep slanting wall and I looked in vain for a more funnel- shaped sand gorge that by some rushing wind action might account for so great a volume of noise. The usual term, 'singing sands,' seems to me hardly appropriate to describe a sound indistinguishable from the siren [65] of a moderate-sized steamship. The noise continued for about two minutes and like a ship's fog-signal, ended as abruptly as it had begun.

A suggested explanation of the phenomenon, that the sand had been heated all day and the fall of temperature in the afternoon set the whole face sliding, came to my notice too late for investigation; the volume and nature of the noise did not suggest it, nor did it occur to me to ask my companions at what other times of the day it happens, though, from the implication of a remark made later to account for a night alarm, 'singing sands' after dark would not in their minds appear to be abnormal.

There are other varieties of sand noises. The sands of Umm Dharta - 'Mother of Wind' - (the name may be generic) to the north-ward of Umm al Hait, I am told, have a springiness which causes

wheezing when camels walk upon them. And I myself was to be startled a month later in the sands of Suwahib on hearing a sharp 'phut'
under my camel's feet like the falling of a spent bullet. It was instantaneous, and I did not hear it again. A Murri riding at my side who was
familiar with the phenomenon, though it was rare, could only suggest
some dark activity in the uppermost of the seven underworlds; but
this has no direct connection with the loud and continuous bellowing
which happens, according to the Arabs of the sands, only in heavy
dune country.

And now, after two long slow days in Shu'ait, we were to bid
adieu to the fair and gentle, if hungry, shivering camps between
steppe and sand. On the 24th December we turned north-west and
struck into the great dune-country, whose near edge stretched away
from us to the west-south- west. Before us rose red mountains of
sand.

The going at once became more difficult, and recalled to me my
struggles a year before in the sands of Mugshin, nearly two hundred
miles to the east-north-east, which I had tried to get through with
mountain-bred camels, and after two abortive days had been forced to
beat a retreat.

Very impressive is a great dune region at first sight -a vast ocean of
billowing sands, here tilted into sudden frowning heights, and there
falling to gentle valleys merciful for camels, though without a scrap of
verdure in view. Dunes of all sizes, unsymmetrical in relation to one
another, but with the exquisite roundness of a girl's breasts, rise tier
upon tier like a mighty mountain system. No contrasting shades are
afforded by the sun's almost vertical rays in this tropical latitude, and
the resulting impressions are soft planes and an exquisite purity of
colour. So smooth from a distance, the sands are in reality lined with
faint coruscations like tiny wavelets on the shore, and what from afar
is a sheet of pure red colour, when approached sparkles with glints of
green and gold. A breeze blowing from the north sweeps up gentle
slopes to spill a filmy wisp of sand over the brink and thus builds up a
flat rim along the upper leeward edges. The effect from near at hand
is that of the Hellenic helmet of Flaxman's Heroes, but in the far

distance the winding ridges of the dunes look like the walls of some
fair city built upon a hill.

The Vigil of Christmas was a night of excitement. We had arrived
late in camp, camels had been hobbled as usual and driven off to. the
scant bushes, from behind some of which came the brisk noises of
merry camp-fire parties. There came a sudden scream. To me it
sounded like the hooting of an owl or the whining cry of an animal;
but it spread instant alarm. My camp was at once in a ferment.

'Gom! Gom!' ' Raiders! raiders!' shouted the excitable Badawin,
leaping to their feet, their rifles at the ready; my servant came running
across to me with my Winchester and bandolier. Our *rabias*, of the
'Awamir and Karab tribes, rushed out shouting: 'We are alert! We are
alert! I am So-and-so [66] of such a tribe. These are my party and are
under my protection.' The object of this was to save us from raiders of
their own factions, if these they were. It is said that the cry is never
abused.

Others ran out on all sides, though in the dark night they were not
in touch with one another, and it seemed to me that friend might
easily be taken for foe.

An hour elapsed and there was no repetition of the sound and,
indeed, no sound at all, though my party were by no means reassured
and the stalwarts who were out remained out to keep night watches.

I was thoroughly tired and hence very ready to believe that the
alarm had been raised by a wild beast and not an enemy, so my vigil
fell short of that of my companions. My assumption was correct. Next
morning the tracks of a wolf were traced near by; its whoop had, it
seemed, been suspiciously like the *awan*, the war cry of raiders
making the attack.

The technique of desert raiding should be studied by all travellers.
An approaching party may be friend, but is always assumed to be foe.
Had the wolf cry betokened what we feared, my party would have
responded with a fusillade in the air in that direction - a procedure
calculated to damp the ardour of oncomers of whatever disposition.
All *rabias* present would have shouted their names and tribes as my
Karabis had done. The shout would have been recognised, for almost

every tribe has some vocal peculiarities. Some friend would have shouted back his name and if reassured, he and the *rabia* of my party would have advanced from opposite sides and the approaching party have been led in.

If two parties meet by day, *rabias* on both sides will ride forward to within a few hundred yards to identify and be identified, while both main bodies halt apprehensively. The discovery of an enemy will send the *rabia* fleeing back to his companions, who will open fire at long range: or in the case of a sudden appearance of a supposed enemy, men will couch their camels and run out in front of them in extended order and fire upon the oncomers. The object in both cases is to frighten away the other party.

The party numerically stronger, better mounted and better armed must prevail, and flight is seldom practicable for the weak. If the raiding party enjoy only a slight advantage a war of attrition will ensue until one or other has no more ammunition, for by desert canons none should submit while he has a round left: but if the attacking party are in preponderant strength there will be no dallying; they will sweep down upon their victims.

Surrender to the first oncomer is the only hope for an individual. '*sellemni!*' is the desert equivalent of the schoolboy cry of *pax*, and as a token of submission the rifle is held above the head, or thrown to one side. '*fi wijhi*' In my face,' is the victor's reply if he wishes to show mercy.

If the would - be prisoner has reason to expect good terms he may say '*sellemni!*' - with my 'rifle, [67] or 'dagger,' or 'camel'; but this is a risk seldom taken; probably his adversary is covering him with a rifle, and the best he can hope for is to be spared to return empty-handed to his kith and kin. But if one of the attackers has been killed, the law of the blood-feud must operate and his life be forfeit. So also if the answer 'by my face' is not returned, he may expect no mercy. Thus raiding parties are of two kinds, that whose tribe and yours have no blood-feud, that where a blood -feud exists. Both want your camels and arms, the second your life as well. 'We would show our "face" to one section of the Sa'ar but not to the other -

God is the All-knowing' - Khuwaitim had said to me as we rode along.

It was Christmas morning as we left behind us the 'alarm' camp (said to lie due north of Wadi Urba) and set out across what was to prove the loftiest and vastest of all the sands met with on my journey - Uruq-adh-Dhahiya. For the first four hours came a succession of mountains, cliffs and intervening gorges of sand. Our camels, wretched beasts, climbed arduously to knife-edge summits and slithered knee-deep down precipitous slopes. Here and there we turned back for very fear and tried a better way, and all dismounted to scrabble with our hands in the soft slopes to make a path for the camels to climb.

As we walked the soft sand came well over our ankles at each step; shoes would have been out of the question; nor was riding any comfort for the body must be bent, now back over the camel's quarters, now forward on the neck, at acute angles. Alarming too it was to look down a steep slope of a hundred feet and more where we must pass, yet our ungainly brutes, resolute and surefooted, braved a diagonal course across its face, their great pads sinking up to the shanks with every step, and throwing up clouds of sand as they were withdrawn.

No horse could possibly negotiate these southern sands, even if it could be brought thus far through the waterless wastes of the borderlands, and for a motor car they would be quite impassable.

Our toil had its compensations. There were moments when we came suddenly upon a picture of sublime grandeur, an immense and noble plastic architecture, an exquisite purity of colour, old rose-red, under the cloudless sky and brilliant light. A winter's day in Switzerland affords a comparison - the feel of the yielding substance underfoot and a glorious exhilaration in the air.

At last, after passing a dune system called Thurub bin Imani, which was said to mark the half-way point between the sweet water of Khor Dhahiya and the brackish water- hole of Bin Hamuda lying to the north-east, the going became easier, for we changed course and steered north for long stretches along the sand valleys that here have a north- easterly axis, between the mighty dunes.

Just before sunset a halt was cried.

'Khor Dhahiya!' shouted my party as we couched our camels. I ran to the brow of the hill before me and, concealing myself, looked down into a mighty sand valley running north-east and south-west, and here perhaps a mile wide. In its bed, three hundred feet below, a green patch marked our objective, the famous water-hole, where Shaikh Salih was to have met me with a fresh relay of camels on the fourth day of the moon. To-day was the fifth, so that I was a day late, but signs of Salih or his party there were none — only silent naked spaces.

For prudence' sake we halted short for the evening, in scanty pastures, while two of our number took their water- skins and at once trudged off by a wide detour down into the valley to spy out the land. I watched with my telescope their microscopic figures at the hole, and wondered whether an enemy lay lurking near. But after a careful search of the whole area they turned back unmolested, while I, waiting expectant for their news, watched their foreshortened figures growing as they climbed the sands until the sun went down and darkness came over the scene. The tidings were at once good and bad news. Neither friend nor foe had recently watered there, tracks made by themselves two moons ago still stood; Mubarak, Shaikh Salih's companion, had visited the water-hole but yesterday, God was the Knower!, and they would show me his footmarks on the morrow.

My Christmas dinner consisted of desiccated soup, made with the water of Dhahiya, which thus needed no salt or pepper, and one of the few tins of baked beans I carried for special occasions - festive fare after a strenuous nine hours' march without solid food. A midday meal was an indulgence I never allowed myself. It would have been quite out of the question to cry a long halt at noon - for the rule of life in the heart of an arid desert demands rapid marching from pasture to pasture. Instead I carried a flask of camel's milk and a daily ration of malted milk tablets, and short stops for our camels to graze or for the Badawin to pray afforded me the opportunity to slake my thirst.

In the desert, halts are always and rightly called in the camels' interests. The poor beasts, which the traveller starts by despising and learns to admire greatly, are the means by which he moves forward to success or away to safety. In remote waste places if the camel die, its master dies. The invariable consideration my companions showed for their beasts was noteworthy. Often I found myself the only member of my party in the saddle, while the others walked for long hours to spare their mounts, and ran hither and thither to collect occasional juicy tufts of camel-thorn with which to feed them as we passed along.

Our camels were tired out. Their humps, large and full at the outset, told a story. The hump is the barometer of the camel's condition, and ours had all fallen miserably away. This was only to be expected after an eight days' journey under loads through these barren and waterless southern borderlands.

On the following morning we were early astir. The Badawin led their camels down as best they could, chanting merrily a promise of the water that the thirsty brutes so sorely needed, in measures the animals most surely under- stood. I went on foot, avoiding their monstrous tracks in the soft slipping slopes, avoiding, too, the sight of camels pushed to acrobatics, carrying precious chronometers on their backs. When I reached the bottom, watering had already begun, to the sound of brisk happy noises that are heard at no other time. The hole, scarcely more than a yard in diameter, was rimmed with a heap of new yellow mud, the debris thrown out by a Badu who at the commencement of operations had descended as always to clean it out. As I looked down into it I saw another Arab standing below, up to his knees in water, replenishing the leathern water - buckets that were lowered to him. Near by a Karabi held bucket after bucket to the lips of his eager animal, talking to her the while, until a raised head and fat belly denoted she had had enough, when he playfully dashed the water that remained over her neck or threw the bucket into the air to catch it as it fell. [68]

But where was Shaikh Salih and my expected camels? I spent an anxious day wondering, though Kilthut, the Shaikh's son, was ready with explanations. Khor Dhahiya was a notoriously unhealthy spot, he said, being known and used by the Sa'ar and other raiders from the Hadhramaut, and there were here no pastures, as I could see for myself.

It was late afternoon before we left the water-hole. Sunset found us on a high sandy flat, thick with *zahar* and *abala*, fat pastures indeed, and even better ones were reported ahead. There Shaikh Salih would surely be. And so an early morning start. The party scanned the immediate sands for signs of his tracks, and soon there arose the now familiar explosive thanks to Allah. I shared their heartfelt joy, for among the footmarks that had been identified were those of Hamad bin Hadi, a son of the Murra whom Salih had mentioned as one sufficient for my purposes, could he be persuaded to turn guide and *rabia*. There were marks of many more camels, twenty others - encouraging discovery - for our animals, exhausted after their forced marches to Dhufar and back, could not have moved on under loads for three more days without a rest.

'Look, Sahib! That is So-and-so,' my men said, pointing to a foot impression that looked like every other footprint to me. 'That is his camel; he was leading her. She is gone with calf. See how deep are her tracks.' I was astonished at the accuracy of my party's description of those that were ahead of us, the amazing facility with which they read the evidence of the tracks we followed. In comparison the finger-print methods of the West seem a slow, laborious, technical process.

The sands are a public diary, that even he who runs may read, for all living creatures go unshod. Each of my companions not only knew at a glance the footmarks of every camel and man of my caravan, but claimed to know those of his absent tribe, and not a few of his enemies. No bird may alight, no wild beast or insect pass but needs must leave its history in the sands, and the record lasts until a rising wind bears a fine sand along to obliterate it. Snakes, hare, a sand fox, and numerous lizards owed their undoing to such tell-tale marks; their hiding-holes were in vain.

And now the sands with the crisp imprints of identified friends became our guide, and led us at right angles to our old course on a north-easterly bearing through rugged dune country, the aneroid steadily falling. As we breasted the tops of sandhills I scanned with eagerness each new horizon for Salih's camp. Suddenly there was merry chatter as black specks ahead were detected and pointed out to me as the object of our quest. A doubly welcome sight! for now our combined strength would relieve the tension of the recent anxious marches, and means become available, I hoped, for the onward march into the sands.

14

A GEOGRAPHICAL NOTE ON RUB AL KHALI

At the cost of breaking into the narrative for a few pages, it may be convenient here, where my route leaves the perimeter of the sands, to refer the reader to my map and consider briefly the shape of these sands and the configuration of Rub al Khali.

The entire area of South-east Arabia, bounded by long.48° 00 north of the 20th parallel, and by long. 46° 00 south of it, is, except for a narrow coastal belt, marked on our maps Rub Al Khali, Arabic words that may be translated the Empty Quarter. The meaning is sufficiently literal to have an application, and the term is one that is familiar to literate Arabs elsewhere who have learned geography from text- books, but the tribes who live in the Rub Al Khali neither use the term nor understand it in its geographical sense.

Rub Al Khali consists of desert, the eastern and southern portions of which to the extent of nearly a third of the total area are steppe lands; the rest an ocean of sands stretching away to the north and west. The southern steppe is known as Nejd, the eastern steppe as Sih in the north, Jaddat Harasis in the south; the sandy region is known as Ar Rami or Ar Rimal. Tribes are within large limits localised and for them particular areas both in sands and steppe have individual names.

A steppe region sometimes derives its name from that of the tribe that habitually occupies it, but more usually from the name of a wadi. [69]

The southern Sands

The southern edge of the sands which in the course of my last two journeys I skirted for nearly two hundred miles, I have already shown to stretch almost parallel with the south coast of Arabia from Mugshin to north of the Hadhramaut, and to be falling from south to north and from west to east.

The eastern edge of the sands runs north-north-east from Mugshin, a four days' march to Qarn as Bahama, thence it turns due north and approximately follows long. 55° 40', passing thus within a day to the westward of Ibri, skirts the west side of Jabal Hafit and extends thence onward as a spur to bisect peninsular Oman.

Within the sand borders, the mountainous gypsum system of Uruq-adh-Dhahiya is said to form a mighty horseshoe range whose base rests on the central south borderlands in the regions of Umm Gharib, Kharkhir, Uruq-adh-Dhahiya, Miniyur and Raga'at; its western arm approximately follows long. 49° as far as lat. 20° N., embracing the regions Ga'amiyat, Huwaiya and Shuwaikila: its eastern arm follows long. 53° E. approximately as far north as lat. 22° 30' N. embracing Uruq Mijora, Tamaisha, Shaiba and Maraikha.

Within this horseshoe will be found only the tribes who are essentially dwellers in the great sands, i.e. (i) the Murra approaching from the north-west; (ii) the Rashid and Bait Imani sections of Al Kathir approaching from the central south; (iii) the 'Awamir and Manasir (to a more limited extent) approaching from the north-east.

Outside the horseshoe and between it and the steppe are the border sands used seasonally by particular sections of the steppe tribes. In the east these tribes are Albu Shamis, Daru', Harasis and Afar: in the south Bait Kathir, Manahil, 'Awamir (southern elements) Sa'ar and Karab, but they severally keep within a safe distance of their own water-holes. [70]

Altitude readings recorded along my four routes covering altogether some two thousand miles in the north, the south- east, the south centre and the centre of Rub Al Khali, together with the recorded direction of wadi beds (either observed or ascertained from Arab information) furnish the means of establishing the slope of this part of the continent of Arabia.

The general configuration of Arabia, which rises abruptly on the west side in the Red Sea and Dead Sea rift escarpments to decline gently eastwards to the plains of Iraq and the waters of the Persian Gulf, does not extend through- out the Rub Al Khali. Here the land mass rises abruptly on three sides: on the north-east, the Hajar range of Oman; in the central south, the Dhufar system; in the south-west, the mountains of Hadhramaut and Najran. Low levels mark the Persian Gulf and Arabian Sea littorals on the south-east side of the desert. That the sands are sloping down to the Persian Gulf on three sides is thus apparent: so also must there be a depression in the central south-east.

The altitudes of the eastern edge of the sands already delineated are approximately as follows: in the northern spur which I crossed in 1926 the reading was 1200 feet. To the westward of Jabal Hafit it is about 1000 feet. Sir Percy Cox recorded Ibri as 1600 feet, so that the edge of the sands in that latitude, bearing in mind the south-westerly fall of its wadi Al 'Ain, must be considerably lower. The height of the sands at Mugshin was about 400 feet. Hence it may be deduced that the eastern edge of the sands is falling from north to south.

East of this long eastern edge of Ar Rimal is a steppe which rises slowly north-eastwards to the great Hajar backbone of Oman, whence the drainage wadis Al 'Ain, Al 'Aswad, Al 'Amairi and Musallim follow almost parallel courses to the south-west to lose themselves in the eastern borders of the sands. To the south-east of Mugshin is another steppe having no discernible slope but said to be bounded on its north-east side by the isolated ridge of Jabal Hugf. On its south-eastern side the wadis Qadan (Ghudun?), Raunib and Haitam (I crossed the mouths at sea-level in 1928) fall south-eastwards into Sauqira Bay.

On its south-western side, Jaddat Harasis receives the system of Wadi 'Ara, the inland drainage of the northern extension of Jabal Samhan. Where I crossed it in its sources on an earlier journey the wadi heads were running north- east, and aneroid readings varied between 1100 feet east and 1400 feet west. To the eastward of Jabal Hugf the only considerable wadis, Halfain and Andam, fall away from the eastern Hajar of Oman and run due south, in part to drain into the Gulf of Masira.

There is thus an area of depression at the south-eastern extremity of the great sands forming a corridor running south-east and extending from the coast of Sauqira Bay through Jaddat Harasis and thence on into the sands, probably in long. 54° E. to 55° E., lat. 20° N. to 22° N. Within it water comes to the surface at Mugshin and Hamaidan. North of this corridor the general slope is upwards towards the north and east, south of the corridor it rises to the south and west.

Wadi Mugshin

An item of much geographical interest is the presence of desert quicksands on the northern side of the corridor, where it meets Ar Rimal. The extent of Umm as Samim, as the area is called, is said to be a two days' march in every direction. In appearance a sheet of salt plain, it gives no indication to the unwary traveller of its treacherous bogs. Many have perished here and only certain Daru' Badawin who come to collect salt on its borders are said to brave its secret passages, raiders, as might be expected, giving it a wide berth.

Von Wrede, the Bavarian soldier of fortune, who in 1843 penetrated the Hadhramaut in Muslim disguise, records a similar phenomenon, its place-name Bahr as Safi. He marched towards one of the white patches armed with a plumb-line of six fathoms. 'With the greatest caution I approached the border to examine the sand, which I found almost an impalpable powder, and I threw the plumb-line as far as possible; it sank instantly, the velocity diminishing, and in five minutes the end of the cord had disappeared in the all-devouring tomb.' While I do not wish to impugn Von Wrede's veracity I should record that most of the companions of my journeys had raided in the sands to the north of the Hadhramaut, in fact the Karab *rabias* hailed from there, but none knew of Bahr as Safi, and all averred that the quicksands described exist to-day only in Umm as Samim, lying between sand and steppe to the north and east of Mugshin and south and west of 'Ibri. Many Omani Badawin and others told me of the Umm as Samim quicksands.

15

THROUGH THE SANDS OF DAKAKA: THE SECOND RELAY OF CAMELS

'Haiya hi wusulkum, sahib!
Marhaba wa haiya bikum!'

This was the desert greeting of Shaikh Salih as I eagerly rode up some distance ahead of my party to the new camp, and couching Gerainha slipped off her back for the last time to grasp Salih's outstretched hand. With him was a man I recognised - fat old Muhammad who had been with me on my last year's expedition. But only these two; the rest of the party of strange Badawin looked on from their sandy eminence a little way off without bothering to come forward to meet me, and I scented a coolness in the atmosphere which seemed to augur ill for my plans. Was this to be the limit of my journey? Was I not to be allowed to move forward? But as my party straggled in the cold faces took on a kindlier expression, and men sprang up to meet their returning kindred and salute them in the manner of Badu meeting Badu. This nose kiss [71] - it is also the lovers' kiss - in its attenuated form before me consisted of three brushing nose to nose movements, left to right, right to left, centre press, while each placed his right hand over the other's left shoulder.

A circle of squatting Arabs was soon formed and I ordered three bowls of dates to be set in the midst and the coffee cup to go round. The new Badawin eyed me silently, giving me a feeling that I was being weighed in the balance as they spoke in low tones to right and left with members of my old party. The last-named disdained the coffee and dates as these went round the first time - unusual for those who had been so insistent for *fuwala* on the march - and it was amusing to me to find in the Rub Al Khali an application of the time-honoured principle of 'family-hold- back.' The delicacies received the nominal patronage usual on such formal occasions and there was plenty left when it came to my party's turn to stick fingers into the common dish.

'*Marhaba wa ehlen ya haiyakum!*'

Thus old Saif, the rightful shaikh of the tribe by blood [72] but an effete branch (and consequently superseded by the Kilut family, not of shaikhly lineage on the male side but resolute, brave and effective) as he took off his ammunition belt and threw it into the circle. This was an invitation to my party whose visit to the coast and hunting activities on the march had brought them a few rounds of ammunition apiece, to spare of their bounty for the titular chief. Now one, now another threw a round into the pool, as it were, and when all had done Saif was ten rounds to the good.

Shaikh Salih had not failed me. He came along bringing a man of consequence for introduction, walking in Badawin fashion hand-in-hand with him.

'This is a shaikh. Sahib! shaikh of the Murra' (it is well to promote your friends thus in the desert, though in point of fact the description was not very wide of the mark). [73] 'No better guide in all the sands than Hamad bin Hadi, no doughtier fighter, no more skilful hunter; and loyal, I call God to witness, for did not my brother take his daughter to wife; none knows the pastures and -the water-holes like Hamad; he knows a way across the sands and agrees to be our *rabia*.

Hamad was a middle-sized man of dark complexion with shifty black eyes, a hawk-like Armenoid face thickly bearded and a curious quick voice which bespoke him a man of greater vigour than Salih, but on first impression not so inspiring of trust. The dweller of the desert, like a child or an animal requires a very slow and careful approach, and Hamad, who had never before seen a man of my colour or heard an accented voice, would not improbably be suspicious; so I decided that leisureliness in coming to the point was the right policy. The first meeting was therefore an occasion only for the coffee cup and amiable conversation about hunting; likewise the second, which was profitably reinforced with the present of a headdress for his son.

A Halt to Graze

'What do you make of Hamad?' said Salih to me the next day.

'The very man.'

'Didn't I tell you so? But he wants a lot. Sahib!' The greed of the Badu is proverbial, but I had made a sworn pact with Salih before leaving the coast, and now he was to observe the conditions scrupulously by persuading Hamad to accept the terms we mutually considered fair.

The new party, now reduced in numbers, had become more friendly to me. The antipathy I thought I had detected in our first meeting was but their native sullenness: in truth they had come here with Shaikh Salih expressly for my purposes. The plan was that they would bear me westwards through these sands of Dakaka to the water-hole of Shanna. There I must dismiss them and engage a third and still further reduced party of men and camels, which Shaikh Salih would go ahead to select and bring to the rendezvous after ten days if God willed, and neither of us met an enemy.

These central southern sands of Dakaka were indeed the key to the problem of my journey, for they had received the rains of last year and were therefore blessed with exceptional pastures so that the herds had concentrated here. This had made it possible for a large party laden with full milk-skins to come to the coast for me; here I could find an escort to take me on, and hence a party would avail at the most advanced point towards the inmost sands for a jump off into the unknown. Had Dakaka itself been hungry, had last year's rains fallen not here but to the north-east, the camel concentrations would have been too far removed for the system of relays by which alone I could hope to cross the deserts in quick stages carrying scientific instruments.

Pay-day was a day of excitement, for a hired Badu is the most diffi-cult person to satisfy on dismissal. His contracted pay was fifty dollars for himself and camel and forty dollars- for a pack animal; of this he had drawn half at Dhufar, in advance; the other half he was getting that day, so that my camp table glittered with Maria Theresa dollars (each worth about 1s. 4d.), the only coin the sands know, and that but infrequently. The chink of silver, a sound rare in Dakaka, was a neces-sary accompaniment to setting up piles of twenties and twenty-fives, which would facilitate payment, for then all I had to do was to put so many piles into each man's hand as he came along. But I was reck-oning without my host. Each laboriously counted and recounted his share and a horrid infection spread amongst them, of each looking up and declaring he was one or two short. A companion would take the money out of his hand and count it back in fives, generally to the man's ultimate satisfaction. My method of counting 6, 7, 8, etc., or even omitting to count at all, appeared to puzzle them. Their practice was to count 1, 2, 3, 4, 5 and then begin at 1 again - an object lesson in the human appeal of the decimal system. At the end of an hour my table was bare, every name on the pay-roll of my escort had been ticked off; two hours later I was congratulating myself that on the whole pay-day had passed satisfactorily, when suddenly there was much shouting; a serious row started and it looked as though the old party, with whom my relations had been so cordial, were going to spoil this record by a free fight on the day of parting. It seemed they had incurred mutual debt obligations at Dhufar and the liquidation of these demanded a standard of mental arithmetic and of patience in discussion not vouchsafed to them; hence the heated words and the possibility of the dagger as an honourable arbiter. Peace only came when Shaikh Salih gathered up all the payments that I had made into a large common heap on his head-dress laid out on the sands, for a complete redistribution by himself. Thus I had to witness all my pretty work of the morning brought to naught.

Peace prevailed at last - but not contentment. For they must have rations, they said, how else were they to get home with their exhausted animals not in milk? They would die on the way. Their demands seemed to me to be three times in excess of their legitimate needs and to be inspired by the approach of Ramadhan, when the fast by day is compensated by gorging at night. Other Badawin, not of my party, also gathered round imagining a vain thing in their hearts. For before me by the most favourable computation was a six weeks' march, and my stock of food represented a bare six weeks' supply and thus had become more precious than gold. To dissipate it must lead to certain failure. I had guarded it most jealously on the march; it was the only matter over which I could afford, when seriously challenged, to show temper, for I knew that the end of my rations meant the end of my journeyings. Normally camels in milk are taken along at grazing speed; not on raids or forced marches, which would run them dry or exhaust them. Thus the great desert before me, with camels of necessity not in milk, would provide, in the last event, nothing but the flesh of our own mounts; and to take that would *propter vitam vivendi perdere causas.*

Camp must be broken with all speed, for so long as I remained my old party and the stray starvelings of the sands that came along would batten on me; so in lieu of food they were sent away cheered with two or three dollars apiece. Similar treatment was accorded to the master of Gerainha - she, patient brute, having carried me from the Qara Mountains, was now returning to her home in the steppes to the south. Her mistress there was reputed to be the most beautiful girl in all the land, one that troubled the hearts of not a few of my escorting Badawin; indeed, she was the subject of a romance of which she would learn in due course after her fate had been decided. She was now nineteen and unmarried, an unthinkable state of affairs in polygamous Arabia, and Bin Aksit, her father, was twitted by the rest of his companions on the march for his selfishness.

'Why not give her to the Sahib?' they would say mockingly, 'he's young and strong, and look at his dollars, why, you could buy all the camels in Rub Al Khali. [74] And behind his back they would accuse him of miserliness for he was passing rich in the possession of fifteen camels, and as he had no close male relatives, the daughter would inherit his all, which made her doubly attractive in their sight.

'How much do you want for her?' I asked him one day in the dispassionate way which a Badu would tolerate from the lips of a man not like himself.

'Three camels,' he said. 'Why, the daughter of Ali brought her father three, and who can compare Ali's daughter with mine? All know she is worth it, but no one has offered me more than two, so I will not agree and she is content to stay with me.'

That was a fortnight before. Later I had seen that Bin Aksit and Ma'yuf sat round the same camp-fire together overmuch, and now and then withdrew from the general circle to engage in rapt conversation, and the gossip of the camp when Gerainha had departed was that Ma'yuf was the lucky man.

Private conversation is achieved by two persons rising from the circle and betaking themselves fifty paces or so from their companions, but even then they are not safe from intrusion. It is amusing to watch a third Badu come along and instead of sitting in the general circle, go up and salaam the whisperers and sit down with them - a flattering if gratuitous indication that he thinks their talk more likely to interest him. There is so much community of life amongst them, however, living as they do in the open, always cheek by jowl for mutual protection from a common enemy, that familiarity, and the impulse to act without too sensitive a feeling for others is ingrained in them, and a European who would travel happily must be prepared to adapt himself to their standards. On one occasion, for instance, a Kathiri, seeing the milk bowl at my side, suddenly held it to his lips and drained its contents; they were dregs, it is true, but a European could not afford to show resentment. Even my heart-to-heart talks with Shaikh Salih were not undisturbed, for one or other of my party spotting us from afar and finding the attraction irresistible would come up with a hearty salaam and sit down without a 'by your leave,' to hear what it was all about.

With my party reduced in numbers to twenty men, nearly all strangers to me, we started off again on a westerly course, meeting no encampment on our way. I suspected that the main body of the Rashid tribe was grazing to the north, and it was essential that I should escape their importunities for food. I should thus also avoid the consequences of any religious objection some fanatic among them might take to my presence on the sacred soil of the Faithful.

The first day, as usual, was a short march - the fresh, untried camels bellowing protests against unusual burdens, and their masters quarrelling among themselves about alleged inequalities of loads. My Bikaner-pattern saddle was the subject of universal disapprobation for its size and weight, wherefore I suffered the humiliation of being given a different camel to ride each day.

In this region of Dakaka the sands were somewhat milder in mood than the mountains and valleys of Uruq-adh- Dhahiyah, for which they form an exaggerated crossing of the **T**. The basic formation was a hard red sand, in immense undulations, like a troubled sea many times magnified. Occasional superimposed sandhills of a paler colour (that became less lofty as we went on) were some- times solid, some- times horseshoe-shaped — termed *hugna*, and of very curious shape. They appear to arise from reversible wind action and in their depressions lay often a white patch of gypsum and not infrequently a water-hole.

Here there was no lack of sweet water - sweet, that is to say, judged by the other waters of the sands — and amidst improved pastures we deliberately made slow going, so that I now found more opportunity for collecting of zoological specimens and photography than during the recent long nervous marches when such things had to be neglected. We dawdled in fact while bin Kilut and bin Ham went scouting the country-side about my business.

The important member of the new party was Hamad bin Hadi, whom I grew to respect as the days wore on. His companions showed towards him much respect, as befitted the son of his father, a Murri known throughout the sands, who had slain eight men of the rival Manasir tribe during his lifetime and had died in venerable old age beside the eponymous well of Bir Hadi, one of many water-holes dug by him. With Hamad came his nephew Marzuq, our *muedhdhin* on the march, and a cousin, another Hamad, of rather unstable temper, who appeared with two strings dangling from his nose (suggestive of the physician's stethoscope with nostrils for ear-holes). This practice of plugging the nostrils with cotton is common throughout Arabia and Persia, as a protection against evil smells which are supposed to aggravate most maladies. Hamad clearly suffered from ophthalmia, which, however, he ascribed to an evil spirit, a *zar*, I attended its exorcism that evening, a simple ritual compared with the elaborate performances practised in the coastal villages of Oman, [75] but presumably of the same nature and lacking nothing in the frenzied display of the possessed. The chief differences were that the desert audience were not women, but men, who did not play a hysterical part in the proceedings; the Master of Ceremonies was a man and not a woman; and fire was used in place of blood.

Hamad, the afflicted, knelt before the fire within a circle of squatting companions, the Master of Ceremonies, Muhammad bin Shughaila, seated himself next to him, and between them on the sands was placed a cup filled with fire. One or two of the party brought their cooking-pots and thus was the stage set.

Hamad now took off his head-dress, folded it once diagonally and used it as a shawl and veil combined, holding the ends with outstretched arms. He began to bob and sway his body, while his companions around chanted, clapped their hands, and drummed with their fingers on upturned pots. The *zar*-possessed put more and more frenzy into his movements as the minutes passed, bowing blindly over the fire on to which he must have many times fallen but for the care of a neighbour, who held out a cane before him; now and then he took up the cup of fire to hold it under his veil and inhale it as though it were the incense burner, an act that seemed to impel him to more feverish activity, and so it went on until his voice became tremulous and his mood hysterical. An hour may have passed thus; and now the Master of Ceremonies began. He had a series of questions to put to the *zar* (who speaks by the mouth of the patient), but the *zar* seemed to share my view that the exorcism had been too summary or so it seemed by the tardiness at first of the answers.

M.C.: 'Are you *afera*?'

Zar: (No answer.)

M.C.: 'Are you *jinn*

Zar: (No answer.)

Chorus of Badawin: 'It's a *zar* oi course. Has not Hamad said it is Saif Shangur [76]

Hamad went on swaying and gibbering. A pause on the part of the M.C.

Badawin: 'Go on, Muhammad!'

M.C.: 'You are a shaikh. What do you want? Tell us.'

Zar: (No answer.)

More vigorous drumming and hand-clapping. The patient whispering to himself: 'Saif Shangur! When are you coming?'

M.C.: 'Do you want money?'

Zar (at last on the move): 'A ring.'

M.C.: 'Must it have a stone in it?'

Zar: 'A ring.'

Chorus of Badawin to M.C.: 'Don't ask unnecessary questions.'

M.C. to Badawin: 'Who has a ring?'

Ma'yuf parted with his poor possession, which the Master of Ceremonies now introduced into the cup of fire and then put on one of Hamad's fingers, and so continued holding his hand while he put his final question.

M.C.: 'Will you remove the evil from the eye?'

Zar: 'Yes.'

M.C.: 'There is no other evil except that in the eye?'

Zar: 'No.'

M.C.: 'Swear that you will remove it.'

Zar: 'Eh, eh.'

M.C.: 'Swear by the oath of a *qabaili*.'

Zar: '*Fi wijhak*.'

M.C.: '*Shered*' — It has fled.

And thus the proceedings were at an end, and the no- longer-afflicted one rose unsteadily and went off to his sandy couch for the night.

We left our camp that lay to the north of the water-hole of Bil Ashush and moving westwards came two hours later to a great horse-shoe hill named Hulaiyil, the red sands here clothed unexpectedly with generous dark green abala. It was our New Year's Day - a festival unrecognised of course by Badawin (indeed, only two of my Rashidi companions remembered the days of the week) - but the place pleased us all for its pastures, and I decided to halt and spend the day shooting. Hamad, the subject of last night's exorcism, came up as I dismounted. His eyes were no better, though he would have me believe that they were, pointing in proof to the nostril wads that had been withdrawn and hung about his neck - but still kept in reserve, I noticed. Perhaps he was of too recent a generation of believers for a faith-cure, for the Murra tribe are said not to practise magic with the exception of the isolated southern groups, having learned it from the Rashid, who use it in common with every tribe of the southern steppe.

I spent the remainder of the day with my rifle under my arm, making a circuit of the camp at some two or three miles' distance, but to my surprise came upon no track of any animal bigger than a hare, for, despite the hungry marches of the southern borderlands, we passed tracks of antelope and fox there every day. Animal imprints became easy to identify, and I soon learned without any conscious effort those of every wild animal of the sands and when it had passed. Dakaka was overrun with the golden hare, and almost every bush bore signs of a recently scraped hole beneath. Into these the passing Badu would thrust an arm and draw out the wriggling creature, while we would often spy one sleeping in some leafy shade and easily get quite near to it upon the soft noiseless sands.

Hare for dinner produced another animal story. If you would hear how the hare became lawful for man to eat, it is necessary for you to know two things: firstly, that in the ancient days the brute creation could speak; and secondly, that it was customary for the women of the time to bind into a faggot the sticks they had gathered and ride it home like the witches of Europe with their broomsticks.

One day, then, the Prophet (upon him be prayer and peace) said to some women: - 'Go and gather me firewood.' And off they went as they were bidden, but in the wilderness they fell to gossiping over-much and dallied.

And the Prophet (upon him be peace), when they did not return, became impatient, and said to the hare that sat at his side:

'Go out into the wilderness and you will see some women gathering sticks; tell them to bind up their bundles, and ride home at once.'

So off the hare went and found the women, but instead of conveying the message as it was delivered to him, he merely said:

'The Prophet says, "Put the firewood on your heads and return home."'

Thus the women, gathering up their sticks, came, returning by the slowest way.

As the hours passed and they did not arrive, the Prophet grew angry; but at last he saw them approaching, and as they came up he cried:

'Why did you not return riding as you always do?'

'Because the hare said you wished us to return this way, O Prophet of God.'

Then the Prophet turned his wrath from the women to the hare, and picking up a brand from the fire, he struck the now fleeing animal on the tail, which to this day bears a small black mark. Then he raised his voice so that all could hear and called after the hare, 'Henceforth you are *hallal*, for all men to eat, every bit of you — even to your bowels.'

We made an early start next day and soon passed two mighty horseshoe hills that marked the water-holes of Mashruma and Dhiraibi. Hamad the *rabia* and I were riding ahead when he suddenly halted, his eyes fixed on some distant object; and he stretched out his hand towards me for my telescope. We dismounted while he pointed out the hill that aroused his fears and motioning me to remain where I was, crept forward towards it, using the cover of the folded sands. Later he returned reassured, for the suspicious thing proved to be a knoll and not an enemy.

Hamad, it seemed, was a marked man. He was famous for raids, sometimes single-handed, into the Sa'ar country; he had in fact shed Sa'ar blood, and so could not expect to survive his next meeting with a superior party of them; this and the Manasir blood-feud he had inherited gave him many ghostly fears. Again and again he held us up while he searched the horizons with my telescope, and whenever we halted for the night, he would slink back over our tracks for some miles lest we were being tracked by an enemy, and return just after nightfall, when tracking was no longer possible, with the glad news that our camp-fires could now be safely lighted.

To our immediate north was reported the water-hole of Waraiga. There my two original emissaries sent from Dhufar to find their tribe had come upon them. [77] And there it was that the main herds of the tribe were now grazing.

The rearing of the camel is in this environment the predestined life to which every man-child is born. He is her parasite: her milk provides almost all his food and drink, her wool his shelter and clothing. Life is the quest for green pastures, rain the gift of God, and lightning man's pillar of fire. The great changing world without; the rise and fall of kingdoms; science and art and learning; spiritual forces at work for human betterment - 'the oppositions of science falsely so-called' and immoral systems making for human degradation; the welter of races, tongues and classes -of these he is unaware. They have no meaning, and therefore no existence for him. He follows the primitive life his fathers have led for ten thousand years, and his sons must live for as long to come. He abjures the soft and sedentary ways of life; his code knows only pitiless ferocity for his enemies, and for his friends the heights and depths of human courage and the milk of human-kindness.

Pastures [78] and water are the two elemental needs of nomadic life. In winter pastures come first for herds require water infrequently - once in fifteen or twenty days perhaps, or where rains have produced sodden grazing they may not return to a water-hole for two months during which time the Badawin never taste water but live exclusively on milk. In summer, [79] on the other hand, when the great heat and glare make the sands almost unendurable, herds are restricted within two days' radius of a water-hole, for they require watering every other day. [80] In the higher altitudes, however, and amidst the perennial pastures of the southern steppe against the mountains, camels are herded into caves by day to escape the effect of the summer sun, and are turned out to graze by night in the cool. In these conditions watering every fourth or even sixth day will suffice.

In the sands themselves man must be for ever on the move. In summer, movement is by night in sharp marches from one water-hole with adjoining pastures to another. In winter, water not being a pressing consideration and pastures being eaten up as they are found, movement is by day with a halt of perhaps two or three days over each; the herds move slowly across the great spaces in unending cycle. The direction of the march is decided by scouting parties of two men (*towuf*), who must ride fast and far. Their reconnaissances in winter may last for several weeks, the men living on milk, with which their water-skins have been filled at the outset. [81]

In summer the great heat of the sands is a torment to them, for it makes sleep impossible once the sun is high, and by night little time avails for sleep, for they must protect their camels by riding in the cool. An honoured task is theirs, given to good guides and men who can be trusted, at need, to calculate not too nicely the time their milk-skins will last, so that they often return a day or two late and fasting. Shaikh Salih and many others of my escorting Badawin had known such experiences. Small wonder that in their minds milk (which alone makes their life possible) should be honoured above every other meat. The Prophet himself held this. Witness the conversation he held with a companion who had returned from a feast:

Prophet: 'And what was set before you?
Companion: 'We had camel's flesh.'
Prophet: 'Your host killed for you.'
Companion: 'And we had rice.'
Prophet: 'He honoured you.'
Companion: 'And dates.'
Prophet: 'He pleased you.'
Companion: 'And we had the milk of the camel.'
Prophet: 'Ah! Enough, he feasted you!'

On the fourth day we continued our westerly course towards the *hugna* of Khudhfiya, a large hill that had been in sight of the camp overnight, and which we passed after half an hour. In its great gypsum-lined hollow facing south-west - as do all these horseshoe hills - was a cluster of straw-like sun shelters beside the water-hole, unusual erections to find in the sands.

Presumably they were relics of some summer watering. Hamad slipped off his camel, as the Badu manner is, without couching her, and handing the headrope to his nephew as we passed on, descended into the hollow to look for traces of watering by possible raiders. He caught us up later with the news that all was well, and only the camel marks of bin Ham (of my recently dismissed party and now on his way to Huwaiya on a recruiting campaign) showed that he had passed three days before. We pressed on to arrive three hours later at the water -hole of Shanna, our immediate objective. My advance guard of two Badawin ran up from the water-hole as we arrived crying, '*Gom! Gom!* Muhammad bin Mubarak the Karabi! Muhammad bin Quwaid the Sa'ari!' (names of two notorious Hadhramauti raiders between whom and my companions there was a blood-feud). Hamad, with whom I now went to the hole, scrutinised the sands and gypsum bed about it, then looked up smiling and reassured. The attempted befooling may have been to tease him or perhaps to encourage me to disgorge a little of my supposedly large stock of ammunition, or it may only have been a joke. In the last event it succeeded, though it reminded us that we were still very much exposed to the raider; indeed, Hamad forthwith borrowed my telescope and made off for the tallest hill and that was the last I saw of him till the hour of evening prayer.

16

AT THE WATER-HOLE OF SHANNA-THE HALT BEFORE THE NORTHWARD DASH

It was the full moon before Ramadhan, and a full moon is a mixed blessing. It makes star observations with an artificial horizon troublesome. It is an ally of the raider, for tropical skies are so bright that he can see to track by night. Its advantage was that I could see to record my notes with no other aid as I lay near a camp-fire.

That night camel flesh was for dinner. One of our camels was found to be ailing, some said mortally, and the one way with a worn-out camel in the desert is to kill and eat it.

The old *fatira's* tribal brand [82] showed her to be of Janaba origin, she had indeed been part of the booty of a raid, a *dhalul* and lady of high degree before coming to this sad inevitable end.

'How does the flesh compare with beef?' I asked Khuwaitim, a Rashidi now domiciled in Dhufar, my original emissary, in fact.

'Incomparably better,' he said.

'And mutton?'

'Likewise it lacks the flavour of camel meat.'

'And what are the prime parts?'

'In a young camel the lower ribs; to-day the legs.'

'What of the marrow of the thigh bones?'

'Delicacy of delicacies! Wait and you shall see,'

'And how are we going to have it cooked - stewed or grilled (In the steppe where a heap of stones could have been gathered they would have grilled the flesh in the Stone Age manner.)

'We shall boil it. But alas! there is no salt. *Wallahi*, if we had salt, you should judge of the soup.'

0, blind lover! I thought. I will also record my own view that camel flesh is very tough and stringy, and that boiled, as it has to be, in brackish water and without fat, it is a weariness both to the palate and to the digestion.

Poor bint Shantuf was brought along and couched. Two holes were hastily scooped in the sand under her forelegs, which were then bound, and one Badu holding her tail, and another twitching her upper lip to bring her head back along her body, made her powerless to resist. Muhammad, better butcher than exerciser, had sharpened his dagger expressly and now bending close to the ground on her blind side, gave her a sharp stab in the pit of her neck. A torrent of blood gushed forth as he quickly slashed across her great throat, muttering as he did so, 'In the name of God, the Compassionate, the Merciful,' and then continued sawing with his dagger blade through her veins and windpipe back to the bone, his hands and arms streaming with blood. After her first desperate lurch and a few feeble gurgling grunts she lay still, with her monstrous neck tilted over like a falling tree, and her eyes of a glassy pallor. Never have I seen Badawin more elated; the prospect of a hearty meal cheered them all and with little axes and knives they all fell gleefully skinning and jointing. Five heaps of fresh meat soon lay on the sands — for the five camp-fire parties composing my caravan, and a shout of joy announced the moment to cast lots for them -- ever the desert way. Five representatives stood forth, one for each party. A head-dress was produced and into it each put a marked round of ammunition. The four corners were bunched together and the contents shaken up. A by- stander was invited to grasp one round through the head-dress, which was then opened and the owner of the chosen round given first choice of heaps. Four times the performance was repeated, each time with a round withdrawn, and when the last had gone so had the body of bint

Shantuf. Eagerly the Badawin scattered in search of firewood, for no sooner is an animal slaughtered than straight it goes into the pot, neither Arab climate nor Arab nature suffering it to 'hang'; within an hour of the time when the beast walked up to the place of execution she was sizzling to content the hearts and noses of the Badawin sitting round' their camp-fires. Not that all of her was to be cooked and eaten that day, for much of the flesh was kept back to relieve our scanty store of food. The surplus meat my companions cut into strips and later dried, like biltong, merely by carrying it on their saddles exposed to the sun, and as they went they nibbled it and declared it to be very good.

As soon as afternoon prayers were at an end the party addressed themselves to the great shining stomach of the beast. It was perched on the top of a convenient *abala* bush beneath which a circular hole about a yard in diameter was scooped in the sands, and lined with bint Shantuf's own neck skin as for a waterproof sheet. The bladder was now pierced and the contents trickled down to make a pool of yellow liquid.

'It is delicious,' they said, as each in turn went down on hands and knees setting his lips to it to drink his fill; 'far better than the brackish water of the sands.'

I was not astir at dawn, but learned later from my servant Muhammad that the *muedhdhin's* call no sooner woke them than the Rashidis made a joyous dash for a drink at the pool [83] before lining up for prayers.

At Shanna one of my party brought me a perfect flint arrow-head saying that he had found it at the water-hole, but this was untrue. The arrow-head, like a large flint spear-head in possession of another Arab, had come from the sands of Sanam. The owners from whom I acquired them had no knowledge of their original use, but I gathered that such flints are sometimes picked up in the sands and used as fire-lighters. Hamad bin Hadi, to whom I showed them, that he might search for others to our common advantage, considered them intrin-sically uninteresting, for he with an eye less for archaeology than for the picturesque, declared that at but a day's march west of Shanna there were 'stones' in abundance and more interesting by far, graven images - 'God was the Knower!' - and the work of the sons of Adam in the Days of Ignorance.

Camels in the Oman Desert

The name of this spot amidst the dunes of Ga'amiyat he called Shag al Masawwar, a name which seemed to promise much, 'the Valley of Images.' It was deemed unwise for me to leave the main party, so I sent Hamad to bring me specimens against the promise of reward. Thirty-six hours later he returned with a rib-like stone two feet in length, another of symmetrical circular shape, one and a half feet in diameter, that looked like the pelvis of some ancient reptile and

various small specimens of quaint shapes, resembling Losspuppen or
Fairy Stones. These were clearly Nature's work. The two big ones
looked like fossil bones, but proved to be mere sandstone concretions.
[84]

'Here you are. Sahib!' said Hamad, as he laid them on the sands
before me, while his fellow Badawin looked at him disapprovingly for
having brought along what must be added burdens for the camels.

'I don't know what they are, Hamad, what do you think they are?'

'The work of Bani Hillal, *Allahu alim!*' said he, and the onlookers
nodded their assent.

Bani Hillal through the length and breadth of Arabia, and indeed
of North Africa, is a name to conjure with, a name that stands for an
ancient but now extinct tribe to which every well or other relic of past
days is ascribed; its name is ever on the lips of men. Bani Hillal is the
fount of the whole folk-lore of the southern desert. Every Badu has
something to tell of its legendary heroes, often in the simple rhymes
of his beloved tongue, and when I have heard one story from different
lips, I have noticed that the version hardly differs by one word.

The great traditional hero of Bani Hillal was one Bu Zaid, so
named not that he was the father of a son Zaid, but because he was
'the possessor of excellence' - a man of superior qualities. The name
Antar was strange to these remote dwellers in the Rub Al Khali, but
legends of Bu Zaid and of his kinsman Dhiyab bin Ghanim, another
hero of the tribe, these they have in abundance.

They place the ancient home of Bani Hillal in Wadi Markha in the
land now occupied by the Daham; there the mighty well Bir Jaufa
with its thirty rigs remains to this day, men tell, as their glorious
memorial. Every member of my party knew some verses - Salih knew
them all - of the poem, a typical heroic, of Bani Hillal in their spacious
days and their decline. It recounts how one hundred thousand, nay,
two hundred thousand, had been the number of their horses; it told of
Bu Zaid's two thousand forbears, of the great drought that befell the
land, so that there was no rain for thirty years and camels ate of the
hair of each other and perished miserably while their masters were
vainly digging in the earth for roots with which to feed them; nor was

there even a breath of wind so that the finely powdered '*waris* [85] they had placed on the Peak of Markha, was found undisturbed a year later; and the sons of the shaikh of Bani Hillal approached their father and said, 'The people die of hunger and we must take from the merchants to feed them,' but he would not, though he himself went hungry and the fort walls groaned with grief.

Most of the stories, however, have to do with a later generation, when Bani Hillal had become a poor nomadic tribe and were waging war with the settled people of Risha, whose king was Zenaiti.

Bu Zaid, their champion at this period, owed a charmed life to his mother's descent from the *jinniya*, which made him impervious to iron, whether it were arrow, sword or the spear, till the day he bore witness '*La Illa, ill' Allah,*' whereupon the *jinns* who had hitherto protected him from front and rear withdrew their protection from the front, so that he became like other men in that he could be killed from that direction. Some of these stories that I thought worth recording will appear in subsequent chapters, as they were told me from time to time on the march or round the camp-fire.

My position here at Shanna I calculated to lie north- eastwards of the Hadhramaut, lat. 19° N., long. 50° 45' altitude 990 feet. Our objective was to be Doha in the Qatar Peninsula on the Persian Gulf 330 miles distant as the crow flies across this barren ocean of interior sands. Hamad claimed to have been there once, pointing his cane in a direction a shade to the east of north, which fitted exactly with my traverse and astronomically worked positions. But I had to be careful not to appear too knowing.

A plan of action had crystallised, thanks to the Murra *rabia*. The size of our party would be reduced to twelve picked men and mounts and five pack animals all in perfect condition. This would make my rations good for thirty days, less the five days which must elapse before the arrival of the new party; but meanwhile to seek relief by reducing my present escort was impossible for fear of raiders. My resources thus allowed none too great a margin, and to loiter in these sands meant death. Perfect health in camel and man was essential; marches must be long and sharp; loss of camels, sickness, treachery or tribal opposition involving a hold up of ten days or too slow progress might spell disaster. The great consideration was to get out of the hunger-stricken wastes as soon as possible. Such were the themes of Hamad's daily homilies.

A successful crossing was by no means certain; if the pastures in our way failed, we should have to face the question whether to tempt the Fates further by going on, or to turn back to certain sustenance, but with men physically fit and fresh camels in good fettle at the most advanced jumping-off point, the problem was well on the way to solution. This was the stage I had reached, Shanna was a strategic point in my crossing, and the starting-post for the last relay.

The improvement in the ration situation which came from the slaughter of the camel was now offset by the arrival of untimely guests - a party of five Karab and Manahil that had crossed the sands by easy stages from Abu Dhabi. Like all their kind on first acquaintance, they maintained an icy reserve and, in answer to my enquiries as to their route, waved a general direction, a matter I found it politic not to press.

I had hoped that they would not dally, but the dates and coffee which they must receive seemed to encourage them to stay for more. It soon became clear that they had no intention of moving so long as my Rashidis' bounty was forthcoming. Hamad the *rabia* alone realised how necessary it was to husband our rations, especially in the light of an approaching Ramadhan, but to withhold food from the passing strangers so long as they chose to remain in my camp would have been to infringe the sacred rules of desert hospitality, if not to incur the odium of my companions. How my men would have wished to regard a parlous situation was reflected in another story to the credit of Bu Zaid, '

'Bu Zaid was most famed of his day for generosity. Camel by camel he had killed his immense herd to feed the stranger and the poor. So the forty sections of Bani Hillal took counsel and said, "We will each give Bu Zaid a camel so that he may possess a herd again." And this they did. But the numbers of his guests and the largeness of Bu Zaid's heart led once again to the day when he had no camels left. The Bani

Hillal saw there was no profit in Bu Zaid having a herd, so they said, "We will make him a present of only one camel on which to mount his wife when the tribe is moving, and this we will do on the one condition that Bu Zaid swears not to slaughter her for the guest, as he otherwise most surely would."

'And Bu Zaid agreed to their stipulation.

'Several moons had come and gone and Bani Hillal were encamped with their vast herds and their numerous tents, when there arrived a party of Arabs from the side of Mecca, and they enquired, "Where is the tent of Bu Zaid?"

'And none would say.

' "Tell us, where is the tent of Bu Zaid?"

' "It is before you," and so they passed on and on.

And Bu Zaid hearing them called to his wife and said, "Bind my eyes that I see not the faces of guests for whom I cannot make a feast." So she brought a strip of date basket and covered his eyes with it.

'And after a while he said to her, "Look out and see has anyone taken them in."

'And she looked out. "No," she said, "they are before the tent of So-and-so."

'And a little later he asked, "See! who has taken them in?"

' "No one," she replied, "they have now moved on to the next tent."

'And again and' again he asked, and again and again received the same reply, so that his heart grew hot within him, and at last able to contain himself no longer he rose, and tore the covering from his eyes, and taking a knife slaughtered his only camel where she stood at the entrance to his tent, and sending for the strangers made for them a feast.'

I could feel no such sentiments for my unwelcome guests from Abu Dhabi, who proved leech-like in their attachment. They were on their way home to the steppes north-east of Hadhramaut, which led me to question them about the mystery of their famous Bir Borhut, supposed scene of volcanic activity, the only one on the mainland of Arabia, and quoted by Dr. Hogarth as 'that great well cursed by Ali, according to the Jihan Numa.' They, like earlier escorts of mine who knew the country, were emphatic that no volcano existed. But various superstitions attach to the wadi wherein the well exists, the most persistent that it was the place of the departed spirits of wicked men, so that to this day none dare approach it by night.

One of the Hadhramautis made a deal with a member of my party - a young camel in exchange for a rifle, ammunition and dollars - but from the noisy arguments that accompanied the transaction, it appeared to lack the grand manner which marked an exploit of Bu Zaid in his boyhood as told me that afternoon:

'Bu Zaid was an orphan and brought up by his uncle the shaikh, Husain bin Sirhan. One day while yet a boy he was grazing a small herd of two bull and seven cow camels, and there came passing by a party of Arabs, and with them was a camel, and on the camel's back was a massive sword, *shahman*.

'And Bu Zaid, regarding the sword, enquired of the Arabs whether they would sell it.

' "Yes, if you wish to buy it," they said mockingly, because it was so large and heavy that no ordinary mortal could wield it. And so the camel was couched.

'Bu Zaid now took up the sword, sighing, "I would have wished it a little heavier, but perhaps it will do."

'Then he laid it aside and went to his camels and brought and couched a cow and over her he placed one of the two bulls to serve her. [86] - This was to be the target for his aim, and the test of the sword. If it cleft through the bull into the camel he would buy it.

'Then he picked up the sword, and standing a little way back he lifted it above his head and brought it crashing down upon the hump of the bull with such force that it severed the two camels into four halves. And turning to the Arabs he gave them his bull and six cows that remained in payment for the sword, and the sword he placed over his shoulder and so came joyfully to the side of his uncle.'

It was the forenoon of 8th January at Shanna and I was sitting exchanging stories with my companions when suddenly a small party of Arabs and camels appeared from behind the shoulder of a hill in the middle distance. My Arabs leapt to their feet and loaded their rifles, though it was only as a protective measure, for we were expecting the Bait Imani Shaikh. My telescope and the leisurely approach of the small party restored confidence and my companions were able soon to recognise Shaikh Muhammad bin Ham and his five companions.

They dismounted a little way off, and leading their camels passed one behind the other along our line of welcomers, for the usual nose-kiss salute; thereafter all sat down in a common circle to exchange the desert news- camels, pastures, raids and the like - over the delicacies of coffee cup and dates that I provided. Amongst them was Musellim, a member of my last year's expedition. His appearance now was a pleasant surprise, but alas! he had not been enlisted among his shaikh's quota, and only came to importune me in the eager hope that I would enroll him separately or instead of another. In the morning he made his plea; he was a typical young Badu with large irregular teeth, tattooed gums [87] and a wealth of long narrow black plaits that fell from under his greasy head-dress; he talked, as the Badu does when excited, in a wild torrent of words, repeating himself over and over again, but never faltering; he knelt at my side, his left hand over the crook of his upright riding stick, his right hand outstretched, the middle finger and thumb making a letter O with which he kept tapping an imaginary door-knocker to emphasise his points, though his voice, which could be heard half a mile away, would never have conveyed to a stranger, unaccustomed to his tongue and mind, that this was his appealing mood. He called God to witness that what he said was true - he was a better fellow than the next, and his mount was my mount! a glory to behold and a joy to ride. His impassioned peroration was typical, so that I thought it worth recording. 'Ya Sahib - *tshuf* - look here - I want to come with you - do you hear me? - I am like your servant Muhammad to fetch your firewood and obey your orders -do you hear me? — I know the sands' (a deliberate falsehood) 'and I'm more favoured of God than others. I call God to witness - Listen! O long of life, I'm not like Sahail or other - Are you listening to me?' (Sahail was!) - 'If you enrol me- pause — *tshuf* - I do not want money in advance, I can be patient - *tshuf* - O long of life, look at my camel, fat, *rahaim*, glory be to God. She will arrive at Qatar or where you wish - do you hear me? - I'm your servant *dhil hin* and *ghair dhil hin - tshuf* - O long of life - if you won't take me take her, *wajain fidak* - I am your servant like Muhammad, you know me - have you thought about it? - I'm a good lad - Glory be to God ' (here he touched my sleeve with his hand which he then carried to his lips and kissed). 'wa hadha! salamtak.'

Musellim's eloquence ended. He sat back looking up for my decision. I liked the wild ruffian, but the ration question forbade my increasing my party without some strong reason, and so against my personal inclinations I told him. No.

Next day Musellim came to say farewell, and so departed to his tribe, smiling as he went, without a semblance of ill-will towards me, confident only in the wisdom of Allah's inscrutable ways.

My party for the onward move was now complete, for Shaikh Salih and his men had already arrived. He too had brought with him an extra recruit, one Talib, a Murri herdsman of the Shaikh of Qatar, thus raising the number of my escort to thirteen. Both Hamad, my *rabia*, and Salih pressed for Talib's inclusion - the number thirteen is not unlucky in Arabia - and so a party of thirteen Badawin it had to be. Talib was indeed a most valuable acquisition for he had crossed the sands this year, whereas my *rabia* had not done so for many years, and the bulk of my escort never at all in this longitude. Talib's still greater qualification was that he claimed to know the recent whereabouts in the Jiban, where our course must lie, of Ikhwan tribes, [88] with whom we must at all costs avoid collision.

These Ikhwan are religious zealots, the puritans of Islam, distinguished amongst their co-religionists for bigotry and intolerance, and the militant nature of their creed. In their eyes even my companions, members of orthodox sects of Islam (the South Arabians, Shafi', the Murra, Hanbali) were heretics, while to me, a non-Muslim, they were likely to be very hostile, and here, being only nominally under the rule of Bin Sa'ud, they might be emboldened to attack us. Smoking is to these Ikhwan a serious and punishable offence, and the nomadic life anathema, because the absence of water it entails must lead to infringement of those religious rules of Islam that prescribe ablution before prayer and after bodily functions. And being for the most part recent converts themselves from Badawin life, they display all the fanaticism of the proselyte.

My own servant, Muhammad, a Muscati and no paragon, put the Ikhwan case succinctly to me one day as his own sceptical view of the acceptability of the nomad's religion.

'These Badawin,' he said of my companions, 'are not fashioned after the manner of God's creatures at all.'

'How?' I said.

'They go for months without water. The sons of Adam would not tolerate it. And their women! they have intercourse with them and do not wash the greater ablution. How can their prayers avail?'

17

THE NORTHWARD DASH

The zero hour for the northward dash had arrived, and at four o'clock on the afternoon of 10th January 1931, my small party set out from Shanna. I should have preferred an early morning start, for I was tired after a busy day spent in settling accounts with my old escort and making advances to a new one. But there were two compelling reasons for delay: firstly, because of the necessity for moving camp before dividing up rations amongst my escort; our Hadhramauti visitors and relatives of my escorting Badawin, who ostensibly came to say farewell, had held on till the last in the hope of profiting; to have issued rations in their presence without giving them a share or allowing my Badawin to do so would have been impossible. Secondly, my *rabia* held Saturday to be the day most propitious for starting a journey, and Sunday entirely unacceptable. [89]

Passing the first high sand ridge sufficed to meet the twin requirements of self-preservation and superstitious belief, and we halted for the night. Camels were unsaddled, hobbled and driven off to the nearest camel-thorn while their masters gathered round to feast their eyes on the rare sight of bountiful food, and to take physical possession of it. Each drew his share of butter in a lizard skin - a receptacle always found in a Badu's saddle-bag, while the other rations were divided up in bulk between the three parties that had been formed. The sight of flour, dates and rice had an exhilarating effect on these habitually hungry men and put them in the right mood for story-telling; so Salih, as he presided over the division of the dates, was easily prevailed upon to tell us another story of Bu Zaid.

'Bu Zaid had a wife but did not allow himself complete coition with her, and so he suspected that the two sons she had borne were not his, but another's. The tribe perceived that they did not resemble him and also had their suspicions, so came privily to Bu Zaid's sister and said that Bani Hillal must have a son from the loins of Bu Zaid. Wherefore one night she went secretly to her brother's bed and he, not knowing her in the darkness from his wife, lay with her. And as he was about to withdraw himself prematurely, according to his habit, she jabbed him with the bodkin that she had kept in her hand in readiness for this moment. The shock achieved its intent and in the fullness of time she bore a son, who came to be known as 'Aziz bin Khala, 'Aziz, son of his uncle. And 'Aziz grew up into a strong youth, endowed with courage and other virtues.

'Many years had passed, and Bin Zaid wished to discover which, if any, of these three supposed sons was his. So he said to the eldest, "Come, we will go a journey." And Bu Zaid prepared a sack of flour and put into the mouth of it a single date. Then the greybeard and the youth prepared their camels and journeyed till they came to a plain which was as bare of pastures as the palm of a man's hand, except for a single *sidr* tree. And Bu Zaid said, "Here we will halt and I will sleep under the *sidr*, while you prepare me a meal."

'And while he slept the young man looked round but could find no firewood, for the *sidr* was green, so he opened the sack of flour, and seeing the single date within, took and ate it, for he was hungry,

'And Bu Zaid awaking, said, "Where is the meal?" "There is none," the youth answered, "for firewood is nowhere to be found, and I opened the sack to find but one date and that I ate."

' "Then we must return," said Bu Zaid.

'And after they had dwelt in their tents some days, Bu Zaid addressed the youth's brother, saying, "Come, let us go a journey." And again he prepared the sack of flour with the single date, as he had done before, and the two set out and came to the same plain with its single *sidr* tree.

'Said Bu Zaid, "I must sleep here while you prepare the meal."

'And the young man looked about for firewood and could find none, then he opened the sack and seeing the date, ate it.

'So when Bu Zaid woke and asked for his meal, there was none, and the youth gave answer as his brother had done.

'And so they returned home.

'Some days had passed when Bu Zaid turned to 'Aziz. "Come," said he, "we will go a journey."

'Once more he prepared the sack of flour and put into it the single date, and the old man and the youth set off, and they came to the same bare plain with its single *sidr* tree.

' "I must sleep," said Bu Zaid, "prepare a meal." So 'Aziz searched the plain for firewood, but finding none, came back and sat down to think, and he saw that only the dry wood of their saddles and riding canes would serve. So he made a fire of these, then chopping branches from the *sidr* with his dagger he fashioned them into new saddles and riding crooks. Thus he baked two loaves of bread and set one for Bu Zaid and the other for himself, and discovering the date, he cut it in halves and set one upon his father's loaf, and the other upon his own. Then he awakened Bu Zaid, saying, "Arise and eat, O father."

'And his father roused himself and beheld what the youth had done, and jealousy entered Bu Zaid's heart, [90] and he said within himself, "I must kill 'Aziz, for he is a better man than I."

'Now it was planned that they should pass on next morning to the water-hole which lay at a very great distance. But at midnight Bu Zaid rose and crept stealthily to 'Aziz's camel and sticking a needle into her foot lamed her, and then quietly preparing his own camel, departed in the dead of night, leaving 'Aziz to perish of thirst.

'And 'Aziz woke in the morning to discover what his father had done, for the camel could not put her lame foot to the ground, and he realised the black design in his father's heart. Then he took a needle and stabbed her other three feet, so that when she put one foot to the ground the sharp pain would make her raise it again, and so bring down her other three feet. In this manner she would pick up one foot after the other and so move forward. And thus, 'Aziz, taking another route than his father, was first at the water-hole; there he lay down to rest, but fearing Bu Zaid, placed his shield, hidden beneath his mantle, over his body.

'Bu Zaid, on arriving, found the youth thus sleeping, and taking his lance, gave a sharp thrust at 'Aziz's heart. The spear point, sliding off the shield, awakened 'Aziz, and he, springing up, wrested the spear from Bu Zaid's hand, saying, "I am stronger than thou, and have thee at my mercy, but thou art my father and my uncle, and so I spare thee."

'Thus did Bu Zaid know that 'Aziz was his own son, and they fell weeping upon each other's necks, and returned home together in contentment of heart.'

The end of the story saw the break-up of the party, for it was the hour of prayer before the evening meal.

The next day was our first proper day's march, and like all first days with new men and camels, was short and noisy. Halts at frequent intervals to adjust camel-loads, and Badawin bickerings about back and girth-galls kept delaying us, so that when we halted for the night we had made scarcely more than twelve miles. Around the camp-fires the wranglings continued until we evolved a system of changing loads from day to day in a regular order to ensure equitable treatment. This restored quiet.

One Badu, more peaceable than the rest, as he collected tit-bits for his camel from the *abala* under which I sat, snapped off a young branch and held it upside down. 'Look, Sahib,' he said, as water dripped from within the stem, 'this is why your Agaba can go for days without drinking.'

Next day we made an early start on a north-easterly course, and passing the large white hill of Abu Akhshaba, came at midday to some isolated dunes which give their name, Gusman, to the locality, and mark the north-westward limit of Dakaka.

Lying inside the great dune bulwark of the southern borderlands,

Dakaka consists of these wide, sweeping red sandscapes of hardish sand with low dunes running in all directions. It falls in altitude from probably 1100 feet in the south to 785 feet hereabouts, and its long axis runs east-north-east for a seven days' march. As we moved westwards the aspect of Dakaka had grown more rugged and water-holes increased in depth from three fathoms in the east to thirteen fathoms at Shanna. Twin water-holes, Zuwaira and Turaiwa, even deeper than Shanna (which was within a day's march of its western extremity) were said to lie to the south-west. Beyond them to the west there was reported to be no water in the sands [91] of Ga'amiyat, Huwaiya and Shuwaikila that extend towards the Najran.

Our march that day had followed the camel-tracks of a small herd, and my *rabia* recognised them as a kinsman's and their direction to indicate recent watering. Soon we came upon the encampment. I was invited to dismount before two small tents to see a sick man, whom I found old and much emaciated; he complained of the almost universal stomach trouble. The Rashid ascribe it to *afera*, the most intractable of evil spirits, but my patient said it was 'from God.' The only palliative in my power was to cheer his heart with a handful of dates, the last I suspected the poor wretch would ever want. The urine of the young cow camel is taken in small quantities for such disorders, or preferably her vomit (said to be less thirst-provoking), which is obtained by ramming a stick down her throat. The urine has a second utility as a hair-wash, in that it kills vermin. All the desert beauties use it.

The only other occupants of the tent were two women and a boy. The women were both veiled, as are all the women of the sands, though they were not averse from talking with the stranger. They were the wives of the old man and of his son. The boy, the son of the younger couple, and aged about four, ran about the tent naked and uncircumcised. [92] Then the younger man came up, carrying a badly mauled hare, with its captor running at his side, a long dog of whippet size and dark brown colour.

The Murra all have these dogs, with which they hunt the hare and occasional rim for the pot (whereas Al Rashid and other South Arabian tribes have no dogs) and on our northward march we passed from time to time the footmarks of a dog, and, near by, the tracks of the Badu master. Sometimes they were in pairs and ab- normally extended, a sign that the animal was then in full course.

A Murra encampment

The miserable tent where I sat was just high enough to give a squatting adult headroom. It consisted of two twenty-foot strips of very roughly woven dark brown and white wool, the dark colour of camel-hair, the light possibly from the sheep's wool of Hasa. Every thread had been spun and woven by the women within. Lying about was the bodkin used in its manufacture, a few iron camp-fire pegs, tent-pegs once the horns of an antelope, the long iron bars used for digging water-holes, a rounded stone from the northern steppe to serve as hammer, two camel saddles and a variety of crude leathern buckets on rough wooden frames, one a water trough, another a receptacle for skins. In such items are comprised the few poor belongings of the nomad folk other than the nobler possessions of camels and firearms.

We passed out of Dakaka (lat. 19° 32') into Suwahib, one of the most extensive regions in the sands. It derives its name from its char- acter, for the word *sahaba* stands locally for parallel ridges, and the plural, *suwahib*, consisted of chains of sandhills in echelon, averaging

perhaps half a mile apart, with a general north-east axis, the intervals
between them bellying sands of red. The ridges seldom exceeded fifty
to eighty feet in height though their feature- less slopes exaggerated
their size. They were reported to stretch south-westwards beyond
Gusman to embrace the western Dakaka and reach to the high dunes
of Ga'amiyat.

The pastures grew scant as we progressed on a north- north-easterly course, crossing the *suwahib* diagonally at long intervals. A twin
giant hill, called Khalilain, was the only noteworthy feature of the
march on the thirteenth, till we came in the late afternoon to the
water-hole of Bainha, the aneroid showing a fall, to the senses imper-
ceptible, of two hundred feet in the march of nineteen miles.

Water was at two fathoms. Its great brackishness and its beer
colour were properties which, I was sad to find, were not disguised by
desiccated soup. Indeed, from this stage onward the water was such
that I gave up drinking it except when desperately thirsty in the
saddle, or occasionally as cocoa when halted, for it acted as a violent
purge. In the marches that stretched down and away to the eastward -
the habitat from time to time of my Rashidi companions - the water
was said to be too brackish for them to drink, while in places even
their camels will turn away.

Camel's milk formed my chief diet, but the supply was limited, for
the two milch-animals I had obtained with much difficulty were
approaching the end of their lactation, and there were days when
their milk had to be watered down to make enough. To these camels,
however, I owed the fitness I enjoyed throughout, though I lost a
stone and a half weight on the diet.

Bainha, [93] where we watered, had been discovered and dug by
my *rabia*, Hamad bin Hadi. I had already appreciated Hamad's great
worth as a guide, for guiding in the desert requires not merely
memory for direction but an intuition for water and pastures, and an
ability to read the sands and avoid the evil that may be impressed on
them. Not every Arab bred in these sands can guide, many in fact lose
their way and die of thirst, particularly when camels stray in summer
and their owners have to track them. To return on his own tracks or

to follow those of others is regarded as a lost man's safest course to water, but a wind arising will obliterate all tracks, and wind is an ever-present menace. About seven years ago a party of Mahra were raided in the steppe by two members of Manahil, who made off with ten camels. Discovering the loss while the tracks of the retiring raiders were still discernible, seven Mahri stalwarts went in pursuit, and the tracks brought them to the sands of Dhahiya, previously unknown to them. On came the bold pursuers, who reckoned upon the pursued having to halt over a water-hole, where they too would water. But the Manahil, fearing pursuit, prudently avoided the water-hole of Khor Dhahiya and went ploughing on northwards through the death- dealing sands, one man alone cunningly going off at a tangent to the water-hole to fill his water-skins and returning by the same track to rejoin his companions. Thence they proceeded. The Mahra, following hopefully on the main camel-tracks of Manahil, were certain that their thirst would soon be quenched, but before they could overtake their despoilers a sand-storm came and obliterated all tracks before and behind them. They were now lost in the sands. Six months later one of my own party of Rashidis came upon the seven skeletons and the bones of their camels.

I was filled with admiration for the consistency of Hamad's direction. Twice and thrice during the hour I would compare my prismatic compass reading and find a variation of no more than five degrees. The shadow cast by the sun at our backs could give no more than a general direction, and I was naturally quick to assume that he was led by the orientation of sand corridors, here 45°-50°. Later, however, in sands that had no such conspicuous tell-tale features, his course showed scarcely less exactitude, and I was driven to seek for some other explanation. Maybe the faint corrugations of sand surfaces, presumably of some constancy from prevailing winds solved part of the mystery, but most I feel is due to an instinctive sense of direction highly developed in particular individuals, of whom Hamad was one. He had not been over this country for many years, and by the very nature of nomadic life, could not have sojourned in any one place for long. Unlike all but one of his companions, he had names [94] for the major constellations and larger stars, and by night to this Theseus the labyrinth of the sands had no mysteries.

On reaching lat. 20° my companions observed with keen interest our arrival into the *hadh* belt, *hadh* being a small, sage-coloured bush, saline in character, which survives longer without rain or dew than any other desert growth - whence, in times of exceptional drought, only the *hadh* regions in the sands support life. There the sand tribes are to be found, unless they are driven clean out into the steppe borderlands, the Rashid in that event retiring south-eastwards to Umm al Hait, and the oasis of Mugshin, the Murra back to the northern water-holes of Jabrin and the Jafurah-Jiban border-line.

Buwah, the first *hadh* region we entered, was well blessed and the signal for an early halt to graze. Full bellies led to an early start, and good going on a bearing of north by east was made all the more pleasant by a light breeze in our faces. The intervening trough of the Suwahib here became red, rolling billows, gentle, but so soft as to occasion dismounting now and then for a path to be cleared by hand that the camels might pass. Hungry and desolate country succeeded, with only sprigs of *gasis*, which grew drooping as wind-blown trees parallel with the ridge-axis in testimony to a prevailing north-east wind. In the afternoon we passed by three shallow water-holes, Bahat Salama, Bahat Hajran, and Bahat Jamal. Water was reported every-where on our right hand at an arm's depth, but so brackish as to be undrinkable by man or beast, and therefore named *khiran* in accor-dance with a practice common throughout the sands.

The Badawin, who had not bothered to fill their water- skins in Dakaka, did so at Bahat Jamal. There also we watered camels for the water was held to be sweet, whereas that before us was saline, that would sharpen the thirst and cause disordered health. The saline pastures of these sands were equally lowering to the camels.

Next day we passed from the region of Buwah to that of Umm Malissa. The intervening sands became more rugged and the long, beautiful ridges grew less definite in character and broke up into small detached chains, which were reported to continue northward a day's march on our right hand, like an inverted letter **S**, through the *hadh* regions of Karsua' and Wasa' to the dunes of Sa'afuk north of the twenty-first parallel.

The heat was most trying even in this winter month of January, and for the first time on my journey I felt very exhausted, doubtless from the combined effects of the hot sun playing down on my back for nine long hours in the saddle, and acute thirst after drinking Buwah's beer- coloured water.

The menace of raiders had diminished as we marched north and was now left behind. True, the Sa'ar had in times past raided as far north as this, but to-day, with the main body of Rashid behind us in the south, a raiding party would come into contact with them there, or, in any case, would not be so foolish as to push thus far and expose itself to the risk of being cut off.

Sa'ar! The name is a word of terror to the Rashid and the southern Murra, whose boys are brought up to live to revenge brothers and fathers, and to redeem lost fortunes. The cause of raids and inter-tribal feuds is at bottom economic. Men kill and are killed in the fight for camels. Peace, or rather truce, alternates with war for periods of a year or two. In time of war it is the greatest shame for a young man to show no disposition to fight, *sharab al khumr*, 'wine-filled,' is a synonym for gallantry applied to the young man who sets out to kill or be killed with a gay heart, but a stay-at-home who shelters his life or makes excuses when the communal interests of his tribe are involved, is regarded as a white-livered craven for whom none will have respect, and to whom none will give a daughter in marriage.

Young Kilthut, Shaikh Salih's son, told me the story of his 'blood-ing' by the Sa'ar which is worth setting down, not merely as a true version of what happens when enemies meet in the Rub Al Khali, but for the light it throws on desert psychology.

War had been going on for a year and more between Rashid and Sa'ar, and the Rashid decided to make overtures for peace. Kilthut was one of four sent as an embassy to try to make truce for a year. They set out and came to the steppe, hoping to meet a Sa'ari *rabia* who would give them safe-conduct into Sa'ar confines.

But the tale will go better in Kilthut's own words, as he spoke them before the camp-fire, his face aglow, and he himself all animation, for a Badu talks with his eyes and hands.

'It was about the hour of the afternoon prayer. Near the edge of a wadi we dismounted and crept up to the edge, and peering down into it, saw five Badawin around a camp- fire and their camels grazing, and we knew them by their double-poled saddles to be Sa'ar. Greed took possession of our hearts, for although we came to make peace we had not as yet done so, and were still in a state of war with the Sa'ar. Also it seemed that Allah had delivered them into our hands, for it was near night and they must soon turn their camels to graze and sleep themselves. Then we could crawl up and kill our enemies and carry away the spoil. But now our own counsels became divided. I urged that we enjoyed a great advantage, having seen them first while they were yet unaware of our presence. However, the two chief members of our party, one of them my Uncle Saif, the Sa'adna shaikh, would not agree, saying that the party below were probably from a bigger body close at hand, and their advanced position here showed them to be themselves on the war-path, so that they would be in no mood for peace parleys; our mission must therefore end, and we must fly. In our pride, we two young men, Musellim, a Bait Imani, and I, said that we would not return except with the camels of our enemies. Our elders strove with words of prudence to persuade us to return with them, but we would not listen and they left us.

'Musellim and I tethered now our camels at a safe distance and crawled to the brink of the gorge to watch the enemy's movements. Presently one of them took the camels off to some grazing down the wadi as we had foreseen, and then returned to his friends. We saw them make up their camp-fire for the night. But with our number reduced now to two against their five, we decided it would be impossible to overcome them; instead we would creep down at dead of night, steal the camels, and depart, thus getting such a start that in the morning there would be no chance of their catching us up on foot. And so we prayed the evening prayer and returned to our watching-places and waited; and about midnight when their fire had ceased to flicker, we crept stealthily down - we could have killed the men in their sleep had there been more of us - and we loosened the hobbles of the camels and thence turned up by an easy slope and found our own camels, and so we started off homewards.

'One of the Sa'aris awoke long before the dawn and discovered that their camels were missing. He roused his companions and they followed on our track by the light of the full moon. Meanwhile we pressed on till the next afternoon, but being then tired and supposing we had many hours' start, my companion and I stupidly halting far a short rest, fell asleep. Suddenly I awoke. There before me, at about one hundred paces, was an Arab, covering me with his rifle. I looked round hurriedly, and seeing no others supposed that he was alone; so I leapt behind a small rock to draw my own rifle from its jacket, [95] but before I could do it he had fired. The shot missed. I had now slipped a round into the breech of my rifle, but thinking that his action might have been defensive, and him perhaps a friend, maybe some Mahri who mistook me for a Sa'ari, I shouted, "We are Ruwashid. Fear not, we are Ruwashid."

'He answered, "By my face. I am so-and-so of the Sa'ar, and we (mentioning his section) are at peace with the Ruwashid. You have my camels, and we are stronger than you; thirty men are behind me."

'And I shouted, "Deliver me with my life, my camel, and my rifle."

'And he answered, "By my face."

'So I got up. But even as I did so his party came rushing upon me, not knowing what had passed between him and me. And one of them drew his dagger and lunged at me' (here Kilthut put his finger in his mouth and rubbed the spittle along his forearm to discover the old wound-mark) 'and another stabbed at my companion, but he, jumping back, was only gashed across the forehead between his two eyes, though he bled much. But now, God be praised, the first man who had given us sanctuary came up and intervened and so our lives were saved.'

'Then you got the worst of it?'

'Yes! They took our two camels as well as their own, and our rifles and daggers, although I had been promised mine. But they honoured their word, for later, when peace was made, I got my rifle back and a camel in place of the one they had taken from me - but not my dagger.' (A most unusual course, as there is no restitution between tribes traditionally hostile, and peace follows the usual formula of, 'The past be past,')

'But,' continued Kilthut, 'this Sa'ar party were themselves to be overtaken by misfortune. They moved on eastwards and came upon a Mahri and his wife and a single camel; they slew the man and took the camel, but when they had reached Manahil country they were caught by a large raiding party of Bait Kathir and Mahra and their shaikh was killed and they turned and fled in confusion, their booty falling into the hands of Bin Tannaf.' [96]

18

THROUGH THE CENTRAL SANDS

Suwahib lay behind us. Gone were the big bellying waves of red sand with their white-ridged crests lit up in the brilliant sunshine, gone the green pastures of the early marches. In lat. 20° 44' a narrow rugged belt was succeeded by a wide expanse of pale sands in the mood of an ocean calm. Relief came here and there in patches of withered *hadh* scrub, which recent strong southerly winds had covered with a film of fine white sand. Otherwise the scene was one of utter desolation, extending over a great part of the central sands of Mazariq, Nuwasif and Munajjar, making them a hungry void and an abode of death to whoever should loiter there. Yet but four years before one of my Murris had grazed herds in this region. In the verbal extravagances so typical of the Badu, he told me these had been the most blessed sands. But the circumstances were illuminating; they explained why the secrets of poor, precarious pastures or water should be so jealously guarded, and why therefore suspicion is the desert man's do min ant characteristic. To such climatic vicissitudes may well be ascribed those early Arabian movements of hunger-driven man, the Semitic invasion of Babylonia, the Canaanite invasion of Syria, the Hyksos invasion of Egypt, and even the Hebrew invasion of Palestine.

A Halt for Prayer

Animal life still persisted in these stricken wastes, indeed by a curious chance two of my most interesting specimens were obtained here, one a sand-coloured fox [97] scarcely bigger than a cat, yet full-grown according to my Arabs and the evidence of its teeth; it proved a new species, probably an Arabian variety of the Egyptian the other find, eagle's eggs, discovered in a gigantic nest, like that of an English rook, but much bigger, and roofing a solitary leafless *abala*. The bird itself I did not see, but the eggs have been found to resemble very closely those of the Abyssinian tawny eagle. My Arabs regarded them as unlawful for food, whereas bustard's eggs are counted a great delicacy amongst them. Bustard the size of young turkeys were met at intervals throughout the southern central sands and were innocently trusting if approached under cover of a slow riderless camel and by a circuitous closing in upon it, but for unfamiliar unaccompanied man they showed a discriminating distrust, so that our many halts in the hope of a meal produced only the back view of birds in flight, and human disappointment over the claw-marks left in the sand - a handsome Prince of Wales feathers pattern. Bird life was scant in the sands, the fan- tailed raven being the commonest and most widely distributed and next after him a tiny pied-wagtail-looking creature.

Generally the birds met were solitary, or at most in pairs. Once I saw four bustard together and once six ravens, but this was unusual.

My natural history collection [98] was made up mostly of small insects, beetles, spiders, a few moths, butterflies, and a single dragon-fly; it included a new mantis and a new locust.

The fox and the hare, both sand-coloured, were the commonest mammals, particularly in the southern sands, and there was a sand rat, wild cat and wolf, though unhappily the last two eluded me. The wolf is said to be small and sand-coloured, and to live chiefly in Suwahib, where it can readily paw a hole to shallow water.

Among reptiles there were twelve varieties of lizards, all alike endowed with pointed snouts for diving in the sands. The most numerous sort was a skink, with a sand-coloured square-sectioned body, and black markings along its sides. Its smooth, shining, snake-like skin did not dissuade one Arab from indulging a childish trick of putting the wriggling tail and half its body into his mouth. The biggest lizard was a monitor, much too strong and vicious to be handled except by being picked up, like a snake, behind the head. The monitor, unlike most of the big lizards of the steppe, is not eaten by Badawin. On cutting one open, I found a skink almost his own size within. The scorpions of the sands were small and of pale green colour in contrast to the big black-and-white varieties of the mountains and steppes. Only three different snakes were met with - all of a sand colour, boa, horned viper, and colubrid.

The stimulus of promised rewards made my Arabs enthusiastic workers for the Museum. Their reduced numbers on this northward journey allowed me to get to know them individually in a way that had been impossible with my earlier and bigger parties. The Badu - unless a religious bigot, in which case he is secretive and sullen - can be a most pleasant companion if you will but simulate a passion for saddle and rifle, praise the virtues of camels and be cheerful. Distant at first, he will after a week or so become, if cultivated, a cheerful fraterniser, and if there is something he wants, ingratiating. His conversations, however, are liberally interspersed with the woes it has pleased Allah to afflict him with - a stomach pain for certain. 'Fever!

there was none in the sands, thank God,' and mv companions were incredulous of the infection by mosquito- bite which evoked only a few and, I thought, insincere expressions of 'There is no god but God,' the usual exclamation when anything that astonishes is encountered. But mosquitoes, Salih agreed, were a great nuisance at Dhufar, so that his visit there had been a mixed pleasure, for while he was used to flies innumerable around some water-holes in the sands, it was only in Dhufar that he and his camel spent nights of torment that made them glad to turn about. Fleas and lice the sands have in plenty, and whenever two of my Badawin found themselves unoccupied at the halt, they would take part in a mutual flea-hunt, each in turn lying face downwards on the sand, while his companion sat by his head and scraped away with a dagger in the long tousled locks.

'You have found none in your baggage!' one would say, looking up at me. And then with pride, 'These bags of straw we use for pack-saddles do not attract them, whereas the double-poled saddle of the Murra is their favourite haunt.'

I was ready to change the subject for a more pleasant one, and found myself listening to a delectable Bani Hillal entertainment.

Would I like to hear how it fared with that ill-starred youth 'Aziz, son of his uncle?

Yes I would.

Then he would tell me the story of the self-imposed immolation of 'Aziz bin Khala to forward his father's amours.

'Bu Zaid loved a girl named Aliya of a neighbouring tribe. One day he set off on a visit to her, taking with him 'Aziz, who had not yet seen her. And Bu Zaid described great beauties as they went along and said, "But you shall know her, O 'Aziz! by this token. If she is sitting other women she will be taller than they; but if stand, she will be shorter than they." And father and son came to a well where women were drawing water, and Aliya was in their midst; and 'Aziz beheld them first sitting over well and then rising to go away, so that he knew her. But alas, for Bu Zaid, Aliya had been affianced by her male relatives to another, and that very night was the nuptial night, when her new husband would come to her. But Aliya was unhappy, for she loved Bu Zaid.

'Now it was that 'Aziz dressed himself in her bridal raiment and set her jewels upon his neck and arms and took her place in the bridal bed, while she went out into wilderness to the place where Bu Zaid was and spent night in the embraces of her lover.

'And the new husband came by night to Aliya's chamber but whenever he drew near to his imagined bride, 'Aziz turned a deaf ear, and a silent tongue to his entreaties, and pushed him away. So the angry bridegroom betook himself next morning to the Alim and explained his plight, adding: "I am not sure in the darkness that it was Aliya, for I strong and never have I met anyone who could resist except 'Aziz bin Khala."

'And the Alim replied, "Go to her again to-night and take with you a needle. And if you receive no better accommodation, pluck a hair from her head and drive needle into the vein *urq al akhal* of her left thigh. If be Aliya or a woman she will live, but if a man he will die and by the hair you will know her."

'So the bridegroom came again that night to Aliya's chamber, only however to meet with the same resistance, and in his struggles he plucked a hair from 'Aziz's head and drove the needle into the vein of his loins, and so departed.

'Before the dawn, 'Aziz rose as was his wont and came to his father's place in the wilderness, and told him of what had come to pass. And Aliya was affrighted, but Bu Zaid plucked a hair from her head and drove a needle into her thigh so that her husband might find the marks, and thus not suspect her.

'Bu Zaid and 'Aziz then mounted their camels and departed, 'Aziz with the needle still in his thigh, for whenever he should withdraw it, he must bleed to death.

'And they came to a plain, and 'Aziz said to his father, "Father, what is this place good for?"

'Said Bu Zaid, "It is a place good for grazing camels."

'And they passed on and came to some other herbage, and Aziz asked, "And what is this place fit for?" Bu Zaid replied, "This, my son, is a place good for raising horses."

'Again they moved on and coming to a place of desolation, 'Aziz asked, "And what, O father, is this fit for?"

'And Bu Zaid answered, "It is a place meet only for a graveyard."

'Said 'Aziz, "Let us dismount here and help me to dig a grave."

'So Bu Zaid and 'Aziz dug a grave and 'Aziz withdrawing the needle from his thigh died, and his father buried him.

'Bu Zaid went on and came to his tents, and his sister, the mother of 'Aziz, saw him a great way off, and alone; and she ran out saying, "Where is 'Aziz? Where is 'Aziz?"-

'And Bu Zaid answered, "We have been raiding and many camels have fallen into our hands, and I have come on ahead bringing the good news, and 'Aziz follows with the spoil."

'Some days went by, and the mother grew anxious; and as more and more days passed and 'Aziz did not return, she moped about the tents and wept for her son's fate, nor would she be comforted.

'And Bu Zaid was sad at heart, and murmured to himself:

' "Have come to thee, old dame, forebodings of evil?

For thou understandest our house

As the wolf knoweth where the flocks are gathered for the night."

'And then aloud:

"'O my grief, if I should say he is dead, she dieth.

And if I should say he lives, I lie."

'And so Aziz's mother knew that her son was dead.'

The story ended, the cry of the *mu'edhdhin* brought my entertainers to their feet and they went off to join the long line of worshippers that habitually fell in behind Hamad bin Hadi for common prayer.

An early start was made on the 19th January, our course still north-west. The absence of grazing in our way and our camels' thirst from their recent saline pastures made for fast marching. Leaving Umm Quraiyin on our right hand -a reported water-hole that marked the northward limit of Munajjar - we came to the sand region of Sanam, white and rolling in a gentle swell. This region - the word itself means camel's hump - is conspicuous for the comparative sweetness of its water-holes and their abnormal depth, [99] an average being eleven fathoms, and some there are of fifteen and seventeen fathoms in the west.

The shallower wells of the southern sands are sometimes filled in after watering to obstruct a possible pursuer. But here the water-holes are roofed to protect them, for great labour, skill and courage have gone in their making. Indeed, the deep water-holes of Tuwal exact a toll of life for the soft sides are prone to slip and entomb the miners, and all that avails for revetment is the coiled branches of some wretched bush of the sands. As we passed Safif, a Murri turned to me. 'Four of my brothers' (i.e. Murra tribesmen) 'lie in the bottom there. Two of them had descended to clean it out and were overwhelmed by slipping sand, and their companions, following to rescue them, were engulfed too. Safif is a tomb; we have abandoned it.'

The fasting month of Ramadhan was upon us. No crescent moon had been seen on the morning of 20th January, so hopes were set upon the evening. We halted in good time, all eyes towards the western sky in the wake of the setting sun. The first appearance of the Ramadhan moon excites intense eagerness on the part of the Faithful, and in Oman its entry and exit are accompanied by the booming of more than a monarch's salute. This evening disappointment was in store for us. The saffron sky turned to slaty grey and then to darkness, but there was no moon; to-morrow my companions would not be glorifying God in the Fast.

Farajja, our next water-hole, lay a nine and a half hours' march distant, and we were obliged to make it because our water-skins were empty. We were thus still in the saddle when just after sunset rifle shots rang out from ahead, and a faint wisp of the crescent moon showed in the pale sky. With cries of 'Glory to God,' my companions couched their camels and prostrated themselves in prayer, one or two of them first sticking their rifles barrel downwards into the sands. Our course had veered due west in the track of our advance party and thus continued until after dark, when the flare of a distant camp-fire was the beacon for our night's halting-place. My companions being on a journey had a right to break or postpone fasting till they regained their homes, but none elected to do so. They all fasted [100] on the march, as my Bait Kathiris had done at Mugshin a year before. Hitherto they had availed themselves of the prayer concession of the march, running the five occasions into three, but now in Ramadhan they observed the entire number. Scarcely in keeping with this increased religious zeal was the change in the food regime. Dinner had formerly followed the joint evening prayer, now it followed the sunset Credo of the *muedhdhin* and was sandwiched between it and the prayer that normally would follow.

Scouts for pastures may postpone the Ramadhan fast, but the rule for the raider is different. He may enjoy the concession only on the return from the raid; during the approach and the attack he must fast.

The sand tribes have also a peculiar marital observance. In Ramadhan sexual relations are only permissible if ablution can follow, that is, when near or carrying water.

At other times of the year the religious injunction regarding this greater ablution is disregarded. When they are away from water, sand is used before prayer, but nothing after the sexual act. It thus comes about that while there is no rule against marriage in Ramadhan such marriages in the sands are rare, if not unheard of.

The months of the desert are lunar months, but known by names not always according with the usual Muslim calendar. [101] The word Muharram, for instance, is never used by them, and they reckon the year, so far as they date it at all, from the Fast month or the Pilgrimage month.

Here in lat. 21° 30' the sands of Sanam must be shallowing because for the first time the hard flat floor emerged in circular patches from the sands.

One of my Badawin found and brought me some potsherds and bits of broken old dull glass from the surface of one such place. I looked but could see no trace of an artificial mound, but only apparently natural undulations, and I was incredulous that the region could have had any considerable settlement, [102] preferring the theory that *dibbis* — syrup of dates - had been brought out here in pots from Hasa, for some bygone Ramadhan, perhaps, before the kerosene tin became the common receptacle of Arabia. The possibility of archaeological remains in Sanam should not, on the other hand, be ruled out. The Murra indeed have a tradition of the foundations of a fort once to be seen but now covered over by sand. Umm al Hadid, a waterhole, is also said to have a tradition of remains - two large blocks of so-called ironstone - whence its name. These, however, may have been meteorites.

I had collected a fragment of black meteorite in the Buwah region of Suwahib. It was found lying on the sands as we passed, the Badu who picked it up calling it an 'ironstone' presumably on account of its great weight. Its nature proved difficult to establish at first on account of its irregular shape and sharp angles for the meteorite is commonly a rounded stone, sometimes pitted with holes. My Buwah specimen is thought to be part of a much larger meteorite which burst into pieces on its passage through the atmosphere. [103]

At Farajja [104] our camels were taken off to water in the forenoon, and this provided me with an opportunity of collecting data for my map - the names and direction and distance of sands and water-holes that must be recorded as we went along and worked out by a process of arithmetical triangulation. But Badawin are apt to fret under too close and long cross-questioning and the most profitable information is obtained when -the Arab can be encouraged to discourse. The occasion was one for a story too - the tale of Bu Zaid and his two brothers Yusif and Baraiga and their encounter with a *Jinn*. It ran in this wise:

'One day Bu Zaid, Yusif and Baraiga set out on a journey and at night they halted at a habitation where a man and his mother and their sheep were. And the man said to them, "I would fain come with you on your journey."

' "No," they answered, "you are not equal to the feats which are likely to be demanded of us on our way, else we would take you."

'And the man, wishing to show what manner of man he was, walked over to an acacia tree close by and seizing it by the trunk in his two arms uprooted it as though it had been tamarisk, and hurled it to one side, saying, "Yet am I strong?"

'So it was decided that he should accompany them and the four set forth. And they came to a place where they met a young girl and she was leading a ram and carrying on her head a dish of rice that was drenched with melted butter. The girl was the daughter of the governor of town close at hand. And they asked her where she was going. Said she, "I am going as an offering to the Jinn in yonder wadi, for the town is under sacrifice, and a virgin, a ram and a dish of rice must be brought to the Jinn each evening; and if these are not forthcoming the Jinn will destroy the town.

'Now Bu Zaid and his companions were famished, and the smell of the savoury dish increased their hunger, so they said to the young girl, "But we want our supper. Give us the ram to slaughter and the rice to eat, and we will attend to the Jinn and ensure that no evil befalls the town."

'And she answered, "The *Jinn* will surely dry up the water and my father's people will perish."

'But they paid no heed to her words, and taking the ram they slaughtered it and cooked and ate it. Then they turned their thoughts to the Jinn; and they divided the night into four watches, that each of them should in turn go and occupy the haunt of the Jinn for an equal space of time,

'The first watch was given to the strong man who had uprooted the *ghaf* by the wayside. And so he went, but as he approached the Jinn, which was in the form of a huge serpent, it cried out, "Oh ha! you who bring my dinner - first the ram!" And the man, full of fear, fled, and returned to the three brothers, Bu Zaid, Yusif and Baraiga, saying, "Surely the Jinn will eat you up," and he ran off and was seen no more,

'Next went forth Yusif with sword, buckler and stick. And the Jinn, hearing someone approach, opened its great mouth, and Yusif making the form of a cross with his sword and stick passed through the buckler handle for a centre, jabbed it into the Jinn's mouth so that the sword stood on its tongue and reached to the roof of its mouth, and the stick lodged between its two jaws, and the Jinn could not close its mouth, or indeed do anything. Thus Yusif spent the whole of his watch until it was time for his relief, when he withdrew his weapons and departed to the side of his brethren.

'Then went forth Baraiga, and Baraiga's skin was so white that he had only to take off all his clothing to become transparent. Thus the Jinn was unable to see him, and spent its time vainly groping about for its prey, and while doing so it bumped its head against a stone, so that one of its eyes was struck out. And thus the third watch was kept.

'Last of all came Bu Zaid, and approaching the Jinn boldly he said, "Close your other eye, stretch forth your neck, and open your mouth that I may enter it for your dinner," and the Jinn did so, and Bu Zaid drew his sword and striking at its neck slew it. Then bending down he wetted the palm of his hand in the Jinn's blood and ran at great speed to the Governor's Fort in the town, and he leapt from the ground almost to the roof and struck his bloody palm against the wall above the doorway, leaving the mark of the Jinn's blood there. Then he returned to his two brothers and the Governor's daughter in the wilderness.

'And when the morning came the people of the town saw the stream of the Jinn's red blood, and the bloody mark of a man's hand on the fort walls high above the doorway. And the Governor called all the people together to discover who had killed the Jinn, saying, *Wallahi!* he who has killed the Jinn shall be governor, and I will hand the fort over to him."

'And there were many present that answered, "I did it," and "I did it."

'He answered them saying, "Come then, leap up and touch the place of blood above the portal."

'But none could do so.

'Baraiga and Yusif now came into the town to see what manner of place it was, for they had left Bu Zaid with the young girl and the camels in the wilderness.

'And the Governor, hearing of the arrival of strangers, commanded that Baraiga and Yusif should be brought before him. And he said to them,' "The town has been under bondage to a *Jinn*, and now it is delivered and no more have we to sacrifice a girl and a ram and a dish of rice. Now which of you brought deliverance? Tell me, for he shall be governor in my room."

'They replied, "We do not know."

'But the Governor did not believe them, and he said, "You must both leap as high as you can for me to see which of you it was."

'Then they did as he bade them, but their hands reached to a point that fell far short of the bloody hand on the fort wall, so the Governor knew it was not one of them. He turned to them again and said, "And where is the rest of your party?"

'And they, fearing evil consequences, said, "We have only a slave" (a part that came easy to Bu Zaid on account of his black colour) - "and he is outside the town with our camels."

'The Governor replied, "I shall detain you till I have seen him." Then he ordered a camel and a slave girl to go out and bring in Bu Zaid. And he said to her, "When you arrive where he is, tell him to mount behind you. If he is a slave he will, but if he is a free man, he will surely desire to come to this place riding in front and will put you behind him."

'So the slave girl set forth on the camel and came to the wilderness where Bu Zaid was, and she said, "I am a messenger from the Governor, and he requires your presence before him at once, and you are to ride back with me upon this camel," and she motioned him to his place behind her. But he brushed her aside and sat her behind him and thus they came to the fort of the Governor and dismounted.

'Then said the Governor to Bu Zaid, "Jump, O slave, and place your hand against the bloody hand above the doorway." Bu Zaid replied, "I am a slave, how can I? I can do nothing."

' "Jump," said the Governor, "you must." So then Bu Zaid leapt into the air, and his hand reached higher than the mark of the Jinn's blood he had left there overnight. So the Governor and all the people knew that it was he who had slain the Jinn.

'The Governor now turned to the people and said, "It is meet that the man who delivered you should be your governor," and then to Bu Zaid, "This fort is yours!"

'But Bu Zaid answered and said, "I want neither riches nor power, give me leave to go about my pleasure."

'And so they gave to him of treasure and horses and *rizk Allah* - the bounty of God - and he departed with his brethren in the fullness of joy.'

Before the story was ended our camels, coming back from water, appeared across the sands. Hamad and I walked out to meet them. As we went we crossed many recent camel tracks which showed Farajja to be a popular water-hole. The grouped tracks of four camels walking in line arrested my companion's attention, and he turned to me and asked me in play which camel I saw in the sands to be best. I pointed - pardonably, I persuaded myself - to the wrong one. 'There,' he said, 'do you see that cuffing up of the toes.? It is a good sign: but not that skidding,' pointing to mine, 'between the footmarks.' 'That,' he said of the third, 'is an animal that has recently been in the steppe. Do you see the rugged impressions of her feet? Camels that have long been in the sands leave smooth impressions, and that' (pointing to the fourth) 'is her baby. Your camel is big with young - see the deep impressions of her small hind feet.' And thus and thus. It was not the least important part of Hamad's lore - a lore shared by nearly every dweller of the sands in varying degree - to read the condition of the strange camel, as yet unseen, from her marks, and hence to know whether to flee or to pursue.

Tracking in Arabia is an exact science, beside which the finger-print methods of the West are limited in scope, for the sands are a perfect medium.

In the more sophisticated parts of the peninsula - Oman, for example, a Court of Justice acts upon a foot-tracker's evidence, though there the *qaffar*, as he is called, has gifts not possessed, as in the sands, by the world at large. A case occurred during my service in Muscat. A Chinaman who had come to buy pearls and sea-slugs was murdered one night while he slept on the roof of his house in the Muscat bazaar. The murderer had apparently been surprised in the act, for he had jumped from the roof (it was a single-storey building) in his flight. The imprint of his foot remained in the lane beneath. On discovery next morning a pot was placed over it, sentries were posted at either end of the lane to prevent people passing that way, and a famous foot- tracker sent for, from up country. Meanwhile the days passed and the town grew nervous, for the murder had been a particularly brutal one - the neck had been cut with a sharp dagger from ear to ear - and the murderer was still at large.

The foot-tracker arrived and visited the footprint two or three times, on each occasion spending some minutes down on his hands and knees over it, as though to memorise it.

The next day the Muscat and Oman Council of Ministers ordered that every male in the town must pass for inspection by the *qaffar*, quarter by quarter sent their tale of men. Some days had thus passed, till at last the *qaffar* gave the sign.

It was a young man in his twenties, an African slave, indeed a Court slave, and therefore not a safe person to charge in error. He was immediately arrested and sent to the Prison Fort, where, charged with the crime, he flatly denied all knowledge of it, and affirmed his innocence.

The clothes he was supposed to have been wearing were sent to the Public Analyst in Bombay and no blood-stains were found, but other circumstantial evidence supported the foot-tracker. The slave was a notorious character; he was the sole occupant of the next house, so that he could have kept a careful watch on the movements of his intended victim; he could also have jumped easily from his upstairs veranda on to the roof where the murder took place, but he could not have jumped back.

The Indian apothecary looked at the foot-impression too. There in the middle was an edge of splintered stone, and his opinion was that the man who had dropped from the roof on to the stone must have a slight cut in the sole of his right foot.

The prisoner was brought before me and I asked him to show me the bottom of his foot. He lifted the left one promptly. Examination of the right foot showed the cut mark there, and my head callipers confirmed that the position of it corresponded exactly with the position of the splintered stone in the foot impression. The slave suffered the prescribed penalty in public at the hands of a firing squad. The foot-tracker had not read the marks in vain.

And now, six months later, in the centre of Rub Al Khali I was enjoying serener moments studying the tracks of the smaller animals. To a Badu, their simple story is immediately intelligible. For a European they have another appeal, the charm of graceful line or subtle invention; the sweep of drooping *gasis* in the wind makes a tiny picture of the prayer-ring the Badu sweeps with his cane towards the setting sun; the straight stride of birds' claws spaced one immediately before the other, a contrast with the earthy meanderings of some small quadruped; the neat little rosette pattern of a rat leads to a thicket, where you will find its tiny hole, a heap of newly turned red sand at the entrance; the crooked but beautiful intricacies of a lizard like a miniature arabesque lead to a sprig of herbage where it has played maypole and rolled over in joyous repletion; that futuristic riot marks the fallen twigs bowled over and over by the whims of the wind.

The morrow was intensely cold. Our course at first due east obliquely across the strong north wind, then turned into the face of it, and I was glad of my greatcoat. A large hawk, the first I had seen in the sands, circled about our heads to sail swiftly down wind as we passed an encampment of Murra with some fifty black camels. The great camel herds of the Murra are said to be mostly black, [105] whence the tents of the sands are generally of that colour, in sharp contrast with the colour of the wild animals of the sands, particularly the mammals, which is that of their environment.

We made a wide detour to avoid these Murra. They were ostensibly a friendly section, but it was declared unwise that I be seen or heard of, lest news of me get ahead with mischievous results.

Shaikh Salih as he rode at my side shivered, but would not bemoan the cold, lest he affront the Almighty, the All Knowing, who had sent it. I told Salih of the cold of an English winter.

'Do you hear that he turned to Mubarak. 'In the Wazir's country the water that is cut off from the sea' (a pond) 'becomes solid with the cold so that the Arabs and horses and donkeys can walk upon it.'

'There is no god but God,' returned Mubarak, and I detected in his expression a fear lest I be the advance guard of a party of invaders, anxious to forsake such misery for their own delectable sands.

Long hungry hours in the saddle and the cold north wind made life at this stage uncomfortable, the night temperature falling to 40° F., and having no tent or other overhead covering, I found it necessary to sleep in all my clothes plus three blankets.

On 22nd January in the red rolling sand-hills of Ubaila we met the first of a series of sandstorms. We were sitting round the camp-fire after the evening meal. Two nights before there had been a heavy dew, our first since leaving the Qara Mountains. To-night a cold wind from the north was blowing, but nothing presaged a coming storm. Suddenly the flames swept this way and that as though the wind blew from everywhere in turn. We all covered our faces with our hands to save our eyes from the smoke. My companions leapt up and rushed off in the darkness to bring in their grazing camels, for the sandstorm is one of their worst enemies. The storm grew fiercer; the Badawin, with their poor mantles wrapped round them, huddled together for warmth.

I slept fitfully. The hissing of the sand-laden wind, the rattling of my camp cordage and the cold of my feet made sleep impossible. When my face was exposed the gritty blast struck it with the sharpness of a knife. The temperature fell to 37° F. dry, 35° F. wet. I dozed off just before dawn and woke soon after to find my saddle and baggage embedded in driven sand. The wind had dropped and round the camp-fires clustered huddled and shivering Badawin. Soon they were rousing their camels that had been rounded up overnight for safety, and the wretched beasts shuffled, shivering, away to feed and to feel the warmth of the rising sun.

To me the night had disastrous results. The sand had got into some of my instruments. My small cinema camera was out of action, and my two aneroids no longer tallied, so that I was obliged thereafter to record two different readings, not knowing which, if either, was right till the end of the journey.

I bring you good tidings of the *shamal!* I bring you good tidings of the *shamal!* ' shouted a young Badu next morning in ironical reference to the bitter north wind, the temperature standing within 5° F. of freezing-point.

'But for the north wind
There would be no increase,'

retorted Shaikh Salih, quoting a desert rhyme upon the wind's stimulus to the bull-camel.

The rolling reds of Ubaila had given place again to the more typical white open spaces of Sanam as we approached the water-hole of Jahaishi. A chill depressing day with the plain a white smoke-screen that swept towards us and past us filming our camels' feet, the wind had stung my poor companions, who, muffled up in their scanty garments, sat shivering as we rode along.

'Couch her. Sahib! Couch Agaba,' they cried, 'it is the hour of the midday prayer.' Here beside the abandoned water-hole of Duwairis were firewood and a little grazing, and I realised we were halting for the day. Sand filled my eyes, and my note-books; sand was every-where; note-taking with numbed fingers was impossible, and all that could be done was to sit idly in the swirl of sand and cold discomfort, and wish for a lull.

The Badawin collected brushwood from the thickets and piled it in a strong hedge twenty yards long. It was *gadha*, a considerable bush which we here met for the first time. Behind this shelter the camels were couched huddled together, only a few hardy brutes electing to stand and graze. Later in the day when the sun made itself felt and the wind dropped a little, they hobbled off to some near pastures, but when the wind again rose they were promptly brought back, their masters fearing to lose them, if left out, for the wind immediately effaced all tracks.

The homing instinct of the camel - if the absence of an established home does not make the term a paradox -is amazing. Her fixed idea apparently is to regain the fat pastures and main herds she has just left. During the preoccupations of marching, she may forget, but when a halt is called and she is turned out to graze unfettered, she will wander back alone the way she has come. Her master means nothing to her. She has no affection for him and never learns to know more of him than the sound of his voice. Yet she is utterly dependent upon him for her watering, being powerless to fend for herself even at the shallowest water-hole. She is excessively stupid except for an uncanny sense of direction, but is none the less 'Ata Y' Allah' — the Gift of God - in his eyes.

If you leave Agaba, [106] to herself,' said Shaikh Salih, 'she will go off across the sands directly under that star back to Dakaka and her companions, though she has never come this way before.'

'But how will she fare for water?'

'She will wander back without water and arrive safely in the winter time, but in summer she will perish of thirst before a quarter of the way.'

Our march during the past two days had afforded an instance of this. A strange camel, a cow big with calf, [107] had joined our party, or rather led the way, for she bounced along ahead of us, making straight for Qatar where her camel brand showed her to belong. She was presumably anxious for dates or sardines, the local delicacies she missed in the sands; lucky for her that the season was winter!

'Do not let your camel eat of this *gadha*,' shouted a Murri next day as we passed through a verdant plain of it; 'it is *jinn* haunted.'

'But only these *gadha* pastures of Al Hirra and Banaiyan,' explained Hamad to me, 'elsewhere it is good enough fodder. Here five camels died in one night, and on another occasion two became ill and their milk dried up.'

I had also found this idea, that *jinns* could affect the wholesomeness of vegetation, at Mugshin, where it caused a magnificent grove of acacias to be largely neglected. My Badawin's invariable habit of picking the juiciest herbage for hand-feeding their camels was there suspended, nor would they shoot the hares of this grove for the pot. [108] The Kathiris had another strange belief, that a camel hand-fed at Mugshin instead of grazing for itself would suffer misfortune.

The famous water-hole of Banaiyan lay but a day's march ahead. An hour and a half after leaving our overnight's *hadh* pastures, we breasted the red sand-hills of Khiyut al Buraidan that marked the northern border of Sanam. The wind had dropped and the pure smooth surface of the rosy sand-hills - here called Hamarur - was in refreshing contrast to the white smoking plains of the recent marches. Patches of vivid green haram lined the gravelly troughs in the sand-hills and our hungry camels occasionally snatched at a tuft as we passed, though without encouragement, for haram is a saline feed which does no good to the animal not used to it. 'Now the Manasir,' said a Badu with a sweep of his arm to the eastwards, 'have little else and their camels are reared on it and grow humps like this' - here he caught the elbow of one arm held out before him, the forearm bent upwards on the palm of the other hand - a favourite gesture to indi-cate a large hump and therefore a thriving animal.

Rare ridges, of red sand in the plain, long and low, and patches of *gadha* growing out of elephant-mask accretions of sand about their roots, formed an area called Qadha Za'aza and brought us to more rolling red hills. In the midst of these we halted over the water-hole of Banaiyan. The caravan had dragged out, as all tired caravans do. Ramadhan was telling on the men, the saline pastures on the camels, and the long marches and cold north wind on both. Hamad and I were the first arrivals.

'Drink, Sahib,' he said, 'the water of Banaiyan is good.'

Hamad, even had it not been the fast month, would himself have forborne. It was their code after a thirsty day's march that when we arrived at a water-hole no drop of water should pass the lips of the advance party until those in the rear had come up, nor would any man eat a crust with me on the march unless his companions were there to share it. If this precarious condition of life produces savagery between enemies, it breeds none the less a fine humanity among friends.

Banaiyan was a real well, stone-lined and therefore unlike the mere pits in the sand that are the water-holes of the south. As my party straggled in there was a visible change in their mood. Cheerful-ness prevailed with the merry shouts and noise of spilling water that they love to make, while their great thirsty brutes with long necks stretched down to the scooped-out water trough gurgled their fill.

The want of pastures forbade a halt in these barren, rolling hills, and the first animals to be watered were already on the march before the last had come up. I delayed to accompany the rear party. Soon we had to halt for the sunset prayer, and after that we found growing difficulty in following the tracks of our advance guard; the failing light soon made it impossible. So with Polaris before our left shoulder -as the Badu has it, with his hand over his corresponding collar-bone so that you shall not err - we made our way through the night. An hour had passed when there was a shout from a man behind me. Turning, I saw the glimmer of a camp fire away to the eastwards. We turned and made camp at seven o'clock. I was thoroughly exhausted after ten and a half hours in the saddle, but comfort came from the realisation that the great central wastes of Rub Al Khali lay behind me, the sea was but eighty miles to the northward, success was in sight.

19

AT BANAIYAN: A RETROSPECT

At Banaiyan I had reached the northward fringe of Ar Rimal. [109] It is a convenient point, therefore, at which to suspend the narrative for a brief chapter to consider in retrospect the shape and structure of the land; its nomenclature, and the sociological aspects of the life of its inhabitants, as revealed by my journeyings.

Arabia is divided geologically by the Rub Al Khali. To the west the preponderating mass of the peninsula is geologically part of the African continent, from which it is separated only by the depressed zone or rift valley of the Red Sea. It has been elevated to a height of several thousand feet, carrying marine rocks to the highest elevation, but within itself has not suffered much dislocation; even the volcanic rocks in the north were ejected without much force, so that no volcanic peaks were formed. On the whole therefore the country has remained relatively undisturbed during the vast spaces of geological time.

The eastern zone, that is, the massif of Oman, on the other hand, forms part of the Persian system of intensively folded mountains caused by pressure from the north against the more stable mass of Arabia Proper, at a time when active earth movements were forming the great ranges of south Persia and northern India. [110]

Dhufar, the starting-point of my journey, lends itself to the study of the geological structure of much of the Arabian plateau. Along the seashore are exposed granites and other crystalline rocks which form the massive basement of the peninsula. They are overlaid by red sand-stones which form the lower slopes of Jabal Qara, probably like the Nubian sandstone found in Egypt, Sinai and Trans-Jordan, and over that again, represented by the high cliffs of Jabal Qara, are limestones of the Upper Cretaceous and Eocene Ages, but the southern face is in reality an escarpment forming the edge of the high sandstone plateau which slopes gently down to the edge of the sands where I found my Eocene fossils.

The great belt of sands lying to the northward for three hundred miles and more did not yield any indication of age, though the sand specimens [111] I brought back from the centre contain grains of pink and white limestone, indicating perhaps that the sand has not trav-elled from a great distance; otherwise they would have disappeared from the friction of the harder quartz.

Along the northern sand fringe to the north of Banaiyan I again found sea fossils of the same age as those in the south, but it is impos-sible to say from my single traverse whether the Eocene Sea once extended all the way across from Qatar to Dhufar, to be covered later with blown sands from the north-east, or whether the points approxi-mately one hundred miles inland on both sides of the Rub Al Khali where I picked up fossils represent the northern and southern limits of invasion of the Eocene Sea.

It is possible that the basic floor of Ar Rimal is of some limestone formation, probably of Eocene or Cretaceous age, with exposures of the Nubian sandstone from which the blown sands have been formed.

The Rub Al Khali has been shown to be a zone of depression between high Nejd to the west and the Oman Mountains to the east, a depression that probably occurred at the time of the elevation of Oman — that is during the Upper Cretaceous and the Tertiary periods.

Of much interest, if of a negative kind, was the gentle character of the topography along my line of march - the general absence of any considerable folding to give rise to prominent features. Just over the Qara Mountains the steppe began roughly at an altitude of 2000 feet, and it sloped gently to 1100 feet at the edge of the sands, making a fall of only 900 feet in 100 miles. So also from this southern edge of the sands at 1100 feet to the northern edge at Banaiyan, 200 feet, the fall is but 900 feet in nearly 300 miles. Northwards of Banaiyan the same gentle slope is maintained towards the sea.

In describing the sands proper, [112] I have already noted that their greatest elevations, the dune country, lie along the southern fringe and swing north, according to Arab report, in about long. 49° and again in long. 53°.

The extension of these wings would approximately trisect Ar Rimal, and a reference to the map will show that it was through the middle section that my route lay.

The belief that the sands would prove waterless has been shown to be unfounded. Water, though very brackish, is found at any rate eastward of 51° E. [113] Indeed, throughout the middle regions in the low sands of eastern Suwahib and elsewhere, there seems to be abundant sub-soil water, but so saline as to be generally undrinkable by man. Such water-holes do not enjoy distinguishing names but are, as already stated, labelled genetically *khiran*. Elsewhere, a water-hole which a camel or man will drink from enjoys a distinguishing name, often that of its digger; when necessary the camel plays the part of a distillery. She drinks the water and man drinks her milk.

Lesser herbage was *Gasis* and *Haram* in the red sands of I., IL, V., VL

Zahar (Tribulus alatris, Del.}.

Hadh [Salsola sp.).

Shinan (Arthrocnemum glaucum, Ung.).

Abala is the most considerable growth of the sands and by far the most useful. The framework of the camel saddle and tent utensils are made from this wood; it is also excellent firewood, unlike *Hadh* and *Shinan*.

So the vegetation lay in zones from south to north

Belt.	Vegetation	Latitude From	To	Altitude From ft	To ft
I. II.	Zahar Barkan Abala	18° 30'	20° 30'	1100	550
III., IV.., V., V., VI.,	Hadh Gadha	20° 00' 22° 40'	23° 00' 24° 00'	600	250
VI.	Shinan	23° 12'	24° 30'	200	S.L.

The sweetest water lay on the westernmost points of my route in western Dakaka and Sanam, where the water-holes were as deep as thirteen fathoms and upwards, but the yield is said to be uncertain. Indeed sometimes, as with Turaiga, they dry up. The most brackish water lay on the eastern- most portions of my route, where it was shallow, as at Buwah, and the supply was apparently inexhaustible; this evidence would seem to support Arab information that the great sands rising towards the west and south-west are entirely waterless.

The regional names of the sands derive very often from some topographical feature, [114] or from some peculiarity of water or vegetation, or now and then from some association with camels.

The mode of human life in Rub Al Khali - the only life that short-lived pastures and inadequate or brackish water permit - is tribal and nomadic, a life economically precarious, politically unstable, but socially fixed and unalterable.

The prosperity of the tribe is measured by the number and condition of its camels. The sources of wealth are good pastures and the manly prowess of its members who will aggressively acquire fresh camels at their enemies' expense.

Camels therefore fall into two classes, herds of milch camels (the assets and reserve) and the less numerous riding camels (working capital). The first may be worth one hundred dollars each, the second from two hundred to four hundred for an exceptional animal. The milch camel never knows a saddle, and is raised solely for breeding and to produce milk and wool. The female is therefore the valued sex, and the cow calf is always reared, whereas the bull calf is a luxury not worth his keep. In consequence he seldom survives the first year of life, and not infrequently is slaughtered for food on the day he is born without his mother seeing him. Normally two or three bulls will serve a herd of fifty cows; they also carry tents and the heavier burdens when on the move. Herds when wandering off to remote inaccessible regions split up over wide areas, each Badu family looking after its own; but the tribe will collect again for self-protection against the raiders of the steppe, whenever the need of grazing draws them southward into danger, as last winter.

The tribes strongest in camels are the Murra, Manasir and Manahil, also, to some extent, the Sa'ar. The Rashid have of late years decayed from the depredations of the Sa'ar, so that to-day a Rashidi with five camels is comparatively well off, with twenty he is rich, and one hundred is the limit of affluence; with the Murra averages are much higher. My envious Rashidi informant in emphasising their wealth, with a simile familiar to us of the West through the Old Testament, picked up a handful of sand and allowed it to trickle through his fingers. '*Wallahi!* so-and-so has four hundred camels,' he said, 'and he is not a shaikh, nor has he money, nor clothes better than mine.'

'What happens to the milk?' I asked.

'Let a man have much milk,' was the answer, 'and he will have many guests. His neighbours expect it of him, and the passers-by. Any surplus milk will be given to the young camels.'

Camel hair provides almost all the few household wants of the nomad life - tent material, ropes, saddle girths, and miscellaneous trappings. Here again the cow is the more profitable sex. Her shoulders and back each year yield to her master's fist or dagger the raw material which his womenfolk will work up, for weaving is a feminine occupation; not milking, however, at least with Rashid and 'Awamir, who share the mountain taboo against the milking of camels by women; on the other hand, the Murra, Manasir, Sa'ar and Hadhra-maut steppe tribes have no such ban.

Two types of saddle are in use in the sands. The double- poled saddle - the *shadad* - placed over the camel's hump. This, the normal saddle of the rest of Arabia, is used in the Rub Al Khali only by the Murra, the Sa'ar, and Karab. By the entire remaining tribes, as indeed in Oman and throughout the whole of south-eastern Arabia, the *zana* is used, a small light frame (without poles) covered with a goatskin and placed behind the camel's hump. The distribution of camel saddles is thus geographical; west of my line of route the tribes use the *shadad*, east of it the *zana*.

So also the sands know two dialects of Arabic, but here the division is latitudinal. There is a northern or Murri dialect and a southern or Rashid dialect, the latter also spoken by the 'Awamir [115] of the north-east. The chief distinctions between north and south dialects are word differences, [116] and a considerable difference of voice modulation. Hamad bin Hadi had volunteered the information that his people's dialect was peculiar, because Murra, he said, had sprung from an infidel; but in the presence of other members of his tribe he corrected himself, and all agreed to a common origin with 'Ajman, thence deriving from Yam. But the original maternal ancestor of the tribe was, God bless you, a *jinni*.

While polygamy is permissible, it is seldom that a Badu has more than one wife at a time, though if he is well off he may have two or may marry, divorce, and remarry. For a man and woman to live together out of wedlock is unknown, and would be impossible in a tribal society in which the liberty of the individual is subordinated to the interests of the clan and its posterity, and whose rigorous moral code is rooted in age-long experience, secure from the philosophical speculations of celibate professors. In theory no marriage is valid, except it be 'knotted' formally by a *Qadhi*, [117] or adequate proxy, with considerable ceremony, doubtless designed to discourage its participants from breaking their bonds.

The prospective bridegroom and representative of the bride, usually her father or brother, go off together to the nearest town,

[118] where a *Qadhi* will be found, for it is almost unknown for a *Qadhi* to come out into the desert. A system whereby certain tribesmen, who have taken advantage of a sojourn in the town to learn the formulae stand proxy for a *Qadhi* and celebrate marriages, has come to have a validity with dwellers in the remoter sands; the office is then hereditary. It is the custom after the 'knot' is tied for the bridegroom to pay over the purchase price to the father. Then he will bring to the bride some silver jewellery and a simple rug for the nuptial couch (and with the Rashid he must also make a feast) before the consummation can take place. The nose-kiss is the kiss of the marital bed. [119]

Man treats woman as an inferior, a chattel. This is perhaps natural in the desert environment, where uninterrupted physical fitness, brute strength, and an aggressive character are qualities which Nature demands and rewards. The beating of women for common, everyday lapses was approved by my Murra Badawin, but not by the Rashidis.

The politics of Rub Al Khali revolve round inter-tribal relationships. Geographical considerations make for three almost separate tribal groupings, the Rimal tribes, their neighbours of the eastern steppe and those of the southern steppe.

The true sand dwellers have been shown to be the Murra in north and north-west, the Manasir and 'Awamir in the north-east, and Ar Rashid and Bait Imani in the south.

Twenty years ago these tribes were at one another's throats. Murra and Manasir were old and implacable enemies; between 'Awamir and Manasir the feud was even fiercer. The 'Awamir, once a very great tribe in South Arabia were the original dwellers in the present, Rashidi sands of the Dakaka, Suwahib, Hibak and Ghanim, but unequal contests with the Manasir have impoverished them; while Murra and Rashid have many old scores. Yet to-day peace, the peace of Bin Sa'ud, prevails throughout the sands. The influence of the Ruler of Central Arabia, wielded through his able Viceroy at Hofuf, Bin Jaluwi, compels peace between all these old enemies, not through direct control, for there is and can be none, but through the immense personal prestige of 'Abdul 'Aziz himself. A belief in his strength and star has swept across the sands. Not love, but awe, serves this wise providence that so directs affairs. My own *rabia* Hamad bin Hadi had not yet made submission, but he was respectful in his fear of the mighty, the belief that the ruler of Riyadh had power to despoil him of his spoils, or make him the prey of an enemy. Upon this conviction is founded peace in the sands to-day. Thus the sand tribes proper are in some degree leagued with Bin Sa'ud. They pay to him a nominal tribute and by that act are ensured mutual protection one from the other. In theory the tribute is an annual levy of one dollar on each camel. In practice, the Rashid have no money, and in any event they escape proper payment by reason of their remoteness. They do, however, send a camel from year to year as occasion offers in token of submission. When, however, rains fall in the northern sands and they migrate thither, the tax-gatherers' demands must be met, and a few camels are sold for the purpose.

Light as is the bond, the tribes grumble at it. They have no sympathy with the Arab proverb, that originated, we may be sure, in a town, 'A tyrannical Sultan is to be preferred to constant quarrelling.' They would rather have unfettered liberty than peace at a price; it is in their blood. They all swear that the existing peace shall last only as long as the present regime of Riyadh. Let Riyadh or Hofuf be thought to have lost its power, and raiding will be resumed immediately, and blood will flow again. This attitude of mind is not peculiar to the Rub Al Khali. The student of politics will recall many instances in the recent history of the British Empire.

It was the knowledge of this unprecedented suspension of blood feuds, springing from a determined but benign autocracy, that emboldened me to launch out across these ancient (and future) battle-grounds of the sands.

The politics of the eastern steppe are not unaffected by Bin Sa'ud's influence, though this varies from year to year. Here the groupings form round ancient hereditary factions of Hinawi and Ghafari already referred to - 'Awamir, Harasis and Afar belonging to the former, Daru' [120] and Albu Shamis to the Ghafari, but their strife has no echo in the sands.

Sabkha polygons

The politics of the southern steppe are completely free from Bin Sa'ud's influence, and the great tribes of Sa'ar, Manahil, Kathir and Mahra, and the lesser ones of Karab, Yam, Nahad and Nisiyin are laws unto themselves. The most powerful single element is the Sa'ar. With them, Nahad and Karab may act in concert, while elements of the others are capable of uniting for a particular raid; but there is no long and sustained or organised warfare. There cannot be, for each man has but twenty rounds or so of ammunition and guards his stock jealously unless he is making a journey to the coast to sell a camel or two. Their wars are consequently sporadic with booty as the end and aim.

The Sa'ar tribe and its allies are to-day the serious menace to peace in the southern sands. Numerically powerful - perhaps two thousand rifles — they derive strength from their remoteness, and have hitherto refused to receive an embassy from Bin Sa'ud.

20

BANAIYAN TO THE SEA: THE LAST STAGE

January 28th was spent resting at Banaiyan after our eighteen days' dash across the central sands -a halt necessary to refresh tired camels and men. We gathered round the camp-fire at nightfall - it proved to be the last leisurely session the march afforded - and with the end of the journey in sight I was able to throw off my habitual restraint.

My electric torch was a source of wonderment to my companions. 'Could a strayed or stolen camel be tracked on a dark night with it?' that was the crucial question. The first Badu to place his hand over the lighted end discovered that there was practically no heat, and brought the miracle to the notice of his companions. They all followed suit and when, instead of feeling heat they saw the red hue of blood and shadowy finger-bones, they burst out in astonished cries - 'There is no god but God. Surely the Sahib's tribe must be a wonderful people?' It was idle for me to declare that I had not made the torch, for did we not make still more marvellous works - rifles and ammunition!

'Who makes rifles?' asked one Badu, fondling his own.

'The Infidels,' said another without looking up.

'No,' I corrected them, 'we are Believers.'

'And if we came to your country. Sahib, would you be our *rabia* so that none should harm us?'

'There is no need for a *rabia* in my country.'

'But,' said Hamad, ' if one should slay me and you were my *rabia* what would you do?'

'But none would slay you. Nobody may carry arms in my country.'
'What a place!' I felt them to be thinking, 'fit only for women and slaves!'

'And should we get camel's milk to drink?'

'We have no camels,' I returned apologetically, for I knew I should get few marks for this.

'Then what have you got? Sheep? Cows?'

'Yes, sheep and cows,' I said, 'but we make ships and rifles and all manner of things from the iron of the earth.'

'True,' interjected Shaikh Salih with a sophisticated air, 'I've heard a Mansuri from Abu Dhabi say that one day a Nasrani came to the shaikh and told him that in his country a bar of iron like this,' and he flourished his camel stick, 'would make five rifles.'

Chorus of Badawin: 'There is no god but God.'

One picked up the torch again. 'It is heavy,' he said.

'God! it's heavy,' said another, as he took it out of his comrade's hand.

Salih: 'They are not an easy people' (i.e, not a weak tribe whose members could be treated as inferiors).

'Inside the torch is *guwa* - strength - (a word they reverence) 'more potent than bullets, and such that it kills men,' I said.

'But why kill them?'

'Only bad men,' I returned - 'murderers.'

'Yes, and very right too - "an eye for an eye and a tooth for a tooth" - 'tis God's Law.'

'But have you no blood-money?'

'None,' I said.

'Then the murdered man's brother or cousin does not profit a single dollar.'

'Not a single dollar,' I repeated, conscious that I was scoring very few marks again.

'But have you no sanctuary?'

'No, our shaikh is strong, and no one would dare to give a murderer sanctuary.'

'But with us,' said Salih, 'sanctuary is honoured, unless there is shame in the murder, such for instance as a *rabia* who has betrayed his companion. What good man is there,' he continued, looking round his companions, 'who would withhold sanctuary from one who had killed his enemy?'

Chorus of Badawin: 'Yes, by God!'

'Which direction is your country. Sahib?' said one of them after a pause.

I pointed with my riding cane in a north-westerly direction.

'How far is it away?'

Hol - a year's march, from Ramadhan to Ramadhan,' I said, 'at our pace.'

Chorus of Badawin: 'There is no god but God.'

'And which direction is it from Mecca?' interposed Salih, one of the few South Arabian Badawin I knew who had made the Pilgrimage. I pointed as before, perhaps a shade more northerly.

'And how far is it from there?'

'Almost as far as it is from here.'

Chorus: 'There is no god but God.'

'Then it is beyond the sea. Sahib?'

'Yes,' I said, 'beyond the sea.'

'And what is there beyond it?'

'The sea again,' I said.

'Where is the Sea of Barlimul?' said Talib. 'I think you must mean the Sea of Barlimul.' He turned to tell his companions that there the world ended. Beyond was nothing. It was the seventh and last sea – *Allahu' Alim!*

I felt I had done my share of story-telling, and was an eager listener when one of them fell to telling a story about Dhiyab bin Ghanim. Dhiyab was from the nobility of Bani Hillal, albeit with the appearance of a slave. And on the black day when Yusif was killed, and Dhiyab, Bu Zaid and Baraiga were made prisoners, his appear-

ance saved him from close confinement, for he was thought to be of
no account.

He was first set to work with the masons repairing Zenaiti's fort.
But such was his lack of skill, that the stones he slung up passed clean
over the fort and landed on the far side in the desert. So his captors
said, 'This slave is no good at this work, we will set him to tend herds.'
And Dhiyab was given cows to look after, but he neglected to water
them properly so that they came near to dying. And his masters,
seeing that he made a bad cowman, sent him with asses to go forth
into the scrub and fetch kindlings. There he cut two long sticks and
sharpened their ends and thrust them through the backs of a pair of
donkeys to make carriers for his firewood. And so he brought a huge
load to his masters. Their first impulse was to applaud, not knowing
by what contrivance it had been brought, but as soon as the firewood
was off-loaded, the asses dropped dead. And the men of Arisha shook
their heads and said, 'Dhiyab's wits are weak, he is fit for nothing but
to tend camels; we will set him to look after the Bani Hillal camels
that we captured with him'; thus did Dhiyab attain the object of his
desire. As the days passed the condition of the camels improved, and
Dhiyab won favour in the sight of his masters. And each time he
watered the camels he chose a more distant water-hole, thus length-
ening his absences by degrees without exciting suspicion until one
day he reached the point that favoured his escape and thence made off
back to Bani Hillal country with the camels. And in order that the
passer-by need bring no alarming news of him to Zenaiti he sat on his
camel, facing backwards towards Arisha, and placed earth upon his
head and under his haunches. [121] And thus he came to the Bani
Hillal. There Shaikh Husain bin Sirhan, after he had listened to
Dhiyab's story, planned to rescue Bu Zaid and Baraiga, and in the fullness of time the tribe set forth and came to a fragrant pool into which
fell three wadis. And Bani Hillal took counsel together and decided to
leave their women and animals with sixty horsemen to protect them,
while the *gom* passed on to the country of Zenaiti, but on the morrow
they changed the plan, saying that in place of the sixty horsemen they
would leave Dhiyab bin Ghanim.

'The camels and the women are in thy protection,' said the shaikh to Dhiyab in farewell, 'guard them with thy life.'

And Dhiyab replied, 'If one of them shall be missing, then is my life forfeit.' That night a *jinn* came wandering down the wadi to see who was encamped there. He carried in his hand a mighty spear, and went in and out among the camels seeking for the biggest and best, and having found it he speared it, and carrying the camel impaled over his shoulder returned up the wadi. The next night he came again so that in the morning yet another camel was missing. And when on the third night there was still another visitation, terror seized the camp, for none had seen the *jinn* except the wife of Dhiyab, and she was loth to speak for fear of the jinn's revenge. Dhiyab, regarding his wife's strange silence, questioned her, but she would not reply. Then he drew his sword and tapped her with it, saying, 'Woman! tell me what thou knowest or I will slay thee.' So she told Dhiyab of the *jinn* that came down a certain wadi and of how he speared the camels and carried them off.

On the following morning Dhiyab despatched his slave to follow up the *jinn*'s tracks and to bring tidings of where *jinn* lived. And the slave came to a well that had been caused by the falling of a star and saw the *jinn* within it, and the remains of the camels strewn round about the mouth of it, and so brought back news to Dhiyab. So Dhiyab mounted his mare and came to the well. As he approached the *jinn* stood up to show his monstrous proportions, for his body was as much out of the well as within it.

And the *jinn* shouted, 'Oh ha! Ya Dhiyab bin Ghanim! hast thou come to eat or to slay?'

Dhiyab replied, 'I have come both to eat and to slay,' and drawing his sword he struck lustily at the *jinn* and cut him in halves, so that one half stood within the well, and the other lay fallen without.

Said the *jinn*'s upper half, 'Hain' - strike a second time. But Dhiyab replied:

'*Ma thinni*, I strike not twice,
Wa la zinni, Nor go a-whoring,
Wa la akl al jins ni Nor am I food for your kind,'

for Dhiyab knew what everybody knows, that whereas one fell blow will kill a *jinn*, two blows will surely bring two *jinns* to life.

And Dhiyab returned to the camp to find that the *gom* was just returning, but alas! knew not that three of his sons had fallen and also Amr bin Khafaiyat, a valiant and beloved warrior whose mother had been of the Bani Hillal. And the *gom* were troubled in their minds as to which among them should convey the ill-tidings to Dhiyab, who would surely strike down with his spear such a messenger of woe. For Dhiyab's spear was never known to miss; once it was launched it must land in flesh; so 'it was written'; and should it not land in flesh Dhiyab would die in that same day.

And none being willing to tell him, it was decided to send Dalaiyan the slave, for they said one to another, 'Should Dalaiyan die he dies; and should he live he lives only to be a slave.'

And Dalaiyan asked for the speediest mare and they gave it to him, and he rode towards Dhiyab's place and drew rein at a great distance.

Dhiyab shouted to him, 'Tell me, O Dalaiyan, as I am of the sons of darkness, how went the fight, and tell me of the gallantry of my sons and how it fares with them.'

And the slave answered:

'Of our camels and our sons, the best have gone. Thy three sons and bin Khafaiyat. Bravest of warriors of their tribe and time.'

And as the slave now turned his mount about and galloped away, Dhiyab seized his spear and hurled it after him; but Dalaiyan bending low over his steed, the weapon passed over him and landed some paces beyond in the head of a snake.

'Great God!' cried Dhiyab, 'my spear has missed. Now must I pass to where the slain have gone.'

'*Selemni*' shouted back the slave, 'save me unhurt and I will give thee good tidings.'

Dhiyab: 'By my face.'

The slave: 'The spear point landed in flesh.'

Dhiyab: 'God be praised! And mayest thou live long.'

We made an early morning start into Wahhabi territory [122] - the home of the Ikhwan (brotherhood) sectaries. Here we moved furtively. Every hour of the day the horizons were scanned for signs of the feared Puritans of Islam, intolerant men who hold it virtuous to fight not merely the infidel, but the heretic in Islam, by whom they mean every Muslim not holding their narrow views. My companions were emphatic that there should be no loitering, not even for my note-taking, between here and the coast, and that if suspicious tracks were crossed, we should take no risks but halt in the wilderness by day, and march by night. Fortunately for my map-making the second course was not imposed upon us, for it was Ramadhan, and the Ikhwan tribes had withdrawn to the regions of Jaub and Jafura for the Fast.

'God is sufficient for their Evil,' [123] exclaimed Hamad the *rabia*.

Our course lay at first through a hard gravelly steppe bright with pebbles coloured like camphor, cornelian or jade; thence through large white salt-fields, with dark damp patches here and there.

Fortunately the recent rain had not been enough to turn the crusted surface into a greasy mire and hold camels up as normally occurs. Beyond we came to light-coloured sands and within them a wadi-like depression with vegetation, [124] Jaub Dhibi, our camping ground and a haunt, as their tracks showed, of hyena, wild-cat, lizards and other steppe animals.

The Jihan tract that lay ahead of us for the next few days was of the same type; alternating ribbons of steppe, salt- plain and rolling sand-hills with a verdant sand depression such as Dhibi at intervals of a half-day's march, Kharit, Thuraiya, Sufaiya and Lizba. The steppes were dusted with gravel of jasper and gypsum, pebbles of black, white, red and green that shone in the sun; the northern salt plains were studded by innumerable small shells in an early stage of petrification; the gullies in the sand-hills were here and there bright green with *haram* scrub, or pink and white with patches of gypsum rubble; and in these same gullies we dug out the shallow holes at which we watered.

Before Lizba, however, was a considerable ridge, the only one of its kind. It stretched east and west as far as the eye could see, rose some two hundred feet on its southern side and fell to the northwards through a quarry-like desolation to rolling sands. In the sands many black-ribbed beetles were crawling amidst sprigs of fresh grass, the green first- fruits of the scanty winter rain. This grass, *ushub*, said to produce the most delicious camel milk, gave us reason to halt from time to time and graze our camels.

Talib, a northern Murri, had supplanted Hamad as our guide in the marches north of Haluwain, a change for the worse, though inevitable, as he alone of our party claimed local knowledge. The compass directions and distances of water-holes that he gave me proved wrong, and when I took him to task, he swore that he spoke the truth 'by Him who created me and created the Sun.' I felt sure he had no mind to deceive us, but the pasture and firewood he promised for our night's halt did not appear. These were the chief considerations every afternoon in anticipation of the night's camp, and my company grew critical. 'Ya Arab,' said one, 'there is only cold and hunger ahead.' We veered to the eastwards, so that the conspicuous sand-hill, Alamat al Nakhala, formerly on our right front, appeared on our left; by sunset we had turned our backs upon it and were actually marching away from our goal in the hope of finding food and warmth that night. Had it been summer- time with its drought the mistake might have cost us our lives. One Badu in ten is a good guide, one in fifty a reliable informant. The mutual suspicion of the Rashid and Murra members of my party was of interest; it showed that neither believed their present peaceful relations to be lasting. So they would not disclose the secrets of their respective districts. Now and then a Murri would slip off to examine the state of some well or pasture, but it would never have done for a Rashidi to follow or enquire. Anyone contemplating such a journey as this is wise to collect all possible information beforehand, then the reliability of any particular informant can be quickly checked.

One day's march was very like another. Always an hour before sunrise I was awakened by the voice of Marzuq, sounding the Dawn call to prayer;

'God is great.

There is no god' but God.

There is no god but God.

I bear witness that Muhammad is the Prophet of God.
I bear witness that Muhammad is the Prophet of God.
Prayer is better than sleep.
Prayer is better than sleep.
God is great.
There is no god but God.'

A chorus of sanctimonious groans from stirring Badawin was their Amen! There often followed Shaikh Salih's parental chiding of Kilthut who was ailing, and in consequence a laggard.

'Rise, O Kilthut!, are you listening? Rise and pray!'

After prayers the Badawin, breaking up, drove their camels off to the nearest grazing, and then returned to breakfast off a handful of dates and a drink of brackish water. For the next eleven hours no food passed their lips, and during Ramadhan no water either; yet they seemed to thrive on it. My own breakfast-lunch, taken also at the first hour after sunrise, consisted of a bowl of camel's milk and a dish of oatmeal - my invariable diet for fifty-eight days on end.

If camel pastures were good I was allowed to finish my meal at leisure and to write up my natural history specimens and other notes before starting off, but if the camp had been a hungry one, then the moment I had finished my meal we would saddle, knowing that during the march we would have to loiter for grazing. My pack-camel was brought first.

'There is no god but God.
O God.
Him whom we supplicate.
O God.'

Thus a Badu picking up his cane lying on the sands between two toes, and leading my pack-camel over to couch her with a *kh kh* and a gentle tapping with his stick behind her knee or over her neck. Another would come to help him load up, and while the animal bellowed protestingly, they broke into a camel-chant suitably *agitato* for the occasion.

Badawin were everywhere loading up and moving off dismounted, each with the first foot forward, muttering some pious invocation to the Unseen. The Rashidi formula [125] was as follows:

'In the name of God, the Compassionate, the Merciful.

Reliance is in God.

Peace upon the *rafiq*.

O God!

There is none other, and none equal to Thee.

And no escape from Thy Will.

O God, by Thy forgiveness

Make easy our path, and guide our rafiq.'

To which one of the party would return:

'There is no god but God.'

The morning routine was that we walked the first three or four miles, leading our camels; but I was usually first into the saddle, except for Bin Ham, a Bait Imani shaikh, and a doughty warrior among them still, in spite of a leg crippled by the old bullet wound of a raid. The camel's great size and lethargic movements make her pace appear funereal,

Shaikh of Qatar's Fort Doha

but the brisk movements of the small man ahead show that her average walking pace in easy- country is about three miles an hour. Couched, her head swings superciliously from side to side and her filthy cud- filled mouth opens expectantly as her rider approaches, for she has been trained to rise instantly she feels the slightest touch to her back. Mounting has therefore to be a quick leap, which she often anticipates by a fraction of a second. Then she must be couched again with more knee-tapping. But so long as her master's riding cane is stuck in the sand by her head or his rifle lies on the sands in her sight she will sit contentedly. It is when he takes these things in his hands that she shows signs of nervous anticipation.

Shaikh Abdullah Al Thani (ruler of Qatar centre), Shaikh Muhammed Al Mana (right) and Salith

Mounted, she is always given her head, the halter being frequently unused, only a tapping on her neck with the cane, and a few guttural noises being required to teach her to obey her rider's will. Her own disposition tempts her to almost every tuft of food in the way; even she will crunch some fragment of white desiccated bone against her ridiculous toothless upper jaw unless her master urges her past in discouragement, as he normally will.

And so the Badu sits jogging along hour after hour with an occasional change of seat. In an Omani saddle he will not ride astride for long, but tuck his feet up under his haunches in a sitting-kneeling position, or ride side-saddle with his legs dangling limply. The double-poled Murra saddle admits of less variety, but is more comfortable to Europeans as the legs can be crossed to rest on her shoulders.

Most Badawin go bareheaded, a great shock of tousled dark brown hair being sufficient protection from the sun. They will draw daggers as they ride along and scratch their own locks unabashed.

The rifle of a mounted Arab is generally carried in one hand across the animal's back; Rashidi saddles lend them- selves to packing it;

with a Murra saddle it leans up rakishly from a bucket, its bunches of tasselled thongs flapping merrily to the jogging. The Badu is a cheerful companion, generally humming some chant to himself. Occasionally he will burst forth *double forte* without any warning to his companions, who seem, however, always appreciative. Sometimes two would sing a duet, in unison of course. These chants vary between tribes; I was curious to record every one I heard so far as European notation would allow. At other times they engaged each other in trials of strength, attempting to unseat one another while on the march, the loser's penalty being a ten-foot drop on to the sands.

Hamad, my *rabia*, was the strong man among them, and I had one or two indecisive tussles; then we tried a wrestling match with no better results, though I was head and shoulders the taller.

To dismount, a Badu will not normally couch his camel but side-slip off her, so also to mount, he will clamber up a fore-leg while she is on the move, gripping it just above the knee between his big and second toe, hauling himself up over, her neck and thence vaulting round by means of the hump into a sitting position.

With such acrobatics were my smaller zoological specimens often collected. Now and again there would be a shout from behind, 'namuna. Sahib, *namuna!* [126] An Arab would come running up with some small creature to go into my killing-bottle and, not infrequently, some fairy-tale about it.

One day a podgy white slug — a repellent creature which lives in the nostrils of a camel till she sneezes it out - was brought along with the remark, 'It is this small creature that has brought camels to the service of man. But for it, the camel would have been as wild as the fox and the gazelle, fit only to be hunted and eaten.'

Another day it was a sand-spider of the kind that had woven a web over the footmarks of the Prophet when he fled before the infidels, so deceiving his pursuers and saving him.

My companions were ever punctilious about prayer, especially Salih, who would in the mid-afternoon look up:

'Is it the hour of prayer. Sahib?'

'After half an hour,' [127] I would say, looking at my watch and pointing to some pastures ahead. Halts for prayer were indeed deter-mined where possible by the presence of camel grazing. Towards the day's end the party was usually stretched out over a mile or more so that my companions on the march would pray in twos and threes wherever they happened to find themselves, and not all together in line as for the camp prayer.

The camel went away grazing as her master made his devotions and ten minutes later there would be shouts of *'Hir-r-r'* (trilled) *'Shom,'* followed by her name. She would look up and wait, statuesquely, for him to come and fetch her; *'Muh'* or *'Ra ra ra'* (rolled) are calls for an unled camel getting out of line on the march.

The boredom of a long silence was often broken by an outburst from somebody. 'God is great and there is none other but He.' A pious answer is always ready.

'The day is cold!' I might say.

'It is from Allah,' would be the reply. To wish it other- wise were blasphemous. From God always, and everything. Never was there a firmer faith in the inevitability of events - murder, raids, disease, all are part of the Divine plan. Each has its written hour.

But there is also a merrier mood. Now and then a Badu will remember some favourite rhyme, perhaps about Bu Zaid or Dhiyab bin Ghanim, or other giant of antiquity.

Salih came riding alongside one day reciting the Bani Hillal's self-satisfied reflections concerning their enemies.

'These are sparrows, and Bu Zaid a *sidr* tree.

Them we put to flight; and to its shade return.

For wolf wound there is medicine.

For Bu Zaid's spear-thrust there is no medicine.

The blood gushes forth as from the well-bucket

Drawn up brimming and swiftly outpoured.'

'And swiftly outpoured,' came from another rider, characteristi-cally repeating the last phrase. Then he turned to me, 'Our Lord Muhammad has said, "Bu Zaid will be found in Paradise."'

I showed no signs of surprise. Then another admirer broke in:

'O Bu Zaid! O Bu Zaid! Bu Mukhaimar!

Thy sword unsheathed, the stricken liveth not.
How many water-holes hast thou passed and not counted [128]
In the watches of the night after the sun had set.
Seen how many waterings with empty bellies [129]
In the day when eyes were closed in sleep. [130] '

I confessed a preference for Arab prose to Arab poetry, and so one fell to telling me the story of the combat of Dhiyab bin Ghanim and Alan the Slave of Risha.

'Alan was the slave of Zenaiti, and, a much feared foe of Bani Hillal, for whoever among them crossed swords with him was surely killed. So they came to Bu Zaid and be- sought him to slay Alan's horse. But Bu Zaid had given his word that he would not, for when he was a prisoner of Zenaiti's, Alan had come to him and said, "Let us swear an oath that if we meet in combat neither of us shall harm the other." And Bu Zaid had sworn. So when he escaped and had raised a *gom* to rescue his brother Baraiga, he could not take part in the attack but must stand aside. And it was the custom for each party to send a champion to fight before the walls of Zenaiti's fort. And the champion of Zenaiti was the slave Alan, and death was the portion of whoever entered the lists against him - thus the three sons of Dhiyab bin Ghanim and the loved one Amr bin Khafaiyat died. And Alan was mounted on a horse the like of which was never seen before or since, and when it neighed the horses of Bani Hillal became cold with fear and their riders powerless to do ought with them. And Alan's strat- agem was to unseat his adversary by means of a long chain that had a hook attached, and this he launched skilfully to catch in the chain- armour of his opponent, whom Alan would drag from the saddle and slay.

'The Bani Hillal took counsel together and they said, "As Bu Zaid will not fight this foe there is only one other who can, that is Dhiyab bin Ghanim." So Dhiyab was sent for and he came. And Dhiyab took three garments and boiled them so that they were reduced to pulp and these he donned instead of chain-armour. Then he filled the ears of his mare with mud so that she should not hear the neighing of Alan's horse. And now the field of combat was ready; it lay before the fort of

Zenaiti and was fronted by a deep moat which Alan, after he had slaughtered a foe, must jump to enter the fort.

'The two warriors came on from opposite ends. And as they approached the centre suddenly Alan's horse neighed, whereupon Dhiyab cunningly turned his mare back upon Bani Hillal and retreated in order to draw his adversary away from the fort. Alan pursued hotly and when he came within striking distance hurled his hook. It caught lightly in the outer mantle of Dhiyab but instead of unseating him, merely tore a piece of the outer garment away; again Alan threw his hook, only to catch in Dhiyab's second garment, and then a third time with no better success. Alan was now discomfited and himself turned to retire with Dhiyab racing after him. And when Alan's horse arrived at the edge of the moat it neighed as was its wont, but Dhiyab's mare, not hearing it, leapt the moat immediately after it and so Dhiyab came up with Alan at the entrance to Zenaiti's fort. Here Alan, who was arrayed in a suit of chain-armour, so that only his eyes appeared, turned his head to see where his adversary was, and as he did so Dhiyab launched his spear and it penetrated Alan's eye and passed through his head and buried itself to a half of its length in the wall of the fort.

'And Alan, as he lay dying where he fell, looked up and asked:

' "Dhib or Dhiyab?" for an Alim had told him that one of such a name would be his overcomer.

'Said Dhiyab: "Dhiyab."

'Alan (with his last breath): *ufi al hisab*" - the day of reckoning.'

The night of 1st-2nd February was raw and cold, and I was awake before the Dawn call to prayer. The big moon in the western sky dwarfed proud Jupiter, whose glory had been unchallenged a fortnight earlier when she was young. From the procession of constellations across the bright tropical sky I had learned to know the hour. To-night were first Regulus and the Sickle (also suffering like Jupiter from a relative proximity to the Moon), then Spica and his Spanker and so on to Scorpio, a magnificent constellation in the east, with Venus to keep him company. I had watched her sliding down his body these last few nights. At midnight I rose to take sights of Polaris, but found that the adjustment of my sextant, a daily requirement after the jolting of the march, had to-night passed finally beyond my power to effect. My star observations (which I had carried out in secrecy throughout) would have been prevented this evening in any case by the presence of a Badu, whose form silhouetted against the moonlit sky, now erect, now kneeling, showed him to be at prayer - surely an act of supererogation at this hour.

At dawn the eastern sky was awash in a sea of blood, crossed by long purple clouds like ledging reefs, amidst which the stars soon paled and vanished.

We made an early start, returning at first on last night's tracks towards the towering hill of Nakhala through rolling sands that now and then obscured it. Two Murra guides, Hamad, Talib and I, clambered up its steep soft sides to the top, and were rewarded with a distant glimpse of the waters of the Persian Gulf. It was a sunny balmy day, and a glorious panorama lay about Nakhala, a waste of low sands stretching westward to the habitations of Jafura, and eastwards over ridges of bare sandhills to the sea. The vast, almost uninhabited wastes of Rub Al Khali stretched for weeks behind us, before us lay but a march of four days to the dwellings of men.

We descended. The aneroid registered below sea-level readings, as indeed it had done on the day before, and throughout the next day. Beyond some sandhills we came to Sabkhat al Manasir, a salt-field several square miles in extent, thickly strewn with sea-shells in an early state of fossilisation. [131]

Keeping the sea a day's march on our right hand, we proceeded on a northerly course through quarry-like country of extreme desolation. A wolf was heard near the bluff of Farhud, where I collected other shells in a more advanced state of petrification.

The water-hole of Khafus gave rise to a dispute among my companions whether our camels should be watered there. The Ayes had it, and a halt of fifty minutes gave me an opportunity of climbing an outstanding crest to take bearings on hill-points said to be over the coast - a bold course that with pay-day now in sight I felt I could afford; also I had, perhaps, after these long weeks with my companions, gained a little of their confidence.

The following day our course, a shade to east of north, had taken us through more of this quarry-like wilderness, when, after a six-mile march, I beheld before me a large silver lake. I had learnt from my Badawin that we should pass on our right hand a certain Sabkha Amra, and had naturally supposed that it would be a dry salt-plain, like the sabkhas of the recent marches. Wherefore a lake some seven miles in length, and perhaps a mile and a half wide, came as a pleasant surprise. As we approached its southern end I picked up two large sea-shell fossils. Thence our course lay in a low flinty plain that edged its north side, its south shore appearing to be low sandhills.

While I photographed it, which I must needs do, straight into the sun under a yellow cloudy sky, my Badawin collected from its margin large chunks of -rock salt, which they would use in cooking their rice. [132]

The border, some twenty feet broad, had a snow-like appearance, and at a distance it was impossible to see where the salt ended and the water began. Within some six feet of the water's edge ran a line of dead white locusts - desiccated specimens probably of the large red variety that is an Arab delicacy. The wretched creatures swarm from the desert in the spring and take a suicidal plunge into the first water they meet. The position suggested that the edge of the lake had receded during the year, but no explanation was vouchsafed by the two Murras, who alone of my party had been here before. The slope was so slight that a little rain, or summer evaporation, would account for the change of level.

After leaving the lake a more north-easterly course towards the hog-backed Jabal 'Udaid led us through a plain sown with jagged splintered stones to another spacious salt plain, here called Amra. It is said to stretch westwards past the ancient sites of Iskak, Salwa and Mabak to the shores of Qatar Bight. Lake salt, and recent shell evidences and aneroid readings suggest that the base of the Qatar Peninsula was at no very distant time depressed below the sea, [133]

Qatar making an island like neighbouring Bahrain, [134] but many times bigger.

My companions had halted in the plain for afternoon prayer. As I came up, Ugaba, my camel, decided the place suited her. She refused to be urged on ahead alone and sat bellowing for bint Riman, her usual companion on the march - an irreverent accompaniment to the audible supplications of the Faithful. I was taken to task afterwards for making an elementary mistake, that of giving her the wrong signal. She had been taught to rise to a tap of the stick on her quarters, and my tapping her neck kept her couched. An unwilling camel is provoking, but no Badu will ever be seen laying a stick about her for fear of spoiling what good qualities she has. If annoyed with her, he will shout:

'Hai! (nasal) Come to thee kharash' - a wasting disease.

'Hai! Come to thee death, lawful or unlawful.'

'Hai! Come to thee a great burden.'

But in his heart he means nothing of the kind. He has a genuine attachment for her which he knows is not reciprocated. And so when she stumbles, it is more likely to be:

'Hai! thy deliverance.'

'Hai! Allah deliver thee' from evil.'

Even when he has tramped for miles in pursuit of his straying camel, he approaches her with the words:

'Hai! God bless thee,' or

Ya hai bish fulana - greeting her by name. [135]

Fresh marks of camels identified with the Manasir tribe induced us to press on, for Hamad, the Murri, was in no mood to meet them.

A few distant grazing camels against the sky caused alarmist exchanges among my party. Talib, who was persona grata with local Manasir, rode ahead to spy out the land and conceal the constitution of our party if necessary, while we made a detour to avoid them.

'There is one thing I want from you when we arrive. Sahib,' said Sahail.

'What is that

'Tobacco.'

'But this is the Fast of Ramadhan.'

'Tobacco is the one thing I cannot do without. Sahib. I fast from everything but tobacco.'

'But is it not a sin?'

'By God it is, but what shall a man do? - and it is only this Ramadhan, in no previous year have I drunk tobacco.'

Formalists would doubtless hold that Sahail had broken the fast by smoking, so that there was no virtue in the rest of his abstinence. Sahail, however - he was the only smoker in my escort - did not avail himself of the lawful privilege of the traveller to break the fast altogether. He was fasting in the spirit, though had any fanatic rebuked him he would doubtless have taken it humbly.

'God have mercy on me,' I heard him mutter as I pushed on ahead.

Talib our *rabia*, who had trotted off to investigate the unknown camels, now came riding back towards us. While yet a hundred yards off he was shouting:

'Have you prayed? Have you prayed?'

'Yes, God be glorified!' my companions shouted back.

He came closer to cry:

'*Ya haiyakum ya haiyakum* good news! if God wills,' and my party crowded round him for the latest gossip of the desert.

A few minutes later Shaikh Salih dropped back to ride by my side.

'Good news!' he said.

'God be praised.'

"Abdul 'Aziz bin Sa'ud is in Riyadh. The governors - a reference also to Bin Jaluwi of Hasa - are in their towns; still they rule!' [136]

'Thank God,' said a third.

'And in Jafura is life' (i.e. pastures from recent rains).

'God be praised,' came a chorus of Badawin, for fresh pastures at hand would let them turn aside on their return journey to rest and fatten their mounts for some weeks preparatory to the long march back to the southern sands.

Rain was indeed falling where we halted for prayer.

Close by on a stone an owl sat blinking, and allowed a Badu to creep up within thirty yards of it, seeming to know how difficult a target it made, for the shot having missed, it calmly perched itself within close range of another rifle, and only took clumsily to wing when that shot also went wide.

My companions remarked the footmarks of asses an hour later when we passed the six-fathom water-hole of Zurga, the water supply of the well-to-do of Doha. Following the beaten track at a sluggish pace, we saw in the distance a large herd of camels grazing - sign that hereabouts were probably the most favoured pastures in the neighbourhood. Talib was sent ahead again to investigate, while my companions talked hopefully of a milk dinner. Unrealised hope - though Talib brought back a large clod of dates from the single slave herdsman he had found in charge of the Qatar camels. To me it seemed likely that he had deprived the poor wretch of the bulk of his food supply - the dates sufficed for the whole of my party that night - but it is desert pride and desert law to give generously to-day to the passing guest, and to-morrow to know hunger and be without the means of appeasing it.

Shaikh of Qatar's Fort Doha

It was a bleak, bitter evening; no stick of firewood anywhere availed, only miserable fires of dung were possible. Drizzling rain fell through the night, and I woke to find my blankets drenched; so that to breakfast in the dry I lay under my camp table. But it was to be my last breakfast in the desert, and so whatever the conditions, they could be supported cheerfully.

We were arriving. The Badawin moved forward at a sharp pace, chanting the water chants. Our thirsty camels pricked up their ears with eager knowingness. The last sandhill was left behind. After the next undulation we saw in the dip of the stony plain before us Na'aija, where we had planned a final watering, and beyond it the towers of Doha silhouetted against the waters of the Persian Gulf. Half an hour later we entered the walls of the fort. The Rub Al Khali had been crossed.

ENDNOTES

1 The adventurous Portuguese of the sixteenth century, in their day the most gallantly ruthless of Europeans in Asia, thought Risut worthy of their steel and blood; a flight of steps and some ruined fortifications still stand memorial to them. To-day Risut is the only possible seaplane base on this stretch of central South Arabian shore for some hundreds of miles during the summer monsoon months.

2 The word Dhufar has also a more limited application. It some-times stands for the capital of the province merely, that is, a group of three villages, Salala, Hafa and Al Husn, in a way corresponding with the Badu habit of the sands where Hofuf is called only Hasa, and Doha, Qatar

3 This movement finds a parallel in two other seasonal movements of man in South-east Arabia — the migration to the gardens for the ripening date-harvest of Oman, and to the Trucial coast for the summer pearl fisheries.

4 The ruins about Khor Ruri— Husn Mirahadh and the entrance of Inqitat (Bent's Khatiya) - occupy the probable site of the ancient port of Moscha of the Periplus (Ptolemy's Abyssapolis as suggested by Bent). The Arab geographers give Murbat as the site of the ancient seaport and capital of Dhufar, which lasted until the tenth century of

our era. Modern Murbat is twenty miles to the eastward of its prototype, which was here. And Murbat in the Shahari tongue is Sik, which
would appear to preserve the important radicals of the name Moscha.

5 *Dhaaf*- Dhufar has a caste system below the noble rank of tribesman. Thus there are the *Bahara* and *Dhaaf* as well as the slave community. The (literally, 'weak,' though the connotation corresponds with
the *Baiyasira* of Oman) are a degree above the *Bahara* in the scale, in
that their women do not appear in public. Also only the *Bahara* and
slaves fish.

6 The blockade applied only to the transport of sardines. The
secret of its success as a weapon lay in the fact that the mountain
wealth is chiefly in cattle, and at certain 'dry' seasons of the year, here,
as in Oman, sardines are the usual fodder

7 A typical feature of the large houses and the mosques is this roof
ornamentation called *tabashir*; it will be found at the corners of the
roof and at intervals along the sides. Its stepped design recalls the
Nabatean ornament at Petra and Mada'in Salih. I was told that it is
met with in Makalla and Sheher and elsewhere in the Hadhramaut,
but I have not met with it in Muscat or Oman. .

8 Coco-nut palm is in universal use in Dhufar for window sashes
and ceiling rafters, and good and enduring material it is, in contrast to
the fibrous and inferior date-palm log of Oman buildings. .

9 The Four Seasons of the Year are called:

- *Kharif*: July to September- the rain months.
- *Surub*: October to December.
- *Shitta*: January to March.
- *Al Gaidh*: April to June.

10 I discovered there was an exception to this rule of a slave wife's
progeny belonging exclusively to her owner, but it applies only to the
Court. In case of a Court male slave marrying a female slave; of a
private owner, the progeny, as a Court privilege, must be shared. The
result is that a private owner will agree only reluctantly to a Court
slave alliance because it is unprofitable for him, and a Court slave

finds it correspondingly difficult to find a bride outside the circle of Court negresses.

11 Although my position was that of Wazir to His Highness the Sultan, and I had introduced the copper currency of Muscat into the Province in 1926 (before that time there was only exchange by barter), I had no jurisdiction in Dhufar, nor indeed had the Muscat and Oman Council of Ministers, of which I was a member. The Sultan treated Dhufar as a Royal Domain. His rule through the Wali was personal and untrammelled by any foreign influence; the regime was tribal, which I think to be the best form of government for tribal Arabia.

12 The most characteristic feature of these ruins is a plain primitive column, with octagonal shaft, square corbelled capital and similar square base, a monolith. It is usually only six feet high, and this and its corbelled cap surest that it supported arches. A raised, plinth, rising in steps to a man's height, supports two columns, or more according to size, and round about lies debris of squared stones, black with age.

13 The infection said to be brought by dhow from the Persian Gulf.

14 This is a feature of the mountain dress. A leather bag, with shoulder straps, hangs dose under the armpit. The variety used for carrying money and clothes is called *haban*. The *anit* is used only for food, dates and water.

15 *Saiyids* are the descendants of Hasan, *Sharifs* of Husain. In reality, of course, they are not the lineal descendants of the Prophet, but of Ali, who married the Prophet's daughter, Fatima. The Omanis, whose sect is 'Ibadhism (the ancient Khuwarij) and to whom Ali's name is therefore anathema, have the apposite saying, 'Ask a mule what his father was.' His reply will be, 'My mother was a horse.'

16 I should here mention that the panther is found in the more unfrequented wooded valleys; the Arabian *Ibex Tar* lives beyond the habitable mountains and in the Jabal Samhan; foxes are found everywhere, and gazelle are numerous in the plains.

17 *at, ait and ai* are the Shahari versions of bait
ir, air, bir are the Shahari versions of bin.

18 Except for the Al Kathir wedge in the central west between Gurzaz and Thifa.

19 Of the four languages spoken, viz. Shahari, Mahri, Bautahari, Harsusi, I have made vocabularies, each of five hundred words, and deduced a few simple grammatical rules. They belong to the Semitic group, but have closer structural affinities with Ethiopic than with Arabic

(i) Shahari is spoken by Qara, Shahara, Barahama, Bait ash Shaikh.

(ii) Mahri by Mahra and Bilhaf.

(iii) Bautahari by Bautahara.

(iv) Harsusi (Aforit) by Harasis and Afar.

Shahari is normally unintelligible to users of the other languages, who, however, can understand one another with difficulty. I was unaware that Mahri and Shahari had been written up by the German philologist Dr. Maximilian Bittner, working on material collected in the Hadhramaut and Socotra by Dr. Muller's Arabian Expedition (1902) and by Count Landberg's Expedition (1898-99).

My Harsusi and Bautahari, which appear to be variants of Mahri, have never before, I think, been recorded.

20 It is not, I think, impossible that the word Dhufar in origin was susceptible of the division Dhu Afar (the medial Arabic article al is not met with in these South Arabian languages), meaning the Red Country. Modifications of the word *Afar* are common, e.g.:

Afar = one of the largest frankincense groves.

Afar = a large wadi: is also the name of a tribe.

Afaur = a large wadi.

Aufur = clouds; and the meaning, 'a cloudy country,' would be just as apt as a 'red' country.

21 The large wadis from east to west are Darbat, Ghazot, Ajarthun, Raithot, Arbot, Nihaz, Gurzaz.

22 A name given to a cow with drooping horns. Every cow enjoys a separate name. They are hereditary names (like camel or horse families) deriving through the mother. The herdsman claims to .know every head he has, so that if one is stolen, he can identify it a year or two later, even in a strange herd.

23 A list of camel chants and mountain chants was recorded as well as European notation would permit.

24 The religious law of Islam prescribes categorically how a man's estate must be divided. The right of bequest is strictly limited, and among tribesmen is almost non-existent. The lawful wives and all children are entitled to a due share of the estate; to a daughter one share, to a son two, and to the wives one-eighth of the estate between them. Where there are no sons, the paternal uncle, or in default of such, the paternal male cousins, receive the son's share.

25 I am informed that chicken, eggs and fish are not eaten by tribesmen in the Medina area.

26 The origin may well have been to drain away the blood, perhaps to feed the god at the altar; cf. Genesis ix. 4 , *'Flesh with the life thereof winch is the blood thereof, shall ye not eat.'*

27 A script worn as a charm is invested with magic virtues. The credulous have no particular concern whether or not it be from Holy Writ, although it is often a verse from the Qur'an, as the scribe knows no other. Venerated Saiyids do very good business, particularly just before the exodus to the mountains, by vending such. A dollar script will protect against the Evil Eyes two dollars for an ailing cow; and more as the price of general immunity.

28 This wood is exceedingly heavy, and sinks in water. It grows only in the mountains of Dhufer.

29 I should perhaps use the word 'colt,' following Genesis xxxii. 15, 'Thirty milch camels with their colts.'

30 This term is used in the Persian Gulf and on the coast of Arabia to denote a British Political Agent. It is said to be derived, by metathesis, from the low Latin *bailus*, Lat. *bajulus*, from Bailo, the title of the representative of the Venetian Republic at the Sublime Porte.

31 I am told that in the Upper Euphrates valley circumcision of males is done at puberty, females never; and puberty is loosely interpreted to mean twelve to eighteen.

32 Usually a shaikh or man of good family, whereas in Oman only a gypsy or menial will officiate.

33 With the Mahra tribe male circumcision at one time was

carried out on the eve of a man's marriage. To-day a decent interval is allowed. Men and women foregather round desert fires. Eight or ten of the most presentable females are paraded and the men declare who is the most beautiful of them, while the remaining ladies protest characteristically, 'No! No! No! No!'

34 The presence of pubic and armpit hair in the female is not permissible. She removes it by plucking, using a wax of frankincense.

35 This is the contrary, as regards cows, of the rule observed by the Arabs of Oman, where a man would lose caste by milking. The Mahra and Al Kathir of these mountains allow their women to milk sheep, but not cows or camels.

36 After cattle are stalled at night, women will sometimes go among them carrying burning incense.

37 The Shara' or Islamic code is distasteful to them, and runs only in the coastal townships where the government imposes it by force. It may be resorted to, elsewhere, in matrimonial cause, but civil disputes and crimes are the province of the *hauz*, who is the tribal law-man, holding office not infrequently by inheritance. He may, or may not, be the tribal shaikh.

38 A *rabia* is a representative of a tribe whose presence ensures protection from that particular tribe.

39 Only within comparatively recent times would the Bautahara recognise a *rabia* at all.

40 The complete list of local shrines in the order of their avenging powers

is as follows :

Name.	Place.
Salih bin Hud	Between Hasik and Ras Nus.
Bir 'Ali	Murbat.
Bir 'Arabiya	Risut.
Shaikh 'Ali '	Afif Taqa.
Shaikh 'Isa	Khor Taqa.
Zahair	Murbat.
Nabi 'Umran	Hafa.

There is in Hadhramaut the famous Qabr al Nabi Hud, the prophet sent to 'Aj, according to the Qur'an, and therefore a personage of the first rank, but perhaps the most famous anywhere is Bin Juwahir in Mahri country. It is so potent that murder will be tried by it. Two lesser local ones are Bin Othman at Rakhiyot and Nabi 'Aiyub, the only one to be found in the Qara Mountains.

41 The story is in the Qur'an, but not, of course, with Christians as the tormentors.

42 *bin* (Ar.), *bint* (Ar.) = son of, daughter of, become in these languages *bir* and *birt*. Sometimes the *b* is elided, whence *ir* and *irt*.

43 A list of chants was recorded as well as European notation would permit.

44 The Prophet himself was the issue, not of cousins german, but very distantly related.

45 My collection from these mountains was composed of the following: Badger 1, Conies 2, Foxes 3, Frog 1, Hyenas 5, Lizards 28, Scorpions 16, Snakes 21, Tree bats 2, Tree rats 2, Wolf 1, Butterflies 96, Centipedes 4, Dragonflies 61, Locusts 50,Various Insects 112 (praying mantis, spiders, hornets, etc.)

46 There are two hostile political factions, Hinawi and Ghafari, to one or other of which every tribe in South-east Arabia owes allegiance. Superficially the terms Hinawi and Ghafari would appear to date from a dynastic squabble over succession in Oman in the early

eighteenth century, but, as I have observed elsewhere, they are of
much deeper significance, for, generally speaking, the Hinawi label
coincides with the tribes of avowed Qahtani descent and the Ghafari
label with those of Ma'adic or Nizari origin, and all other non-Yemeni
stock. Within limits, therefore, the division is in origin racial. These
labels apply as far west as the Sa'ar tribe, who are regarded as Ghafari,
whereas Al Kathir, of which Ar Rashid are a section, are Hinawi. So
also is the central bloc labelled Ghafari, though in South Arabia as
distinct from Oman, there is no factional solidarity, and these labels
have no political significance.

Ma'arab and Mishgas are used in South Arabia as regional terms
for westwards and eastwards of Dhufar respectively. Thus the Sa'ar
and all other western tribes are Ahl al Ma'arab.

47 Ant-hills are *sidr* in Shahari, the ants themselves *izdirit*,

48 *subaigha*.

49 Groves are graded by size into,

(1) *manzila*, of great extent, of which the most famous are Afaur,
Asug, Afar, Gizilaut, Zuwa, Ata, Tanshit, Qaim and Amaut;

(2) *hawil*, of a size that can be worked by five collectors or fewer.

There are three varieties of frankincense: *negedi (nejdi), shazari* and
sha'abi, their quality descending in the same order. *Negedi*, the silver
variety, is the product of the intra-montane uplands of the Samhan
and Qara mountains; *shazari* is the product of the mountain region of
that name at the junction of the Qamar and Qara ranges; and *sha'abi* is
a poor quality of the plain around Risut. The frankincense ports from
west to east are Jadhib, Rakhiyut, Risut, 'Auqad, Salala, Hafa, Taqa,
Murbat, Sudh and Hadhbaram.

50 Sahail = Canopus, a name common among Badawin.

51 This name is commonly given to water-holes supposed to have
been formed in this manner,

52 The antelope's other virtues are its skin for leather; its blood
for snake bite; its flesh for exorcism (*hamara*, to be described later); its
soup for joint pains; its flesh for meat. They rate it better food than
any other beast, a view I could not subscribe to. Perhaps they reckon
by the after-effects of gluttony upon an empty stomach, for though

their diet is usually frugal, moderation on such an occasion is an unknown virtue, and my medicine chest was always in requisition after a night orgy following a 'kill.'

53 The Hebrew word used is *rim*.

54 On every journey I have made during the past six years in Oman, and in South-east and central South Arabia, I have heard the same story. The natives avow that there has been a falling off of rains, scant though they ever were, within their lifetime. The date crop of interior Oman is but a half of what it was a generation ago, and many plantations, have perished of drought.

55 Wadi Mugshin, surely the Prince of Wadis in all South-east Arabia, for nowhere have I met its like, consists of a belt of giant acacia (*ghaf*) jungle thirty miles long (east and west axis) on the south-eastern edge of Ar Rimal. At its eastern extremity (altitude about 400 feet) drinkable water comes to the surface at 'Ain or 'Ainain. A considerable date grove growing wild and unattended lines the banks of a marshy bed, and to the eastward is a trough-like pond a few hundred yards long and some fifteen wide.

56 The tributary wadis are systems in themselves. Thus Wadi Katibit has affluents Andhaur, Dhahibun, Ingudan, Ghazal and Rakibit draining the eastern part of the Qara Mountains and the western part of Samhan. The eastern limit of the system in Andhaur which rises approximately north of Murbat Peak (whose alternative name shown on the chart as Jabal Du'an is unknown to the inhabitants, by whom it is known as .Zairutun). Wadi Dauka rises in the longitude of Salala and receives Al Hauf, Dha'arfit and Ista. Wadi Ghudun rises slightly to the west of Dauka and receives Hila, Dhuhair and Haluf on its right bank and Ghara on its left. Wadi Aidan rises in the longitude of Rakhiyut and with its two large tributaries Difin and Habarut, rising respectively north of Jadhib and Damkut, drains the whole of the Qamr range. Wadi Shihin and Wadi Hat are shorter systems rising at the respective eastern and western extremities of Fatk-Shaghuwat

57 Tribal distribution is as follows: the Umm al Hait system is the habitat mainly of two tribes, Mahra and Bait Kathir; they also extend

to the west. Nominally the lower wadi reaches of Dauka, Ghudun, Aidam and Hat belong to Bait Kathir, though the Mahra use them freely; the upper sources of the wadis (except Ghudun) are largely in Mahra hands, particularly Habarut, Ghazal, Ingudan and Dhahibun, as well as the individual wadis immediately to the west. Scattered about amidst the Mahra and Bait Kathir are a number of small Hadara tribes, non-Arab survivals. Thus to the westward of Hat in its lower courses is found the Bilhaf, a rather nondescript tribe owing allegiance to no faction, but Mahri in speech. A distinguishing feature of their dress is that they carry a knife, not a dagger, in their belts. They neither raid nor are raided, and like the Salub of Nejd are accepted as a *rabia* by all. They are also servants of the Shrine of Jauhari (Umm al Tabbakh) where the Mahra pay pilgrimages and make sacrifices. At the eastern extremity of the Umm al Hait system Wadi Andhaur is nominally a possession of the Bautahara (Bit Bohor) though the Mahra tribesmen are usually in evidence there. The Bautahara, a now dwindling and *declasse* tribe, most of whom are fishermen, with an exclusive language, were once the reputed possessors of the whole eastern steppe from Wadi Ghudun (of the Kathir) to Wadi Qadun (?) (of the Harasis), while the western steppe is reputed to have belonged to the now legendary Bin Dhurbut. Elements of another small tribe, 'Afar, live in Habarut with the Mahra and the equally obscure Bait ash Shaikh (Bit Istait or sometimes Insakht), and thought to be collateral with the Shahara, occupy Wadi Ingudan near the water-hole of Hanun. To the westwards of the Umm al Hait system the Mahra tribe extends to Wadi Rama, thence Manahil to Wadi al Jauf; 'Awamir succeed as far as Wadi Khadhra, whence commences the Sa'ar habitat.

58 With the Harasis and Mahra a curious custom obtains — that of never milking their sheep into a cold receptacle. A hot stone, heated in a fire, must first be introduced. The explanation it suggests, that the warmth thus applied to the udders encourages a facile milking, is not wholly satisfactory, because the practice is observed only in respect of sheep, not of camels. A shepherdess of the Bait ash Shaikh tribe, from whom I purchased a sheep in Wadi Dhikur, would not agree to its being slaughtered in sunlight because of the fear that it would bring

misfortune to her family, and this also was a common belief. A Harsusi of my escort informed me that in no very distant times past the Harasis would not only not slaughter, but not milk their flocks in sunlight, and to this day there are two breeds of sheep, *banat al murtal* and *banat al muqtuf* which no tribesman of whatsoever tribe would dare slaughter until after dark.

59 The Kathiri tribesmen use a formula in the Shahari dialect of the mountains. This I have recorded but not yet translated.

60 The configuration of the accretions of sand curiously resembles the front of an elephant's head.

61 The notion must be modern, for the sun helmet has not been in use among Europeans in the East for more than a century; it is unknown in the Americas, and not, I believe, worn in Australia or South Africa.

62 I am indebted to Mr. Philby for drawing my attention to the similarity of Ubar with the form Wabar, None of the 'serious' Arab geographers mention the place, but Yaqut gives a copious selection of local tradition, all to the same purpose. The place is generally defined as lying in the sands 'between Shihir and Sana'.' It was a great city in a fertile oasis belonging to the tribe of Ad, and its inhabitants were punished for their sins by being turned into *nasnas* — a kind of monkey with only half a body, one eye, one arm, one leg and so on. Since then it has been inhabited by *jinn* who endeavour to prevent approach to it and destroy those who reach it. The Mahra camels are descended from the offspring of the camels of these *jinn*. In some stories the people of Shihir are represented as hunting the *nasnas* and even eating them. The South Arabian archaeologist Nashwan bin Sa'id d/573 AH/1117 A.D., says only: 'Wabar is the name of the land which belonged to 'Ad in the eastern parts of Yemen; to-day it is an untrodden desert owing to the drying up of its water. There are to be found in it great buildings which the wind has smothered in sand. It is said also that it belonged to the people of Ar Ras.' It is possibly more than a coincidence that Arisha (the land of the Ruler Zenaiti of the desert folklore) is the Shahari equivalent of Ras (Arabic).

63 In the Rashidi dialect of the southern sands, as distinct from the

northern dialect of the Murra, **J** is pronounced **Y**, thus Jaub = Yaub, and Jiban = Yiban. It is possible that the **Y** in Miniyor, Yadila and Yibaila is a **J**.

64 *Hanaina* = bellowing. The two tribes of the sands use different terms for singing sands. The Rashid call it *Al Damam*, and the Murra *Al Hiyal*.

65 The modern use of this word is equally unfair to the enchanting voices of the Sirens of the *Odyssey*.

66 *abu fulan*. In Arabia a man will often call himself be known as 'the father of a son's name,' a commentary on the honour in which parent- hood of males is held. Indeed, Saiyid Taimur bin Faisal, the Sultan of Muscat, almost invariably signed himself in private correspondence, Abu Sa'id,' his son, Saiyid Sa'id, being the heir apparent.

67 I found the word *bunduq* (pl. *banadiq*) in common use in the sands for 'rifle.' This confirms Yule's note in Hobson-Jobson that the Hindustani derives through the Arabic.

68 I have heard that the local gypsum is used to build a water-trough in summer round these water-holes.

69 The word wadi, i.e. 'valley,' or here a 'dry water-course,' is used by these Badawin not so much in a topographical sense but as a term for pastures. *Al Wadi al kabir* (there is a Moorish relic in the Spanish Guadalquivir), meaning the big wadi, often stands in the colloquial tongue for good pastures, and not necessarily for a huge valley, or stream.

70 There is an isolated island of sand to the eastwards in the Ja'alan triangle, which is the habitat of the Yal Wahiba tribe.

71 Between desert men the nose kiss takes the place of hand-shaking. With Bait Kathir under the mountains it is observed after a five or six days' separation, but seldom oftener; here in the sands Badawin salute each other thus if separated for only one day. The Mahra in the steppe, though a Badawin tribe, are peculiar in using amongst themselves not the nose kiss but a triple cheek kiss, right, left, right.

72 If Bait Imani is excluded from Ar Rashid (and they are now regarded as having achieved autonomy}, the tribe consists of two

sections, Mat'ariba and Sa'adna, the latter the shaikhly house of which Saif was the head,

73 Hamad was the headman of the Hathalain, a subsection of Al Ghuferan, one of the divisions of Al Murra.

74 This marriage price would go entirely to the father. With Bait Kathir in the mountains the marriage-price of a virgin bride may vary between twenty dollars and three hundred dollars, according to her family, face and fortune, but a half only goes to her father, the remainder being divided between the other near relatives. I have met a case of a two-hundred-dollar bride (which places her high in the scale of social values) where the division was as follows: father (half), one hundred dollars; brother, thirty; mother, twenty; sister, nothing; paternal uncle, twenty; maternal uncle, ten; paternal aunt, five; maternal aunt, four; paternal grandfather, four; paternal grand-mother, three; byes, i.e. unaccounted for, four. A widow or divorced woman on remarrying would herself get the marriage-price. In Oman the bridegroom pays half the marriage price in advance to the father, and the remaining half after marriage by slow instalments. In theory it goes to the bride for her jewels, bedding and personal adornments.

75 See my book Alarms and Excursions in Arabia,

76 There are many *zars*. This is one of the most popular of them.

77 The route they took is of interest in showing the Rashidis' probable line of retreat before Sa'ar depredations. From Shisur my messengers had moved north-eastwards along the Umm al Hait, struck through the sands of Umm Dharta to those of Ghanim, where they watered at Khasfa and Ablutan, thence north-westwards through the salt-pans and sand-mountains of Mijora to the sands of Hibak, watering at Zughain, thence south-westwards to the bordering water-hole of Fida, on through the sands of Dakaka to the water of Waraiga.

78 Pastures = *mar'a, akl* but generally *ma'ash* (Rashid dialect). To the Badu the best camel-fodder is the *samr* acacia found in the steppe at altitudes above 1200 feet. Next come *abala* and *zahara* shrubs of the sands and *gasis* after rains or dews. *dhu'ya* and *dha'ut* both steppe flora, follow, and then *markh*, found between steppe and sand. Next in the order are *ghaf* acacia and *selem* (known locally as *hardhai*). There are

many other kinds of camel fodder, but these are the mainstays of the southern deserts.

79 Parties of Murra are said to come from time to time and spend the summer in Dakaka on account of its comparatively sweet water.

80 Camels which are frequently watered are called *shuwarib*. Camels away from water in winter for long periods; *jazi* (sing.) *juwazi* (pl.) by Murra or *nash (neish) nuwash* by Rashid.

81 After the first few days, of course, the milk curdles; where marches are long, it is diluted with brackish water.

82 Each true Badu tribe has a particular mark, usually very simple in design, but with significance of an armorial bearing: it is branded on each camel of the tribe on the face, neck or quarter as may be the particular tribal custom. Sections within the tribe sometimes have their own particular *wasm*. A complete list of those met with in Rub Al Khali is given in Appendix V.

83 *Ilfadh*. The Murra, according to Hamad, contrary to South Arabian tastes, do not greatly relish it, and drink it only when suffering from thirst that cannot be satisfied in any other way. The Rashidi word for it, *althudh*, seems to have substituted *th* for *f*, a peculiarity I noticed in other words.

84 W. Campbell Smith of the British Museum received samples

85 A vegetable product of South-west Arabia used in Oman as a skin-dye; it is brought as a fine powder, canary-yellow in colour,

86 Camels are thus, like the llama and the lion, rare in the animal kingdom in the performance of the act in a sitting position. The Badu master is necessary to the operation, scooping the sands round the cow's legs for her comfort, inserting the penis - the formation of which is in reverse axis to nearly all the rest of mammal creation, and interfering after a few minutes to drive the bull off. After ten days if no result is apparent, the cow's master will find another bull to serve her. The sign of pregnancy is the flag-wagging of her ridiculous tail when approached by a rider to mount.

87 A series of short black tattoo lines on the upper and lower gums between the teeth. It is a universal practice of both sexes in

South Arabia, carried out in childhood, and is said to arrest the growth of long teeth and to prevent them from becoming loose:

88 The elements we feared were Bani Hajar and two sections of the Murra - Fuhaida and Al Adhaba.

89 Propitious and unpropitious days were constantly met with in South Arabia. The second and fifth days of the week were held to be good: Friday only moderately so. Sections of the Mahra tribe will never start on a raid or journey on a Sunday at all, or on a Friday until after the midday prayer. The first day of the moon is held to be a good day if it falls on any other day of the week.

Karab and other Hadhramaut Badawin have told me of the following superstitious, beliefs which may or may not hark back to ancient star worship in South Arabia:

{a) During a period of five days, when the moon is in the constellation of Scorpio, action is unpropitious; no raid, journey or the like will ever be undertaken.

{b) The age of the moon is taken as a guide in the direction of a journey. The first, eleventh and twentieth days, called *duwar*, are propitious for movement in any direction.

The semi-circle east-south-west is divided up into ten divisions (bearings) coinciding with the ten days between the duwar. It is unpropitious to move on a bearing that coincides with its day, e.g. third bearing from east on third, thirteenth or twenty-second of the lunar month.

90 Bu Zaid could not tolerate a rival; in his later days he murdered Dhiyab bin Ghanim, a mighty hunter and fighter, though Dhiyab had taken one of Bu Zaid's sisters to wife. Dhiyab's son, when he grew up, slew Bu Zaid to revenge his father, in the traditional Arabian manner.

91 The route of raiders from the sands into the Hadhramaut is therefore restricted, to the westwards, to a north-south route through western Dakaka and Kharkhir. It thence turns west along the southern borders of the sands through a famous corridor called Shaggag al Ma'atif.

92 Circumcision with the Murra takes place at the age of about five or six. Ar Rashid, and to some extent Bait Imani, have of late

years adopted the same practice, giving up the adult circumcision found among their Mahra neighbours to the south, but they still maintain certain rites, the boy being taught to hold his head up bravely during the operation while the onlookers say 'Karim! Karim!'

93 Bainha, so named because it lay midway between the water-hole of Bir Hadi and the Buwah.

94 The identity of his star names with ours, in the case of: Altair = Nasir al Tair; Rigel = Rijl; Scorpio = Al Agrab, i.e. scorpion (Ar) recalls the fact that many of our star names are derived from the Babylonians through the Arabs. I record below some star-names given me by a dweller in the Rub Al Khali who had not been out of the sands;

English	Arabic of Rub' al Khali	English	Arabic of Rub' al Khali
Altair	Nasir al Tair	Regel	Rijl
Vega	Nasir umm Wuga	Betelgeuse	Yid Sa'ad
Polaris	Al Jedi	Bellatrix	Yid al Kesha (Rashidi)
			Yid al Tib (Murri)
Great Bear	As Seba'		
A star called	Banat Nash	Sirius	Mirzem
Capella	Al Imbari	Canopus	Sahail as Saduq
Pleiades	Al Thuraiyya	Achernar	Sahail al Kadhib
Aldebaran	Kelb al Ghanim	Scorpio	Al Agrab
Auriga	Ghanim	(Its tail)	Shola
Orion	Sa'ad	Venus	Zahra
Orion's Belt	Janbiya		
Three small stars	Ausa (penis)		

Venus was the only named planet. They had no name for Jupiter or Mars

Venus was the only named planet. They had no name for Jupiter or Mars

95 Every Badu in the Rub Al Khali carries his rifle in a rude leather case to prevent sand from getting into the mechanism. He makes this case himself, usually from the skin of the antelope or other beast of the chase. Its tip is often decorated with a gay bunch of leather thongs. The well-to-do Arab of Oman decorates the stock of his rifle with bands of silver and gold from the same affectionate sentiment for it.

96 Bin Tannaf is the hereditary tide of the shaikh of the Manahil

tribe. The present holder is one of the most famous of leaders of the raid. The leader has always the perquisite of two or three of the best camels taken, otherwise there is equal division of the spoil as in 1 Samuel xxx. 25.

97 The fox was called *hirr*, which is classical Arabic for 'cat.'

98 The specimens collected in the sands numbered one hundred and twenty-five and were received by the British Museum.

99 A crude pulley-block formed part of the Murri kit: its use is nowhere necessary in the south.

100 The Sa'ar, according to the Rashidis — perhaps a tainted source in view of their relationship - neither pray nor fast. And they mock a Rashidi visitor (in times of peace) who does so, though they swear by Allah and claim to believe in Him, 'They say, God is the Knower! that their ancestor saved the Prophet from the hands of infidels who were intent on slaying him, and the Prophet granted to him and his heirs exemption from prayer observances. They say so! May God forgive them!'

101 The months of the Arabs of the sands are: Ramadhan; Id Fitr al Awwal; Id Fitr al Thani; Arafa (pilgrimage month); Ashur (or the month of Zakat); Sifr; Tom al Awwal; Tom al Thani; Tom al Thalith; Mithalil (sometimes Tom al 'Urba), called Tuwam; Rijeb; Qusaiyir. Qusaiyir and Mithalil are held to be unpropitious months for the raid or a journey. Ramadhan also unless a start has already been made.

102 Salwa, Iskak and Mabak, ancient sites in the base of the Qatar peninsula are ascribed to *Fuwaris*, that is, the Persians. They are now in Ikhwan hands, and for this reason I could not explore them.

103 A description was given in a Note by Mr. Campbell Smith of the British Museum

104 Farajja, named after its digger Faraj, a Murri, who is said also to have dug Shanna.

105 A herd of camels is called *jaish* by Murra, nishera by the Rashid, and *bosh* by Oman tribes. The Badawin of the sands have five colours in camels: white, red, black, yellow, green. These are the dictionary equivalents. In reality: white = fawny cream colour; red =

gazelle colour; black = a black- brown colour; yellow= between fawny cream and gazelle colour; green=a dark wood-smoke colour.

106 Every camel has an individual name by which she is known to her master, but a disinterested party will know her by one of nine names, according to her age: first to seventh month, Huwar (suckling); seventh month to second year, Inferid (i.e. fending for itself); second year, Bint al Bun or Weled al Bun; third year, Madhriba (may be covered by bull); fourth year, Yadha (able to calve); fifth year, Thiniya; sixth year, Raba; seventh year, Sidis; eighth year. Shag al Naga or Nufi.

107 A cow in calf is known as *midini* (Rashid) *al algaha* (Murri). The period of gestation is twelve months. She may go thirteen months, or sometimes eleven, but in the latter case the calf seldom survives. Where it does it is called *saham*, the mother *jaret*. The cow calf, as yet uncovered by a bull, is a *bakra*. The Murra call a bull and cow calf *ga'ud* and *hashi* respectively.

108 A curious taboo peculiar to the Manasir tribe is that they will not eat hare or any other animal that has been shot in the head, i.e. presumably if its brains have been disturbed.

109 In this longitude 51° E., Banaiyan is regarded as the northward limit of Ar Rimal. To the eastwards the sands continue northwards through the regions of Batin, Liwa, Qufa and Bainuna to the shores of the Persian Gulf; to the westwards they continue through Jaub and Jafura to Hasa. But in the mouth of the true son of the sands these regions are not Ar Rimal.

110 The reader interested in the subject is referred to 'The Geology and Tectonics of Oman and of Parts of South-Eastern Arabia' (Quart. Journ. Geol. Soc., 1928), by Dr. G. M. Lees, to whom I make acknowledgments.

111 A list of sand specimens with analyses was made by H. W. Parker, of the British Museum.

112 A resume of the belts of main sand-shape I encountered from south to north is as follows:

I. High, red, dune country - 20 miles

II. Elevated, less rugged, red sands, with horse-shoe hills - 40 miles

III. Parallel white ridges with intervening red valleys - 100 miles

IV. Flat or gently undulating white sands - 70 miles

V . Flat or gently undulating white sands, with transverse red hills - 50 miles

VI. Steppe, salt plain, and red hills alternating - 100 miles

113 A chemical analysis of the contents of every water-hole I used was made by Mr. B. K. N. Wyllie, Anglo-Persian Oil Co. Ltd

114 Mention has already been made in this sense of these categories of Dakaka, Suwahib and Sanam. So also are:

Buwah, plural of *Bah* a shallow dipping-hole.

Munajjar from *Minjor* where a water-hole has to be bored through hard rock.

Hadh al (Ga'ada), a region where hadh vegetation is predominant.

Khila(t Ajman), a region where *hadh* vegetation is not found.

Umm Matlissa — 'mother of smoothness,' a region in which neither *hadh* nor *zahar* grows.

Jaub, a wadi-like depression in sands -region Banaiyan-Jabrin.

Jiban, plural of *Jaub.*

Jafura from *Jifr* — , deep hole,

Shuwaikila — 'strings of the udder bag' - hence two flanking areas of Huwaiya,

Tuwal — 'length' - abnormally deep water-holes of western Sanam.

Aqal — 'camel hobble' — the hdf-fathom holes of eastern Jiban.

115 Kathir and 'Amr, the respective ancestors of Rashid and 'Awamir were, according to their traditions, brothers and the sons of Hamdan. A common expression on the lips of Shaikh Salih was: 'By the sunnat (i.e. rules) of 'Amr and Kathir.' The Hadhramaut tribes also have their separate dialects.

116 E.g.

Unleavened bread Girus - Rashidi / Gadama - Murri

Wild cat Khawenga - Rashidi / Idfe - Murri

Steppe Jadda - Rashidi / Hadeba - Murri

Digging tool 'Atela - Rashidi / Ilhim – Murri

. . .

Reference has already been made to **Y** taking the place of **J** in the Rashidi dialect. The *chim* for a *kaf* is nowhere met, though common with the Ikhwan tribes of Mutair, 'Ataiba, 'Ajman, Dawasir, etc.; the **G** takes the place of **Q**, a *qaf* sound is never met with amongst Badawin; the participle *qad*, noticeably absent in 'Iraq dialect, is universal in South Arabia. (In the Mahri and non- Arabic dialects its equivalent is *bir*.)

117 An interpreter of Holy Law, sometimes a preacher among Sunnis, but among Shi'ahs, in Persia and 'Iraq, a priest. The institution of a priestly hierarchy is foreign to Islam, and is anathema to the orthodox, and especially to Wahabis.

118 The Manasir tribe uses Abu Dhabi.

The Awamir tribe uses Ibri, Dhank and Biraimi.

The Rashid tribe uses Dhufar or Raidha.

The Murra tribe uses Hofuf or Jabrin.

119 Intra decern primos matrimonii dies pudori habetur interdiu coitus. Corpus feminae ab umbilico usque ad genua nunquam detegere licet: si vir pannum qui ei pro tegumento est, removere velit, ilicet femina questa e tabernaculo excurrat. Pro lecto arenas habent; nam lectus, qualem nos habemus, eis ignotus est. Maxime usitatum est a latere vel a tergo cum femina coire, id quod etiam cum muliere praegnante vel paucis ante partum diebus nonnunquam fit.

120 Daru' and Manahil, supposed to have had a common origin, now by some odd chance belong (in name) to opposite factions.

121 I record the story as told, but the allusion is not clear to me, and to have questioned my narrator would have broken the thread of the story.

122 So named by us after the followers of the religious rules of Muhammad bin Abdul Wahhab of Nejd, a religious reformer of the eighteenth century. The Ikhwan, their twentieth-century successors, have taken their place and revived their doctrines.

123 The word evil is used to mean every kind of misfortune, e,g, raids or disease.

124 The vegetation consisted of *shinan, gadha,* the stunted, bulrush-like *tarthuth,* and *sa'adan.*

125 When starting out on a raid, the formula is sometimes as follows: 'God give to her back' (i.e. his camel's) 'good luck, and guide us so that we may return.'

126 *Namuna* = a specimen. With the Badu it often became *lumuna* or some- times just *muna*, which is illustrative of the resilience of the desert tongue,

127 The word 'hour' is meaningless to these Badawin. The only unit of time smaller than a day is the interval between prayers. Generally speaking, time is expressed in terms of distance.

128 Viz. from the speed of the raid.

129 Viz. camels famished and able to go no longer.

130 Viz. the enemies

131 The fossils collected were examined by Dr. J. A. Douglas, palaeontological adviser to the Anglo-Persian Oil Co., Ltd.

132 Water, sand and salt was analysed by Mr. B. K. N. Wyllie, Anglo-Persian Oil Co. Ltd.

133 It is perhaps not unreasonable to suggest that Gerrha, the ancient Gulf port of Ptolemy, if it is not to be identified with Bahrain, may be looked for, not under the sea, as has popularly been supposed, but some miles inland.

134 The name Bahrain- 'two seas,' applied originally to the whole area from Doha to Qatif. The islands that are to-day called Bahrain were in early times known as Awal.

135 The Murra welcome of a stranger is, '*marhaba wa mas'hala*'; the Manasir, '*marhab-kum*.'

136 The significance of this was that my Rashid and Murra companions felt secure from one another and from the Manasir.

Historic Journeys in Arabia

ALARMS AND EXCURSIONS IN ARABIA

BERTRAM THOMAS
ALSO WITH MODERN B&W IMAGES

ISBN 978-1-8380756-5-1
A remarkable account by Bertram Thomas
of his life in early 20th c Iraq & Oman.

ARABIA FELIX

BERTRAM THOMAS
ALSO WITH MODERN BLACK & WHITE IMAGES

ISBN 978-1-8380756-3-7
The ground breaking first crossing of the
Empty Quarter in 1930, by a non-Arab.

MEMOIR ON THE ISLAND OF SOCOTRA

JAMES RAYMOND WELLSTED
ALSO WITH MODERN B&W IMAGES

ISBN 978-1-8380756-9-9
The first comprehensive account of
the island of Socotra from 1834.

TRAVELS IN ARABIA
TRAVELS IN OMAN

THE 1835 VISIT BY
JAMES RAYMOND WELLSTED
ALSO WITH MODERN B&W IMAGES

ISBN 978-1-9989970-2-2
Travelling extensively through Oman in
the early 19th c, James Wellsted give us
an insightful account of the country

SHIPWRECK IN OMAN

The Anashed Account of the
Remarkable Escape and Sufferings of Author
Daniel Saunders, Jun.
ALSO WITH MODERN B&W IMAGES

ISBN 978-1-8380756-8-2
Shipwrecked during 1792 in Oman,
Daniel Saunders survived and walked
several hundred kilometres to safety
in Muscat.

INDEX

English names – by family name

Arabic names – by first name

Tribes – name first with definitive article 'Al' after – so Ghassan, Al

An individual of a tribe usually will have an 'i' as a suffix – so Al Rashid / Al Rashidi – the tribe and non-specified individual of that tribe are listed together as Rashid(i) Al,

Bait – in the context of tribes is usually a sub-section of a larger tribe and again their name is listed first and the Bait (house) subsequently.

INDEX FOR INTRODUCTORY PAGES

IMAGES

IMAGES

Majority of Black & White photos – Bertram Thomas

Muscat 1902 – unknown photographer

Sultan Taimur – unknown photographer

Bertram Thomas – unknown photographer

British Embassy - Brian Harrington Spier - Wikipedia

Maps – Bertram Thomas adapted Arabesque

Colour images - Arabesque

Lightning Source UK Ltd.
Milton Keynes UK
UKHW020658190722
406066UK00009B/900

9 781838 075637